THE GREAT PHILADELPHIA SPORTS DEBATE

Also by GLEN MACNOW

The Great Philadelphia Fan Book

Glen Macnow

THE GREAT PHILADELPHIA SPORTS DEBATE

Angelo Cataldi

Middle Atlantic Press

Manufactured in the United States

1 2 3 4 5   08 07 06 05 04

Library of Congress Cataloging-in-Publication Data

Macnow, Glen.
    The great Philadelphia sports debate / Glen Macnow, Angelo Cataldi.
        p. cm.
    1. Sports--Pennsylvania--Philadelphia--Miscellanea. I. Cataldi, Angelo.
II. Title.
    GV584.5.P46M33 2004
    796'.09748'11--dc22

                                        2004016743

Cover Design: Vicki Manucci and Terence Doherty
Interior Design and Composition: Vicki Manucci

For information write:
Middle Atlantic Press
10 Twosome Drive
Moorestown, NJ 08057

DEDICATION

To my parents, Angelo Sr. and Ida, who inspired my love for sports and then provided me the education to pursue it.

—Angelo Cataldi

To my grandmother, Dorothy Goodstein, who played catch with me when I was seven, and still has my back in every debate.

—Glen Macnow

CONTENTS

FOREWORD

By Ray Didinger

One of the great sound bites in the NFL Films library involves Philadelphia and Bill Parcells. The New York Giants were warming up for a 1989 game at Veterans Stadium and a large group of Eagles fans had gathered behind the visitors bench to, shall we say, welcome them to South Philadelphia.

Parcells, the Giants head coach, glanced over his shoulder at the jeering fans. Finally, he turned to Lawrence Taylor, his All-Pro linebacker, and said: "You know Lawrence, they call this 'The City of Brotherly Love,' but it's really a banana republic."

It just so happened Parcells was wearing a wireless microphone for NFL Films that day, so his comment about the Philadelphia fans found its way onto network television. Thus, it became part of this city's sports history, along with the snowball attack on Santa Claus and the Vet court with Judge McCaffery.

There is no doubt, Philadelphia is a tough town. It is a wonderful city, with its rich history as the cradle of American freedom and its thriving arts community, but it is still a hard-knocks kind of place. It is a blue-collar, row house town where most folks scuffle to make a buck. And rooting for the home team—loudly, passionately, sometimes angrily— is part of what defines them as Philadelphians.

Other towns have their Yankee Clippers and Galloping Ghosts. Here, it is Concrete Charlie Bednarik and the Broad Street Bullies. Brotherly Love? Yes, there is some of that, but don't push it. Don't walk into an Eagles game wearing a Cowboys jersey and expect a warm greeting. It doesn't work that way.

Philadelphia may not be a banana republic, as Bill Parcells claimed, but it isn't all that kind or gentle either, especially when it puts on its game face.

The fans here are tough, but they are knowledgeable. They support their teams, but they will not tolerate players who give less than their best effort. They have been called "boo birds," yet no fans embrace their teams more lovingly than the Philadelphia fans when they feel the players have given all they have to give, even in defeat.

Philadelphia fans take their sports seriously and, for that reason, they have serious sports debates. Who was the greatest coach in the city's history? Who was the most dominating player? What was the most exciting moment?

The debates help stoke the interest and keep alive the history. For two decades, they have fueled the conversation on WIP, Philadelphia's sports-talk radio station and now they are here in the pages of this book.

Angelo Cataldi and Glen Macnow are the author/debaters. They have been in the city for more than 20 years, writing sports for the *Philadelphia Inquirer* and, more recently, talking sports on WIP, so they have a solid grasp on the subject.

More importantly, having lived through the many disappointments of the last 20 years—the Joe Carter home run, the Eagles' NFC championship game losses, Game 7 against Edmonton—Angelo and Glen have the same emotional scars as the fans who grew up with these teams and therefore, they bring the same passion to these debates.

You may agree with them, you may disagree with them, but you won't doubt the fact that they are arguing in the booming—and often anguished—voice of a Philadelphia fan.

I know all about this because I grew up listening to similar debates. My grandfather, also named Ray Didinger, owned a bar on Woodland Avenue in Southwest Philadelphia. As a youngster, I spent many afternoons there, drinking Cokes, playing shuffleboard and listening to the arguments. Who was the better pitcher, Robin Roberts or Bobby Shantz? Who was the better fighter, Gil Turner or Joey Giardello? The Phillies never should of traded Del Ennis. Whaddya mean, he was a bum.

I absorbed it, all of it, and I know it helped shape my career in sports journalism. When I heard my grandfather talk about going to the 1948 NFL championship game in a blizzard, how he drove as far as 33rd and Girard and, when his car wouldn't go any farther, how he wrapped burlap bags around his feet and walked the rest of the way to Shibe Park, I knew this was serious stuff.

I never asked why he did it. To me, it was understood. The Eagles were playing for the world championship. Of course, you would go. A foot of snow? A four-mile walk? So what? You go, because you know if the Eagles win—which they did, defeating the Chicago Cardinals 7-0—it is a day you will cherish forever.

The whole notion of being a Philadelphia fan—fiercely loyal, but also fiercely opinionated—was passed down to me in such a way that I could not imagine a life without it. The winning, the losing, the elation, the disappointment and, of course, the debating. If you're like me, it is a part of who you are. And if you're like me, you will want to read this book.

FOREWORD 2

You may both be right.

—Al Morganti

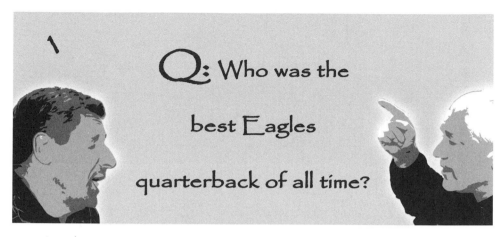

Q: Who was the best Eagles quarterback of all time?

Angelo says: Two years after Ron Jaworski ended his long-running feud with Buddy Ryan by leaving for Miami, the greatest quarterback in Eagles history received the ultimate indignity by an ungrateful organization.

The No. 7 that had adorned Jaworski for a decade in Philadelphia was not retired. It was besmirched. The green and silver No. 7 uniform was assigned to placekicker Roger Ruzek.

That's right. A stinking *kicker!*

It was an appropriate postscript to a tenure unlike that of any other Eagles quarterback, before or since. Jaworski, the embodiment of gritty perseverance, has just never gotten his due in Philadelphia—not from the fans, not from the team and not even from the historians.

So let it be said here for the first—and possibly only time: Ron Jaworski is the best quarterback in the history of the Eagles.

For the purposes of this argument, let's not go all the way back to the leather-helmet days, though I'll concede that Norm Van Brocklin was a great leader and winner. It's just that the game he played in the 1950s barely resembles the sport played today.

Jaworski was extraordinary by all means used to measure quarterbacks. He was prolific; his 26,963 passing yards with the Eagles is a record. He was successful; the only Eagles team in the modern era to go to the Super Bowl was led there by Jaworski in 1980-81. Above all, he was durable; his team record of 116 consecutive starts was an NFL mark until Bret Favre broke it in 2002.

I was there near the end of his career in Philadelphia, and no player has ever impressed me the way Jaws did. By his own count, Jaworski had 32 concussions in his 17-year career. In his final years, he would laugh off the latest bell-ringing with a shrug and his trademark cackle.

"Will you be ready next Sunday?" I'd ask.

"Dumb question," he'd say. "Of course I'll be ready."

Jaworski didn't have the athletic ability of successors like Randall Cunningham or Donovan McNabb, but he was more of a leader than either of them—and he had a better arm to boot. They didn't call him the Polish Rifle for nothing.

In the years since his decade as a starting quarterback in Philadelphia, Jaworski has been treated more like a Bobby Hoying or a Roman Gabriel than the greatest QB in team history. And I don't understand why. The Eagles have refused all overtures to retire his number. The best they could do was to give him status in the team's Honor Roll. Big deal. And when he asked to be considered as a general-manager candidate, he was treated like a door-to-door brush salesman.

Buddy Ryan with the greatest quarterback in Eagles history. (You decide.)

The fans haven't been much better. They booed him through much of his career, and their response to his exemplary work as an Arena League owner and an ESPN broadcaster has been tepid at best.

Granted, Jaws didn't provide the highlight-reel material of Cunningham and McNabb. He didn't bring the championship that Van Brocklin did. He spoke his mind more than most, I guess. More than what was good for him, obviously.

But if there is one athlete in Philadelphia who personifies the blue-collar, never-say-die attitude of Philadelphia, it is the greatest quarterback ever to play for the Eagles.

No. 7 is No. 1.

And I *don't* mean Roger Ruzek.

Glen says: No doubt, Angelo, that Ron Jaworski has been disrespected by this organization—and often by its fans. And I'll give you that Jaws was a leader, a gamer and a smart guy. I, too, enjoy his television work.

But the best quarterback in Eagles history is Randall Cunningham.

For the sake of this debate, I've limited nominees to quarterbacks who started at least four seasons for the Eagles. That takes out Norm Van Brocklin and Sonny Jurgensen, who are in the Hall of Fame largely for years spent away from Philadelphia. In truth, they weren't really ours. I'm also omitting Donovan McNabb, whose career is still unfolding, although I'm laying claim to him when we do the sequel to this book in twenty years.

So who's left? Well, Tommy Thompson, Adrian Burk, Bobby Thomason, Norm Snead and Roman Gabriel. Plus Jaworski and Cunningham. Not exactly a murderers row, eh?

Of that group, I'd take Randall, the most spectacular player I've ever seen. No quarterback in history could move like Cunningham, and few could unleash a buggy-whip arm as he could. *Sports Illustrated* dubbed him "The Ultimate Weapon," and for good reason. He could beat you with his arm (30 touchdown passes in 1990, which is more than Jaworski ever threw), his legs (4,928 rushing yards, the NFL record for a quarterback), or his foot (I was at the Meadowlands that frozen day when he uncorked a team-record 91-yard punt).

You threw out a few stats, Ange, to make your argument. Well, if you want stats, I've got them: Randall's passer rating as an Eagle is higher than Jaws's (78.8 to 74.0). Randall's ahead on completion percentage, lower interception ratio, and touchdowns-to-interceptions. Here's the biggest one—Randall's career record as an Eagle starter was 64-43-1, a .594 winning percentage. Jaworski's was 69-67-1, a .507 winning percentage. And don't you even think about arguing that my guy was blessed with better teammates and coaches.

He made three Pro Bowls to Jaworski's one. Even you wouldn't disagree that, at their peaks, Randall was the more outstanding quarterback.

Do you remember the highlights? Randall taking the hit from Carl Banks on Monday Night Football, somehow keeping his balance, and tossing that touchdown pass to Jimmy Giles. Or his five-touchdown game against the Redskins that ended with him finding Calvin Williams with the back-of-the-end-zone game-winner in the final seconds. Or the 95-yarder against Buffalo, when he sidestepped three sacks in his own end zone before launching a howitzer to Fred Barnett that went 60 yards in the air.

With all due respect to Jaws, the pass he may most be remembered for is the first one he threw in Super Bowl XV—right into the hands of Oakland linebacker Rod Martin.

Of course, you say, Jaws took his team to the Super Bowl and Randall never did. True enough. I will concede Randall's lackluster post-season record (1-4 with the Eagles, compared to Jaworski's 3-4), as well as his wiftiness, his poor leadership skills and his affection for gold-tipped shoelaces. Still, there's a part of me that still believes that if stinking Keith Jackson could have held the stinking ball in the Chicago gloaming of 1988, the Eagles would have won the Fog Bowl and gone on to the Super Bowl. Randall passed for 407 yards in that playoff loss—a franchise record.

Jaws may have been too candid for his own good, but don't count against Randall his out-and-out loony-tunes approach to life. There has never been a less-Philadelphia athlete than my guy, who once implored teammates to hold hands in the huddle to "show a little love." He never quite got the hard-boiled East Coast mentality. He was much more comfortable in his homeland—deep outer space.

One more thing, Angelo. I agree that Jaws's number should not have been given out, especially to a kicker. But, in case you haven't noticed, Randall's No. 12 has not been recycled since he left town in 1995, not even in training camp. I have it on good authority that it will never be worn again by an Eagle. That's got to mean something.

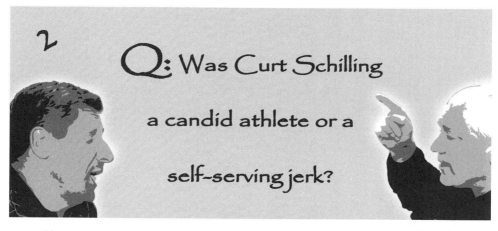

Q: Was Curt Schilling a candid athlete or a self-serving jerk?

Glen says: Here's what we ask of our athletes in Philadelphia: A full-tilt effort on the field, plus the ability to throttle it up for the big game. A civility to fans and media, maybe even a sense that they actually understand us. Honesty—and an occasional controversy doesn't hurt. Throw in a charitable streak and we'll build a statue in your honor.

Curt Schilling provided all these attributes during his nine seasons as a Phillie. He was the most accessible, candid, fan-friendly player this side of Charles Barkley.

And yet there are critics—led by you, Angelo—who twist Schilling's openness into something smug and self-serving. Hey Ange, did you prefer the Scott Rolen approach?

The true nonsense here is that, while Schilling is criticized as a phony, his two-faced teammates on the 1993 Phils are memorialized for being a great group of guys. We love Macho Row for its Regular Joe image, but those of us who covered that squad know the truth. Unlike John Kruk, Schilling did not get snarly once the TV cameras left. Unlike Lenny Dykstra, Schilling didn't make a drunken idiot of himself in nightspots around the nation. Unlike other teammates, he was not a bully, a homophobe or a serial adulterer.

What did he do wrong? He wrapped his head in a towel when Mitch Williams threw wild pitches all over the park. Gee, let's shoot him.

Curt's biggest problem was that he was too honest for his own good. He couldn't understand why others in the Phillies organization—management and players alike—didn't share his commitment to winning. Sort of like a fan.

He groused that ownership wasn't spending enough money to build a winner. That prompted general manager Ed Wade to say, "Curt is a horse every fifth day. The other four days, he's a horse's ass." You want to take Wade's side here, you go right ahead.

Schilling had been taught his terrific work ethic as a young player by Roger Clemens. He just couldn't tolerate a teammate who didn't care as much as he did. Once, he laid into young Phils pitcher Garrett Stephenson for ignoring his homework. The dress-down came in front of others, which wasn't very tactful on Curt's part. But what do you prefer, the guy who demands excellence or the guy who takes the lazy route?

I had the pleasure of being around Schilling away from the ballpark—and so did you, Angelo. I recall one time he drove way out to Exton, Pennsylvania to appear on our old TV show, *The Great Sports Debate*. Didn't ask for a dime. Brought his two rottweilers onto the set. He even goofed around by playing in a street hockey skit we had planned—putting a few pucks past you, as I recall. Quick, Angelo, name two current athletes you could ask to kill most of a day for that kind of nonsense. Okay, name one.

Then, try to name the local players who devoted as much time to charity. Schilling became a lead man in the Phillies campaign to raise money for the fight against

An extremely rare photo of Curt Schilling with his mouth shut.

Amyotrophic Lateral Sclerosis (ALS, or Lou Gehrig's disease). He started an annual fundraising golf tournament in 1996 and continues it all these years after leaving Philadelphia.

I was a guest auctioneer at Schilling's 2003 tournament in Blue Bell, Pennsylvania. A middle-aged woman in the advanced stages of ALS was wheeled in to meet Curt. The poor woman's condition made her speech loud and slurred and, truth be told, made many of the people listening a bit uncomfortable. But as the insurance agents and business executives who paid to play in his golf tournament waited, Curt held her hand and spoke gently with her for 15 minutes.

Yep, you couldn't find a more self-serving guy.

Angelo says: As soon as I wipe away the tears, I'll try the impossible here and give a more accurate portrait of the most self-serving, selfish, self-absorbed player in baseball history.

Just one question, Glen, is that your speech for when Curt Schilling is inducted into the Hall of Fame, or are you aiming higher now and shooting for his sainthood?

Yes, I did have a chance to get to know Schilling through our old TV show, and yes, I did pet his dogs and he did score a couple of goals against me in street hockey. I enjoyed all of that. I also have talked to his wife Shonda many times, and she is a fantastic person.

I'll add something that was even more important to me and my career. At a time when no one from the Phillies would ever call WIP, Schilling called us every morning, win or lose, in the latter stages of the 1993 run. There were days when he would be waiting on the phone as we came on the air at 6 a.m.!

All of which should tell you something, Glen, if I don't like a guy after all of that, there must be a reason. And I have more reasons than space here will allow. So I'll just go through a few of the major ones.

Curt Schilling was all about himself from the day he arrived in Philadelphia. Everyone in the Phillies organization, from the top reaches of the front office to the lowly batboys, could not stand Schilling. They knew, right at the beginning, that he was selfish. They knew that his lip service about the fortunes of the team was just that. He didn't give a damn about the Phillies, or about winning.

Remember the towel-draping act in the ninth inning of games he pitched in '93, Glen? Let's analyze that for a minute. Here was a young pitcher openly showing up a teammate, Mitch Williams, and distancing himself from the possibility of failure.

The towel over the head was saying to the fans: "Hey, if we lose this, don't blame me. I'm not any more comfortable with this guy on the mound than you are."

Macho Row hated Schilling for that unprofessional, grandstanding tradition, and Curt knew it. But he didn't stop because it got him some face time (or, in this case, towel time) on TV. Even back then, it was all about Schilling.

His final years in Philadelphia were among the ugliest in the history of our sports town, Glen. You know that. The diatribes about commitment to winning, the trade demands, the media wars (with me, among others). . .they were all just an updated version of the towel-draping. Again, he was distancing himself from failure. If the team lost, it was the owners and front office, not Curt. Never Curt.

He won a world championship in Arizona, although people may forget that he left the seventh game of the 2001 World Series *losing* 2-1 because he gave up a huge home run to Alfonso Soriano in the eighth inning. The Diamondbacks won long after Curt had left the mound. But this was one time when he did not distance himself from the team. Oh, no. There was no towel draped over his head when Luis Gonzalez blooped the game-winner. As I recall, Curt was one of the first Arizona players on the field. More precious face time.

Now Schilling is a member of the Boston Red Sox, after more open politicking for a trade once Arizona stopped winning. He milked those contract negotiations right through the Thanksgiving holiday in 2003. In the end, he got a huge contract and vowed to end the curse of the Bambino. Who was going to mention that a week earlier he had waived his no-trade clause because he was going to join Boston's evil rivals, the New York Yankees. Not you, Glen.

A few weeks into the 2004 season, Schilling told his teammates that they should take less money to stay in Boston. Lots of them were in the final year of their contracts, and he said they should stop worrying so much about money.

Hey, he got his. Screw them.

Curt Schilling is the biggest phony I've ever witnessed in 30 years of covering and talking about sports. Even your heartwarming story about the sick woman leaves me cold, Glen. I know better.

I guarantee you—absolutely *guarantee*—there was a TV camera somewhere nearby, recording this act of sentiment. The fact that you were watching, ready to broadcast this latest example of his greatness, cannot be discounted either.

Even that story wasn't really about the woman, Glen.

It was about Curt Schilling.

It's always about Curt Schilling.

Q: Who would you most want to share a beer with?

Angelo says: Can I lodge a protest before I choose someone, Glen?

I think it's a terrible idea for anyone in our business to share a beer with a sports figure they might have to criticize next week or next month or next year. Lots of media people are nothing more than athlete wannabes who are trying to insinuate themselves into the sports culture by any means possible. The *dream* of most of these phonies is to have a beer with a player or coach.

(If this description calls to mind any of our colleagues—especially one with facial hair —that's your conclusion, Glen, not mine.)

Also, a better question might be: Who the hell would want to share a beer with *me?*

But I'll play along. My choice is a no-brainer: Pat Croce.

I came up with this name very easily. Most baseball players are insolent jerks. Football players are either too busy during the season or living too far away in the off-season. Basketball players all have posses, and I hate crowds. And hockey players, I'm told, have short arms and deep pockets.

Pat Croce is the single most impressive person I've ever met in sports. I first encountered him in 1983 when he was a trainer for the Flyers. At least that was his title. Pat wasn't like any trainer I'd ever met. Amid all of those great hockey players—including Bobby Clarke, Bill Barber, Tim Kerr, and Mark Howe—Pat's personality was the biggest in the locker room.

He was known back then as a maniac; in other words, nothing's changed. Players who would agree to go through a Pat Croce workout invariably would complain for weeks about the torture he imposed. Back then, Pat would say you weren't really trying if you didn't vomit at some point in the workout.

It was inevitable that Pat would take his unorthodox training methods and turn them into an empire, which he did as a founder of the NovaCare rehabilitation facilities. After he sold that business for millions, he turned to his true calling—sports ownership.

And that's where I'd start the conversation at the tavern, Glen. I'd tell him that he blew it when he left the Sixers, even though he has become a famous author and motivational speaker. I'd tell him that, for a guy who constantly preaches about setting high goals and achieving them, he fell a little short himself with his basketball team. I'd remind him that his team *lost* the NBA Finals in 2001.

None of us will ever know exactly why Pat burned the bridges that he did on his way out of professional sports after that incredible run. Obviously, Ed Snider was driving him nuts, with notable assists from Larry Brown and Allen Iverson. Still, the job wasn't done. If he really wanted to run Comcast Spectacor, he had to wait his turn.

My basic strategy during this beer would be to get Pat spouting his "I feel great!" credo, and then turn the tables on him. I'd do to him exactly what he did to convince Harold Katz to sell the Sixers. I'd tell him that *my* dream was to have him run another pro franchise in Philadelphia. I'd tell Pat to go after the Phillies first, and then maybe the Eagles.

Then I'd turn into the motivator myself. I'd tell him about all of the fans who've endured one disingenuous jackal after another owning and running our teams. I'd tell him that the reality TV projects and Slamball diversions are fine for other people, but he has a higher calling. I'd try to appeal to his love for Philadelphia, and for a real challenge.

If he said no, I wouldn't accept his answer. I'd talk about his early days as a trainer, when he loved to tell people that the only way to get stronger was to suffer a little. He suffered with Brown and Iverson. Now he was stronger. Now he was ready.

There is nothing I want more for Philadelphia than another run at a championship with the most popular and inspirational man who ever ran a sports franchise in our city, Pat Croce, leading the way.

I'm willing to go to extremes, Glen.

At the end of that beer, I'll even pick up the check.

Glen says: Well, Ange, I've downed a few with Croce over the years. And despite your generosity, I know this much: He always insists on picking up the check.

But I'd be willing to buy rounds all night to hear the wisdom of Dallas Green, former Phils pitcher and manager, and consigliore to the current administration. No one knows like Dallas where the bodies are buried and—as you and I have learned—Mr. Green is never reluctant to speak his mind.

So I'm bringing enough to buy a six-pack. Here's what I'll ask:

Beer one: Why did the Phils choke and die in 1964?

Green was a 29-year-old reliever on that team, and still shakes his head over Gene Mauch's mishandling of the pitchers. One of Mauch's mistakes, he says, was relying on a washed-up mop-up man named Dallas Green. I love that candor. Plus, he's got a few good Richie Allen tales. Did you know that Green and Allen were former high school basketball stars who battled in savage one-on-one games every spring training?

Beer two: As manager, how did he turn around the underachieving 1980 Phillies?

Dallas's infamous outburst between games of an August doubleheader in Pittsburgh is often credited for transforming a listless team into world champions.

As I've heard it, Green was incensed at his players taking their emotional lead from self-absorbed cool guys Mike Schmidt and Steve Carlton. After a third straight loss, he locked the clubhouse door and delivered an obscenity-laced tirade that reporters could hear through the concrete walls. In the second game that day, he nearly got into a fistfight with reliever Ron Reed.

Regardless, his angry players won nine of their next 11, and finished the season with a month-long burst of passion to capture the franchise's only title.

Beer three: Why did he launch into a 1981 news conference with the words, "F— you, Jayson!"

It was right after the players' strike ended, and Dallas was in a lousy mood. His Phils had been playing great before the strike, but reported back fat and lazy. Green hoped out loud that it just meant the pitchers were ahead of the hitters, like in spring training.

But those pitchers got rocked in their first three post-strike games, and Green was incensed. So, when the *Inquirer's* Jayson Stark opened questioning one day by asking, "Does this mean the pitchers aren't ahead of the hitters anymore?" Dallas went off.

His 4½-minute tirade set the international record for vulgarity. He wasn't mad at Stark. Jayson had just served up the hanging curveball Dallas needed to shred his players. He even stomped out of his office and into the clubhouse—mid-rant—to make sure they were all listening.

Beer four: How did he steal Ryne Sandberg from the Phils?

Dallas left town after 1981 to run the Cubs. His first trade with his old club was a swap of veteran shortstops—Ivan DeJesus for Larry Bowa. He cagily insisted that the Phils throw in an overlooked prospect from their farm system.

Sandberg's path to the Phillies was blocked at third base by Schmidt and at second by Manny Trillo. Near as I recall, Dallas figured out a position for him in Chicago.

Beer five: What prompted him to rip Scott Rolen?

You recall this one, Ange, because it occurred on your show. Rolen was whining his way through the 2002 season when Green took aim at his work ethic. "Scotty is satisfied with being a so-so player," he told you. "In his mind, he probably thinks he's doing okay, but fans in Philadelphia know otherwise."

Great stuff, candid stuff. Rolen went ballistic. Within a month he was traded to St. Louis. Personally, I don't miss him a bit. Thanks, Dallas. Let me buy another round.

Beer six: What does he really think of the Phils future?

I don't trust Ed Wade, Ange, and I know you don't either. So, now that I've loosened up Mr. Green, I'll try to get him to speak candidly on this team, its management, its line-up and its farm system. Yo, Dallas, is the future as bright as the new ballpark?

My six-pack is gone. But my questions aren't. I want to hear the Paul Owens stories, the Tug McGraw stories. I want his opinion on Jimmy Rollins and Brett Myers.

Tell you what, Dallas. If you stick around, I'll graduate into buying Johnnie Walker Black.

Another round?

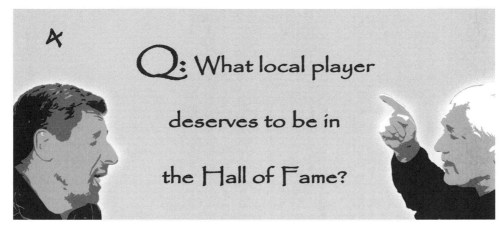

Q: What local player deserves to be in the Hall of Fame?

Glen says: Here are some defensemen inducted into the Hockey Hall of Fame: Leo Boivin, Phat Wilson, Fernie Flamen, Hoo Stuart, Hooley Smith.

Here's one who isn't: Mark Howe.

Viacheslav Fetisov, who played nine NHL seasons and scored 36 goals, is in. Howe, who played sixteen seasons and scored 197 goals, is not.

Winger Bernie Federko, whose career plus/minus was a minus-132 is in. Howe, with a career plus-400, is not.

Am I missing something?

I watched Mark Howe play for most of his ten brilliant seasons as a Flyer. I can honestly say I never once saw him make a mistake. He never coughed up the puck in his zone, never got caught out of position, never took the wrong man on an odd-man rush. He was the key to the Flyers' transition game, intercepting a pass and moving the puck forward with poise and creativity.

Howe's numbers speak for themselves: Three times he was runner-up for the Norris Trophy as the league's top defenseman, finishing behind immortals Paul Coffey and Raymond Bourque. He was first-team all-star three times. He played in three Stanley Cup finals, two with the Flyers. In 1985-86, he finished second to some guy named Gretzky in the voting for MVP.

What an incredible season that was. Howe scored 24 goals and added 58 assists—both still franchise records for a defenseman. He scored 7 short-handed goals, a number surpassed in history only by Coffey among NHL defensemen. His plus-minus for the season was an astonishing plus-85. That means, simply, that for each game he dressed, the Flyers were likely to score one more goal than they gave up.

Howe came to Philadelphia in 1982 as a converted winger with a reputation for being a bit of a whiner and difficult to motivate. He was just the opposite. After home games,

Howe would sit in his den with a cup of coffee and a notebook, watching 2 a.m. Prism replays of the contest he had just played in. He looked for ways to improve his game (good luck), and, while he didn't push ideas on teammates, was always ready with a suggestion when asked.

"I've threatened Mark that if I ever really want to punish him, I'll put him behind the bench," Flyers coach Mike Keenan once joked. "The guy has such an intrinsic knowledge of hockey, it's incredible. I guess it must be the genes."

Ah, yes, the genes. The son of Gordie Howe was blessed with the skills and instincts —if not the sharp elbows—of the man nicknamed Mr. Hockey. Some sons shy from following famous fathers, but Mark insisted he never felt any pressure. "From when I was a

Hall of Fame genes were just part of Mark Howe's greatness.

toddler I spent my time watching Dad play," Mark said, "and always figured, what could be more fun?"

He broke in as an 18-year-old, flanking his dad and brother Marty on a line for the Houston Aeros of the old World Hockey Association. Three years later, the family business moved to the WHA's Hartford Whalers, who in 1979 were accepted into the NHL. Like his father, Mark had staying power, playing until he was 40.

Quick trivia break: Mark Howe is responsible for what major change in hockey rink design?

Answer: Goals that easily break away from their moorings. Before 1980, nets were affixed to the ice with long spikes, making it nearly impossible to dislodge the goalposts.

Playing for the Whalers in the 1980 playoffs, Howe slid into the net, which didn't budge. His backside was impaled on the blade-like piece of metal on which the net used to sit. The injury nearly cost him his career. The next year, the league—and soon the rest of hockey—moved to tear-away moorings.

That's not exactly why I'd put him in the Hall of Fame. Instead, I'll go with hockey's stated criteria: "Playing ability, sportsmanship, character and (a player's) contribution to the team or teams and to the game of hockey in general."

Mark Howe played twenty-two professional seasons, including ten as a Flyer. He certainly fulfills the sportsmanship and character requirements, and he has all the statistics and honors to meet any playing standard. He is the best defenseman ever to play for the Flyers, and the best defenseman not yet inducted into the Hall.

Angelo says: Philadelphia baseball players have always had a terrible time getting voted into the Hall of Fame. It took a campaign by a *New York Times* writer to get Robin Roberts voted in. Jim Bunning had to wait 25 years before the Veterans Committee finally pried open the door. Richie Ashburn had given up all hope before a fan protest finally nudged him into the hallowed grounds a few years before his death.

And need I even mention the man with the most hits in big-league history still considered *persona non grata* in Cooperstown, New York. After his insincere 2003 book, all bets are off for Pete Rose. As far as I'm concerned, Rose should never get into the Hall. His greedy, lying nature is not worthy of celebration.

But if the guardians of the gates are going to punish players like Rose for their ethical shortcomings, shouldn't they reward others whose character was so strong that it changed the game forever?

The man I propose for admission to the Hall of Fame was not, technically, ever a Philadelphia player, though I'm pretty sure you'll grant me an exemption on this one, Glen. This player was traded to the Phillies, but he refused to report. Ultimately, his courage and conviction triggered a new era of baseball, an era of unprecedented contractual freedom for players.

There may be no player in the history of baseball who accomplished more than Curt Flood.

On the field, he is worthy of some consideration, if not automatic entry. He won seven Gold Gloves, batted over .300 six times, was part of the champion 1967 Cardinals, went to three World Series and played 15 seasons of consistently exceptional baseball. He was a pro's pro. Some would argue that he was the best defensive center fielder in the history of the game.

But to judge Curt Flood on his statistics is like weighing the value of Jackie Robinson by looking at his baseball card. Flood's contribution to the game transcended his efforts on the field. His impact was felt from the day he began his crusade in 1969 to the day he died in 1997. And every time in the future that a player signs a big free agent contract, he should nod up to the heavens in honor of Curt Flood.

Marvin Miller, the former executive director of the MLB Players Association, once said, "There is no Hall of Fame for people like Curt," because he challenged authority and tirelessly fought the injustice of the reserve clause.

Well, there should be. Flood knew when he was fighting his trade to the Phillies that he would be sacrificing the last great seasons of his playing career. He knew that he would be tied up for years in court while baseball trained its best lawyers at his resolve. But he never wavered. Even though he ultimately lost his case in the Supreme Court, he broke the system. His noble struggle led to the dawn of free agency.

What amazes me more than anything, Glen, is that baseball writers—like most media people—are liberals like yourself who admire this kind of crusading, and yet there has never been a serious movement to get Flood elected to the Hall of Fame. If the baseball writers had voted him in, there is nothing that the game's hierarchy could have done to stop it.

Yet his best vote total was 71 in 1996, a year before his death. He needed 353 to get in.

Why is it that when the writers pound out their annual screed about the injustices in the Hall of Fame, no one ever mentions Curt Flood?

I don't really expect to get much support even from Philadelphia for my proposal here, Glen, because in refusing the trade, Flood also branded our city as racist. He said he had no interest in inflicting on his family the kind of discrimination Richie Allen had endured in his final days as a Phillie.

Maybe Flood had that part of his crusade all wrong. Maybe he should be criticized for indicting a city without ever getting to know it first. And maybe—probably—he savored the role of martyr.

Does any of that really matter, though? By all accounts, Curt Flood had an extraordinary impact on the game he played and loved. He was a fabulous player, and he was so much more.

If there's no place in the Hall of Fame for a man like Curt Flood, is there really any reason to have a Hall of Fame?

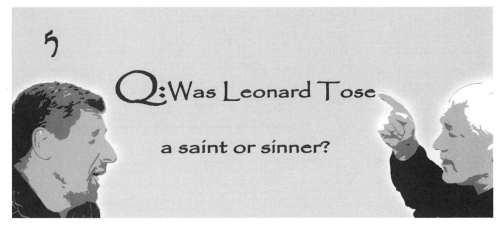

Q: Was Leonard Tose a saint or sinner?

Angelo says: The year was 1984, and Leonard Tose was about to do the worst thing an owner has ever done to the sports fans of Philadelphia. He was going to move the most beloved team of all, the Eagles, to Phoenix, Arizona.

For more than a week, Tose was a pariah in the same city where, five years earlier, he had been a hero. "From the Super Bowl to the toilet bowl" is the way he himself described his descent. He is gone now, but he left behind a legacy of success and excess—of cheers and booze; of an exhilarating Super Bowl and a fatal gambling addiction; of wine, women and wrongs.

The truth is that a more loyal, more caring owner has never occupied the front office of a Philadelphia sports franchise.

What other owner created a charity for the sole purpose of helping those less fortunate than him? Tose started the *Eagles Fly for Leukemia*. What other owner handed a blank check to his GM and coach and told them to build a champion? Norman Braman? Jeffrey Lurie? Please. What other owner remained revered by his players and coaches long after the last dollar had been spent and the last drop of liquor had been drained?

Leonard Tose was a great owner because he was not ruled by a ledger sheet or a board of bureaucrats. His general manager back then, Jim Murray, has said many times that Tose never—not once—rejected a request for a player because of money. The owner would always ask just one question: "Will this player help us win?"

Tose owned his team the way he lived his life. He shoved all of his chips into the middle of the table and rolled the dice. It was inevitable that, one day, he would roll snake eyes.

I got to know Tose personally in his final years, and a sadder story has never been told in Philadelphia sports. He lived in a barren hotel room, his only solace an ever-present bottle of Dewars bought with handouts he received from his old coach and friend Dick Vermeil. He had a girlfriend about half his age then, after four failed marriages. He rarely spoke to his only daughter. He was flat broke.

And still I saw a great sports owner, if not a great man. I asked Tose many times why he even considered moving a team he knew was so loved by the fans, and he said, just as many times, that he never could have or would have done it. He just wanted a better lease on Veterans Stadium, which he got after the Phoenix threat. Months later, he sold the team.

Then I asked him the question that haunted him for 17 years from the time he sold the Eagles until he died in 2003. Why *didn't* he move the team? Nothing meant more to him in his life than owning the Eagles, and the move would have replenished his bank account and assured his continuity of ownership.

This man who had so many vices had more morality than all of his predecessors and successors combined. He said it was never an option.

So instead, he made the ultimate sacrifice. He put up for adoption his only son, the Philadelphia Eagles. With emphasis on *Philadelphia*.

Today there are still many people who see Leonard Tose as a villain. These people were not at his funeral. On that day Leonard Tose was called a drunk, a gambler, and a lothario by the people who loved him the most. It was not like any funeral ever held. His own children and grandchildren openly discussed his many weaknesses, as he himself did for so many years.

But Tose was also called something else that day, something that will outlive all of his foibles. He was called the last great sportsman to own a franchise in Philadelphia.

And he was.

Glen says: You surprise me, Angelo.

Hell, you covered Leonard Tose's attempt to sneak the Eagles out of Philadelphia. You were there when that con artist put a gun to our heads (his other hand jiggled a pair of dice) and threatened to move the team—our team!—to Phoenix. You wrote the stories when he extorted his ransom in the form of luxury boxes.

And now you tell us how much he loved us?

Come on, Angelo. I never thought you'd be the type too reluctant to step on some Tose.

So allow me to refresh your memory. It was right before Christmas 1984 when word came that Tose and his evil daughter, Susan Fletcher, were in the process of loading up the U-Haul for Arizona. In a few short days, Tose's public stance changed from "The Eagles will move over my dead body" to "No comment" to "We'll have a statement soon." A city whose fans had forged a 52-year public trust with the franchise lived in fear that the legacy of Bednarik and Brookshier would be relocated to a part of the country where people go to die.

Ultimately, of course, they stayed. Not because of Tose's civic devotion, mind you, but because Mayor Wilson Goode reluctantly offered up $10 million in taxpayers' money to bail this drunkard out of his personal debts. At least until the next time he crapped out.

I'm supposed to believe Tose was displaying high moral character? That he did this for *us?*

There are really two ways to look at this. Either Tose was really planning to kidnap a civic treasure, or he was just preying on our loyalty. Is one really better than the other? Either way, he played us for saps. As the great Ray Didinger suggested at the time, Tose was "the millionaire who rolls down the limousine window to spit in our faces."

Then, I might add, he excused himself by saying, "Hey, I was just kidding."

Look, we've had a lot of hideous owners in this city over the years—scoundrels and cheapskates, liars and snobs. But only one ever put us through the genuine fear of losing our passion and our history. And then, for good measure, he sold the Eagles to Norman Braman. Right after he hired Braman's Mini-Me, Harry Gamble. Gee, Leonard, thanks for the parting gifts.

I will not deny Leonard Tose's loyalty to his players or his charitable streak. Often, those traits came together—like when he vastly overpaid mediocrities like Anthony Griggs or Kenny Jackson.

And I'll give Tose credit for owning the team the only year it went to the Super Bowl. Let the record show, however, that Tose said he discovered coach Dick Vermeil while nursing a New Year's Day hangover watching UCLA upset Ohio State in the Rose Bowl. I suppose if Ohio State had won, the next Eagles coach would have been Woody Hayes.

Somehow, Tose's drinking and gambling got him cast this city's Jay Gatsby, a lovable rich-boy rapscallion who apparently couldn't count to 21. That's fine, except that *he* had the addictions and *we* all had to suffer from them.

Don't buy it from me? Here's what a few local literary giants wrote back in the day:

Stan Hochman: "Scorn outweighs pity because of Tose's elegant lifestyle. He needed help and was too muddled or too belligerent to listen."

Didinger: "A relentless bumbler who pushed an NFL franchise worth $65 million to the brink of financial ruin. . . Tose and Daughter Dearest, Susan Fletcher, offered a rare blend of deceit, arrogance and incompetence."

John Schulian: "The NFL's reigning lowlife, an overgrown child of 69 . . . if life were a locker room floor, he would be the fungus that grows on it."

Wow!

Look, all these years later, we know that sports is a dirty business. We've seen our owners hold us up with profit grabs and PSLs. We've seen a city with broken-down streetcars and substandard schools commit zillions to sportsmen's palaces. But don't forget that it was Leonard Tose who first taught us how dirty it all was.

He was the one who stole our virginity.

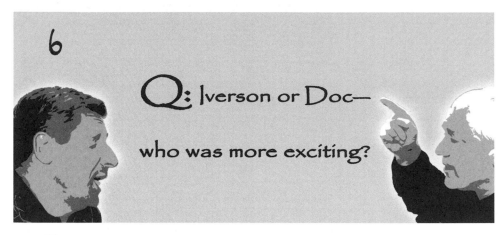

6

Q: Iverson or Doc—
who was more exciting?

Glen says: I never saw Wilt in his prime. I did marvel at Doc, as well as Andrew Toney and Charles Barkley. Thrillers, all of them.

But the most exciting player ever to wear a Sixers uniform is AI.

Ignore, for a moment, the soap opera and the histrionics and the, "We're talkin' 'bout practice!" Focus instead on the times this undersized warrior prompted you out of your seat (which, in your case, Angelo, probably required a forklift).

Iverson—listed at 6 feet, but who's kidding—is the shortest scoring leader in NBA history. He got there not by standing outside the fray, but by daring to enter the realm of the giants, where he got bounced around like a Superball. He'd take a knee to the groin, a forearm to the head and still ricochet off the seven-footers to scoop up a feathery lay-up. We'd gasp every time he got knocked down, and cheer like mad every time he rose back up.

Remember the Eastern Conference Finals against the Bucks in 2001? He caught an elbow in the mouth—loosening a tooth—and swallowed his own blood so the refs would-n't notice and make him leave the game.

Dr. J played with an unparalleled elegance. He soared and then always stuck the landing. Iverson, meanwhile, landed in pieces—first the knees, then the rump, then the elbows. His fearlessness—admired by adults, adored by children—would make you shake your head and wonder aloud, "How does he survive?"

I'll compare them in terms of another sport. Doc was Joe DiMaggio, all charm and aloof grace. Iverson's more like Pete Rose (with corn rows replacing Rose's Three Stooges haircut), spit and gristle and 150 pounds of heart. He cried when the Sixers lost in the playoffs. No way Erving lets the people see that emotion.

Like Rose, Iverson beat you any way necessary. Some nights he'd arc shots that seemed to come from the Walt Whitman Bridge. He was never the most accurate shooter, but when he got on a roll (especially in the playoffs), he'd hit three-pointers with Reggie

Miller's hand in his face or Sam Cassell tugging on his jersey. Then, he'd run back down court, his hand cupped against his ear, imploring the wild Sixers crowd to cheer louder.

Other nights, he'd pause at the top of the key, yo-yoing the ball while some unfortunate defender waited for him to make a move. Iverson's eyes would go one direction, his head another and his feet yet a third. Tyronn Lue or Charlie Ward would flinch, and here would come the crossover dribble, followed by a supersonic drive to the basket. He'd make the lay-up, take the foul and turn it into a three-point play.

Recall that famous ankle-breaking move on Michael Jordan during his rookie year? At

A.I. shows local traitor Kobe Bryant how it's done...

the time, Jordan was regarded as the league's top defender.

I'll remember that, as well as the time he slam-dunked a rebound over 6-foot-11 Marcus Camby. The laws of mathematics say that could never happen.

And I'll remember the night Iverson scored 26 points in the fourth quarter to pull the Sixers back from a 19-point deficit to Milwaukee. There were many times he'd load the whole team on his skinny shoulders and carry them to victory.

Julius Erving is one of the top 20 players ever in the NBA and, ultimately, better than Iverson. But the question here is which guy more often made you shake your head in wonderment, high-five your friends and say aloud, "I can't believe what I just saw." That's AI.

I started this debate by citing Wilt. So let me finish it by quoting what the Dipper had to say about Iverson shortly before his death:

"I knew he'd be incredible, totally exciting, even more so than Pete Maravich because of his quickness and his desire. What I like about Allen is his drives to the basket. He gets thrown up against the pads, brushes himself off and goes in there again. He's one of the few players I truly enjoy watching."

Yep. Me, too.

Angelo says: This comparison between Julius Erving and Allen Iverson is intriguing because it is difficult to separate the myth from the reality. Just as their talents are hard to define with mere words, so, too, are their personalities elusive.

Think about it. Dr. J was arguably the most elegant basketball player in history, a man who glided over the court with the regal wingspan of an eagle. AI is the lunch-pail superstar, preferring the rugged terrain under the basket as his stage.

Your comparison of Joe DiMaggio to Pete Rose is inspired, Glen. And it goes beyond that, too. Joe D once said that he gave everything he had every night because he didn't want to disappoint the fan who might see him in person only that one time. Dr. J was the same way. He never presented himself in anything but the best possible light. He cared about what people thought. His image was paramount to him.

On the other hand, Iverson—like Rose—couldn't care less about the fans who have cheered him every day of his career in Philadelphia. He's a rebel. He'll bend his ear toward the crowd to incite them, but only under his terms—only to celebrate himself and his teammates. Those same fans can expect not even a half-smile from him if they bump into their hero later that night.

I've never been very good at separating the person from the talent, Glen, so I might be at a disadvantage in this debate. I have no respect for Iverson, because he has no respect for me. His style of play is a vivid reflection of who he is: defiant, fearless, dangerous.

...while Doc soars over another anonymous Laker.

More than that, his play is an enigma. Here's breaking news, Glen: Iverson is, at best, a mediocre shooter, not exactly a plus for someone who's barely six-feet tall and plays the position of *shooting* guard. Yes, he's capable of a crossover move that could break a defender's ankles—Michael Jordan, for example—but most of the time that is not his game.

When Iverson is succeeding, he's braving the forest of redwoods under the basket. That might be exciting to you, Glen. It's grueling to me. For every highlight-reel reverse layup, there are five ugly misfires, followed by the thud of Iverson's body as he crashes onto the hardwood. Yes, it's fun to watch Iverson. It's also fun to watch the car crashes in NASCAR. For a while, anyway.

Julius Erving is superior to Iverson in every way on the court, Glen. You even concede he was a better player. He was a more exciting player, too. Do you forget the astonishing leaps from the foul line that ended with a smooth, delicate finger roll at the basket? Or how about when Dr. J would palm the ball and, while in mid-flight, dangle it before his defender, then pull it back without his feet touching the ground. Nobody else even tried that one.

Here's the best difference I can offer to support my argument. Iverson is good for one or two highlight-reel plays a game. Erving *invented* the highlight reel.

I would be remiss if I didn't get back to my original point before I close here. As I stated, the hardest part of comparing Iverson and Dr. J is separating the myth from the reality.

By most accounts, Iverson is a first-class jerk. He hates to practice, he ignores rules, he sulks when he gets benched and he's prone to outbursts of stupidity. Yet I'd take him any day over Erving off the court, because Dr. J was a total fraud. You can look it up.

The paternity suits, the extramarital trysts, the trashing of Iverson when AI was a rookie—all of it speaks of a man who didn't deserve his role-model image.

As it turned out, Dr. J was just as deceptive off the court as he was on it. And maybe more exciting there, too.

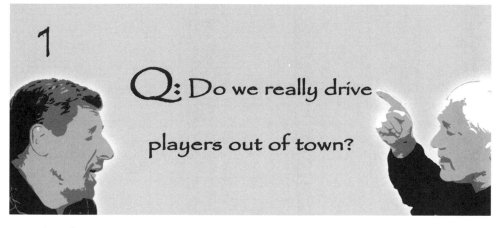

1

Q: Do we really drive players out of town?

Angelo says: Most media people would cringe at the allegation that they ran a player or coach out of town.

I consider it a compliment.

After 20 years in Philadelphia, I can say with absolute conviction that I helped move one player, one manager, and two owners outside the city limits. And we're all much better off that they left, believe me.

Would you dare to suggest that I had nothing to do with the firing of Phillies manager Terry Francona in 2000, Glen? Maybe I should refresh your memory.

Near the end of his fourth consecutive season of glaring incompetence, I decided to do a little research. I looked into what effect Francona's managing had—not just on the fortunes of the team, but also on attendance. I figured that bad baseball had become bad business. Then I invited his boss, general manager Ed Wade, onto my television show.

Within minutes, I was jowl to jowl with Wade, who staunchly defended his butt-kissing, strategy-impaired manager. At one point, when Wade suggested that I had no idea what I was talking about, I flashed onto the screen the attendance numbers as they related to the team's declining record under Francona.

I really didn't have to say anything else. The numbers finished the job for me. In the space of three weeks, Wade went from supporting Francona to firing him. Now I can't say that our exchange on TV completely swayed Wade, but I can say that it swayed someone —probably the owners of the team, who cared a lot more about the bottom line than the standings.

In any event, Francona was shown the door. He later referred to his time in Philadelphia as "a mulligan." I'd say it was more like a triple-bogey.

And then there's the odd case of Eagles lineman John Welbourn. Now this might not fit a precise definition of "running out of town," Glen, but the incident definitely led to his sudden departure.

Welbourn was sick of playing for an Eagles team that he felt did not reward its veterans. He wanted out. So he called me at home one night and said he wanted to appear on my radio show. He even told me his intention was to infuriate coach Andy Reid so much that there would be no choice but to trade him. Reid had been quoted that week in the papers saying he would not consider a deal for Welbourn.

Sure enough, the next morning, the big lineman came on the air and ripped into the team's front office, the recent drafting record of Reid and the Eagles' insensitivity to players reaching age 30. (He conveniently played down the fact that he had signed a long-term deal that he no longer wanted to honor.) He also promised to come on my show after every game and talk about the inner workings of the Eagles.

Two days after that appearance, Welbourn was traded to Kansas City.

In my long tenure on WIP Radio, I led fan revolts that resulted indirectly in many trades and releases. Shawn Bradley, Izel Jenkins, Mitch Williams, Keith Van Horn, J. D. Drew, Chris Gratton, James Thrash . . . the list is endless.

But I am most proud of creating an environment that led to the departures of two boils on the ass of Philadelphia sports: Norman Braman and Harold Katz.

Braman was a pompous, money-vacuuming Eagles owner who loved money and hated dissent. The only way to loosen his grip on the ownership of the team was to have the criticism seep into his pretentious little world of champagne and villas. For the final four years of his seven-year tenure, we were all relentless at WIP in painting him as a greedy, baguette-eating dilettante. His image was stained forever. Eventually, he gave up and sold the team. (Of course, for much more than it was worth at the time.)

Meanwhile, Katz hated the incessant drip-drip-drip of criticism so much that he actually moved back to Florida near the end of his 16 years as owner of the Sixers. By then he was vulnerable to the overtures of a determined salesman, and so he really had no chance when Pat Croce talked him into signing on the dotted line. Yes, Croce was the point man in the transaction, but it was the media—and especially WIP—that set the whole process into motion.

If it sounds like I enjoy ridding our city of these scoundrels and ne'er-do-wells, Glen, please understand. I *do*. Philadelphia has a reputation for being a tough media town. We don't suffer fools well.

Goodbye to Terry and John, to Norman and Harold, and to all of the others that we sent packing.

I'd like to say we miss them, but we don't.

Glen says: You flatter yourself, Angelo. Gee, you ran John Welbourn out of town?

Get serious. Welbourn used *you* to hack his way to Kansas City. All you did was serve as a caddie.

Who else are you taking credit for? James Thrash? A no-talent God Squadder, whom Eagles management stubbornly held onto for too long. Do you really believe Andy Reid took his cues from WIP when he replaced Thrash with Terrell Owens? Gosh, thanks for showing him the light.

Terry Francona? If the media (or fans) really had power, we wouldn't have suffered through four full years of that bumbling idiot. C'mon, Wade just didn't want to publicly cook a lame duck on your TV show a short time before canning him.

J.D. Drew? That's pretty good. Now you're applauding yourself for driving out a guy who never even showed up in the first place.

Your list is chock full of underachievers and journeymen who never had a prayer of a long stay in Philadelphia. The thing that really ran Izel Jenkins out of the Vet was a Michael Irvin post pattern, not the power and venom of some big-nosed radio host.

And, as for the owners, while I'll concede that Katz and Braman probably grew weary of the bleating of the masses, they didn't depart until they found rubes willing to overpay for their franchises. If you actually influenced Braman, I hope he takes some of the $196 million he got from Jeff Lurie and sends you an annual Christmas card from his villa on the Riviera.

No, any argument about Philadelphia chasing away its players has to focus on the talented ones, not the mediocrities. Because our national reputation is based not on what we may have done to Van Horn, Gratton and Williams, it's based on what we (supposedly) do to our superstars.

It comes from moronic statements like this: "The media ran Scott Rolen out of town. Scotty was a good guy, but when he turned down the money, they turned on him. They ran Eric Lindros out of town, and they ran Randall Cunningham out of town. They're good fans, but what happens is that when the press turns against you, they kind of roll with the punches. Once they turn on you, you've got no chance."

That nonsense comes from the yap of Charles Barkley, who's also frequently put on the list of our alleged victims. But no one packed Charles' suitcase but Charles himself (well, I'll give Katz an assist there). The fans here loved Charles, even after he branded us stupid and racist.

Let's look at the other guys that Barkley cites:

Rolen: Here's another guy who forged his own path to the Midwest. Rolen never fit on the East Coast, never wanted to play here. The fans and media had nothing to do with this *miserable* ending up in St. Louis.

Lindros: Most Flyers fans stayed loyal to Eric to the bitter end. The media appreciated him, as well. It was Bob Clarke—and Lindros' parents—who caused this relationship to sour. I still see more than a dozen No. 88 jerseys every time I go to a Flyers game.

Cunningham: The most ridiculous charge of all, although our critics continue to allege it. Randall spent 11 seasons with the Eagles, a tenure surpassed by just six players in the franchise's seven-decade history. If we were really trying to chase him away, he was a better scrambler than people even give him credit for.

The supposed crucifixion of our superstars remains one of those horrible myths that people spew about Philadelphia fans (I hear a couple of guys wrote a bit on the topic, Ange. You may want to check out, *The Great Philadelphia Fan Book*.) That you not only buy into the myth, but want to promulgate it, shows how misguided you are.

Hey, if you really have that much power, how about turning your attention to something more important? See if you can do something about removing Mayor John Street from office before he does further damage to our great city.

Oh, that's right. You tried mightily to do that the last time Street was up for re-election. So much for all that unbridled influence.

8

Q: What's the worst move ever by a Philadelphia coach?

Glen says: No debate here, Angelo. My nominee is so egregious that it probably cost the Phillies a trip to the World Series. The crime was committed by one of the dumbest managers in history, Danny Ozark. It even has its own nickname—"Black Friday."

You remember the setup. The Phils and Dodgers were tied at one game apiece as the 1977 National League Championship Series came to Philadelphia. Game 3 started perfectly—63,000 championship-starved fans literally heckled Dodgers starter Burt Hooton from the mound in the second inning. We goaded the Dodgers' fidgety starter into four straight walks and a public nervous breakdown.

The Phillies had a 5-3 lead heading into the ninth. When Gene Garber retired the first two Dodgers, the fans rose up, ready to celebrate. Remember, the NLCS was a best-of-five series back then, and with Steve Carlton set to pitch the next night, well, who had reason to fear anything?

Except, then . . .

First, pinch hitter Vic Davalillo beat out a perfect two-strike drag bunt.

That brought up 39-year-old pinch hitter Manny Mota. No big deal, we all thought. In fact, how many among us realized at the time that the bumbling Ozark had already committed the gaffe that would make him infamous?

For the entire season, Ozark had removed leftfielder Greg "Bull" Luzinski—who ran with all the speed of a glacier—in the ninth inning and replaced him with defensive ace Jerry Martin. Except on this night, Ozark didn't.

Why not?

Ozark later explained that he wanted Luzinski in the lineup just in case the Dodgers rallied. Yo, Danny, way to let yourself be ruled by negative thinking.

His own players heard a different story. Recently I asked Phils manager—and 1980 shortstop—Larry Bowa about the game. He tersely spit out his recollections. "I didn't get it," he said. "I remember running out the short for the ninth inning and waiting for Jerry Martin to go by, and here comes the Bull. I said, 'What's he doing out here?' A teammate told that Danny wanted Bull to be on the field to celebrate the win."

Nice sentiment, bad strategy. Pinch hitter Mota sliced a pitch to deep left. Luzinski took a step or two in, and then realized the ball was going over his head. The big man lumbered back, groping for the ball, which glanced off his glove for a double.

"No rap against Bull," Bowa told me, "but Jerry Martin catches that ball every time."

Instead of ending the game, Ozark's stupidity opened up a box of bad karma. A couple of bleeding hits, a questionable umpire's call, an error, and the 5-3 lead quickly turned into a 6-5 loss. The *Daily News'* Bill Conlin called it "the most devastating single defeat in ballclub history, a 10-minute collapse that was a half-inning version of 1964."

The next night, in a gloomy rain, the Dodgers' Tommy John out-pitched Steve Carlton, and the pennant was gone.

"It was the toughest loss of my career," Bowa told me. "It just took so much out of me, out of the team and out of the fans. I still believe that 1977 team, talent-wise, was the best I ever played for."

Somehow, Ozark survived his own stupidity. Phils fans showed their feelings early the next season by hanging the manager in effigy in leftfield—Luzinski's post, ironically. In a later interview with the *Daily News*, Ozark conceded, "Maybe Jerry Martin would have caught the ball. Who knows?"

Jerry Martin knows. "I can still see the ball," Martin said in the same story. "I can see it plain as day. In my heart, I believe we would've gone to the World Series had I been in leftfield for just that one play."

One play. One inning. One game. One big, fat, bumbling gaffe by a village idiot of a manager.

Angelo says: You've got the right sport, Glen, but the wrong year. Let's try to approach this question with simple, deductive reasoning. Here are a series of questions all leading to the same conclusion:

What was the worst failure in Philadelphia sports history?

How responsible was the coach or manager for that disaster?

Did the coach or manager do something so ridiculous that it was never repeated?

Now I realize that I'm showing my age, but it is widely accepted that there has never been a collapse like that of the 1964 Phillies, nor a managerial meltdown ever to approach Gene Mauch's in the final weeks of that season.

To this day, people are incredulous when they hear that a manager with a 6 ½-game lead and 12 games remaining would opt for a two-man pitching rotation in the final two weeks of the season. That's right, a *two-man pitching rotation*.

Jim Bunning and Chris Short were those two pitchers, and by the end, they literally could not lift their arms over their heads to comb their hair. At 32, Bunning ended the year with 284 innings, Short with 220. They were probably relieved they didn't have to pitch in the World Series.

By nature a nervous, ill-tempered man, Mauch simply didn't have any faith in 24-year-old Art Mahaffey or young phenom Rick Wise. Mahaffey had made the fatal mistake of allowing Chico Ruiz to steal home on September 21, costing the Phils what appeared to be a meaningless late-season tune-up for the Series.

But Mauch was not able to shrug off the mental error by his pitcher, so he opted instead for the two-man rotation. Even in that era, when pitchers routinely went to the mound every fourth day, it was unheard of to try to run them out there every *other* day. But Mauch wasn't going to blow that big a lead.

Of course, that's exactly what he did. The Phils went on to lose ten straight, sending the franchise and the city into a tailspin that took more than a decade to overcome. The subsequent verbal attacks by fans against star first baseman Richie Allen developed racial overtones, the Ruiz blunder became a metaphor for an entire city's futility and Mauch was justifiably vilified throughout the land for his insane plan.

Mauch would never win a championship, despite a 26-season career as a manager. And to the very end, he would defend his strategy, though he never used it again.

"When I think back, I think about what a wonderful that season was," he said in 1989. "I refuse to think about anything else."

Now let's compare this historic mistake with the glitch you chose, Glen. Granted, Danny Ozark was no Einstein, either. He will forever be known more for his malapropos than his mental acuity, but how can you even compare what he did to the 1964 collapse?

Can anyone say with absolute certainty that Jerry Martin would have caught that ball even if he were in the game instead of Greg Luzinski? OK, so maybe Larry Bowa can say it, but maybe Martin wouldn't have been positioned exactly where the Bull was. And while it was incredibly dumb, Ozark's desire to have Luzinski on the field for the celebration at least contained a tinge of sentiment.

Since that gaffe in 1977, there have been countless times when equally inept managers have used the wrong outfielders or made bad pitching decisions (Roger Mason in 1993, for example), but how many times have managers used only two starting pitchers and blown a huge lead in the final weeks of a season?

The answer, of course, is none. Mauch's stupidity that year has never been replicated.

When I was about to send in this piece to be included in the book, I bumped into one of the greatest sports journalists in Philadelphia history, Stan Hochman of the *Daily News*. Stan covered the 1964 collapse and was also there in 1977 for the Martin mistake. I asked Hochman to decide this argument.

Do I have to tell you who wins, Glen?

Mauch, by a mile.

9

Q: Has Bob Clarke been a failure?

Angelo says: There will never be another player like Bobby Clarke. He was the perfect Philadelphia superstar—ruthless and relentless. Elegance and sportsmanship are for the West Coast teams. In blue-collar Philadelphia, we like our Stanley Cups smeared with a little blood.

There will never be another general manager like Bob Clarke. Who else would be given 16 seasons to win a championship, all the while receiving the blind support of management and a limitless bank account? Who else would fail that many times and still hold the same job?

Let's face it, the relationship between the Flyers father figure Ed Snider and his prodigal son has been disastrous for many years now. Snider is like a poker addict who keeps playing the same hand—and keeps losing. He's positive the cards will be different the next time, but they're not.

The boss doesn't know when to fold 'em.

He doesn't know when to walk away from Bobby Clarke.

And therein lies the real problem. Snider sees *Bobby* Clarke, not *Bob* Clarke. He sees the wide, toothless grin and the Stanley Cups. He never sees the gray hair and the barren trophy case. Snider is living in the past.

But this situation, like the relationship behind it, is more complex than just the loyalty between two men. How strange is it that Snider's surrogate son was fired once by the organization, and that was by Snider's real son, Jay. How weird is it that Jay is out of sports now while Bob labors, year after year, with no sign of an end to the title drought.

This may be the first case in sports history of reverse nepotism. The son got one chance. The surrogate son got two.

People ask all the time what it will take to convince Snider to get rid of Bob Clarke for good. These questions usually crop up in the spring, right after another respectable regular season is followed by another playoff ouster. The answer is: NOTHING.

Look at it this way: If the 2000-01 season didn't seal Clarke's doom as GM, what will? After performing his usual mad-scientist routine with the roster, Clarke also managed that year to conduct, simultaneously, a bloody feud with the Philadelphia media, a bitter public battle with his star player, Eric Lindros, and Lindros' parents, and the GM still found time to denigrate the reputation of a head coach, Roger Neilson, who was dying of cancer.

That was a full season by anyone's standards. When it was over—when Clarke had changed coaches yet again—Snider saw fit to give Clarke a vote of confidence.

Now *that's* loyalty.

But enough is enough. There has to be a statute of limitations on everything, including two Stanley Cups. There has to be someone—maybe the Comcast executives who are footing the bill now—who is willing to stop this madness before we have to wait another 30 years for a Stanley Cup.

Bob Clarke had his chance to bring another championship to Philadelphia. Sixteen chances, to be exact.

It's time to go, Bob. The statute has finally run out.

And so has our patience.

Glen says: Failure? No, failure means losing. In his second turn as general manager, Clarke's Flyers have strung together a decade of winning seasons. Failure in the NHL means not making the playoffs. Clarke's team has done that 10 years in a row, a feat matched by just three other franchises.

Look, Clarke's got his warts. I'll grant you that, Angelo. His feud with Eric Lindros showed his vindictive side—although even you must concede that some blame for that fiasco goes to Bonnie and Carl Lindros. The Roger Neilson affair was handled horribly from a public relations standpoint, but I'll still agree with Clarke that Neilson, wracked with cancer, was in no shape to go back behind the bench during the 2000 playoff run.

Bob Clarke lacks diplomacy. He will never win the Lady Byng Trophy for executives. He makes enemies and plays dirty. Just like he did as a player.

None of those shortcomings, however, prevent him from being one of his sport's most respected general managers.

Yes, the Flyers have not won a Stanley Cup in 16 years under Clarke's tenure—a drought that runs concurrent with the three other Philadelphia teams. They have, however, won eight division titles and been to four Stanley Cup finals. They are 244 games above .500, averaging 98 points for every 82-game season. Can any other local sports executive

46

boast of that success?

You focus a lot on Clarke's snarly demeanor, Angelo, but ignore the nuts and bolts on which GMs are judged. Start with the draft. In the past five years, the Flyers picked Simon Gagne, Antero Nittymaki, Roman Cechmanek, Justin Williams, Joni Pitkanen and Dennis Seidenberg. Some have been swapped for veteran players, some are now part of the Flyers' nucleus. Not too shabby.

Now, let's look at trades. Years ago, Clarke sent Mark Recchi to Montreal for John LeClair and Eric Desjardins. You like that one? Then, he got Recchi back from the Canadiens for non-entity Dainius Zubrus. A steal. Or, how about trading the overrated Brian Boucher to Phoenix for Michal Handzus and Robert Esche? Clarke must have been wielding a gun and wearing a mask when he pulled off that robbery.

He even got the best of the Lindros deal in the end, sending poor Eric to the Rangers for rising star Kim Johnsson, winger Pavel Brendl (whom he then swapped for Sami Kapanen) and Jan Hlavac (whom he spun into Donald Brashear).

I've also got no complaints about him signing free agent Jeremy Roenick. How about you, Ange?

Is Bob Clarke the best GM in hockey? No, that title goes to Lou Lamoriello of the New Jersey Devils, who does more with less. I'd also rank him behind Montreal's Bob Gainey (formerly of the Dallas Stars), Colorado's Pierre Lacroix and Detroit's Ken Holland.

After that first tier, Clarke's right there, prickly side and all. Now, you could fire him and bring back your pal Jay Snider, Angelo. But recall that the Flyers managed the near-impossible by missing the playoffs four straight years during his tenure. Maybe there's another available genius out there like, say—Russ Farwell.

Impatience is understandable. But sometimes stability makes more sense. Given enough time, perhaps Clarke will even cure his blind spot with goalies.

10

Q: Who's the enemy, the Cowboys or the Giants?

Glen says: I can't believe you're even attempting to argue this, Angelo. The enemy of the state around here has always been, and will forever remain, the Dallas Cowboys.

The Giants may be the annoying next-door neighbors, while the Cowboys live a few blocks farther away. And the Giants-Eagles rivalry may have the edge in longevity, although I don't recall much about those Tommy Thompson vs. Frankie Filchock classics from the 1940s. What I do know is that the greatest highlights—and lowlights—for current-day Eagles fans always involve the Cowboys:

Wilbert Montgomery off right tackle in the 1980 NFC title game. Fourth-and-one – twice. The Bounty Bowl. The Snowball Game. Troy Vincent's 104-yard interception return. The Pickle Juice Game. The cheap hits on Timmy Brown and Harold Carmichael. Tim Hauck's kill shot on Michael Irvin.

The Cowboys are a loathsome legacy of hardened criminals and preening psychopaths, from Hollywood Henderson to Nate Newton. The black hat passes from Landry to Johnson to Switzer to Parcells. From Meredith to Staubach to Aikman to . . . hey, does Dallas even have a quarterback these days?

Meanwhile, who has been worth hating on the Giants all these years? Nice-guy Phil Simms?

The anti-Dallas passion engulfed the Vet on all those "F— Dallas!" T-shirts and in Judge Seamus's courtroom. The frenzy would start the Monday morning of Cowboys week and build right up through the final whistle, as McNabb (or Randall or Jaws) took a knee in victory and we hoarsely threw whatever invective we had left at those blue-starred losers running off the field. You know that passion well, Angelo. You led the fans' cheers before one Monday night Dallas affair on a WIP pre-game show that lasted 15 rowdy hours.

And fans are what this rivalry is all about. Giants loyalists—at least those in our area —are mostly older, quieter North Jersey refugees who know enough to clam up in mixed company. But Cowboys fans are as abrasive and irritating as that pebble stuck in your wing tip.

The seeds of our hatred were planted during an awful earlier era, when the Cowboys routinely tortured our guys. Dallas won 21 of 23 games between the teams from 1967-1978. Most were blowouts. Good Eagles fans toughed it out through those years, but weak-willed front-runners bailed. They joined the Evil Empire, dressed in those hideous blue-and-white Starter jackets and strutted around town nasally crowing, "How 'bout them Cowboys!" Sadly, they still turn up in the best of families (not mine, however). They are traitors who must be disowned.

Let me quote that eminent psychologist James David Ryan, who once said, "The first thing you learn about Philadelphia fans is that to get on their good side, all you have to do is beat the Cowboys twice a year. So I made that my goal, just to please the people."

Dr. Ryan, affectionately known as Buddy, came through on that pledge. He never won a playoff game, but he whipped the Cowboys seven straight times between 1987 and 1990.

Ask any Eagles fan why he still adores Buddy, and he'll start by talking about 1987. That was the year of the NFL players strike, and the two teams met for a scab game in Dallas. Landry rubbed our noses in it by using his star players who had crossed the picket line against a bunch of junior college dropouts dressed as pseudo-Eagles.

The first game after the strike ended happened to be against the Cowboys at the Vet. Playing with his regulars now, Ryan built up a 10-point lead. With a minute to play and the Birds in possession, Randall Cunningham twice took a knee as Dallas used up its timeouts. The end of the game appeared imminent. But on third down, Randall faked the knee, dropped back and launched one into the end zone for Mike Quick. Dallas' cornerbacks panicked and drew a pass interference call. On the next play, Keith Byars plunged it in from the one, giving the Birds a needless extra touchdown and giving us all sweet revenge.

It was vindictive, and we loved it. Landry called Buddy a man of "no class," but we knew who the lowlife was. Sometimes, you get the bully back.

Oh, and one more thing, Angelo.

As I've heard even you say:

"Dallas sucks."

Angelo says: The hatred that Philadelphia has for New York is unlike any city in America. As someone who has lived in both places, I totally understand it. New York is the phoniest, most pretentious city on earth. Philadelphia is home to me—tough, feisty and honest.

When they don't like you in New York, they wait for you to turn your back. Then they plunge the knife right between your shoulder blades.

In Philly, they'll just spit in your eye.

I'm no psychologist like your brilliant Dr. Ryan, Glen, but I think this hatred extends to the rivalry between the Eagles and Giants. And again, I speak from a position of knowledge. You see, I was a Giants fan. My son still is. I take no pride in either of those statements.

When the Giants take the field to face the Eagles, the rancor is bitter. Those who populated the sorely missed 700 Level at Veterans Stadium would tell you there was simply no better motivation for a brawl than the sight of someone wearing a New York Giants jersey. There was so much blood spilled at those games, some Philly fans actually believe red is part of the Giants color scheme.

The Cowboys are an entirely different story. Yes, they are hated, too. All of those memorable moments you cite, Glen, are truly among the best highlights in Eagles history. But how many of them signify a championship?

Uh, that would be none. The Eagles haven't won a championship since 1960, when the Cowboys were in their very first year of existence.

If you want a really meaningful moment, you'll have to go back a little further than Tim Hauck's "kill shot" on Michael Irvin. You'll have to travel back to the days of Chuck Bednarik, where you will need a new definition for "kill shot."

You might recall, in that championship year of 1960, Concrete Charlie greeted Frank Gifford with a shot over the middle that was felt by Frank, Frank's father and three generations of Giffords before that. It made Hauck's hit on Irvin look more like a smooch.

Bednarik's devastating blow is the single most revered moment in the history of the Eagles. Nothing else comes close, and you know it, Glen.

And that's where you and many others make your mistake. You value style over substance. You measure the volume of "Dallas sucks!" chants instead of studying the shallow emotion behind it. You make proclamations about today without looking at yesterday.

The hatred of the Cowboys is as deep as the threadbare turf of Veterans Stadium and as enduring as the latest chant. The hatred of the Giants is at the very deep roots of the emotion between the two cities. To New York, Philadelphia is a mosquito buzzing around the head of the Statue of Liberty. They swat at us. We want to bite them.

We don't just hate the Giants. We hate the Rangers and the Knicks, the Mets and the Yankees, the Jets, the Islanders, the Empire State Building, Rockefeller Center, New York delis and Manhattan.

Dallas does suck, Glen.

But if you really want to sink your teeth into something, try a Big Apple.

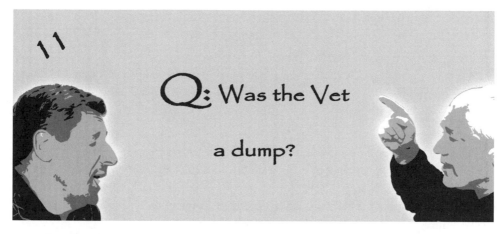

Q: Was the Vet a dump?

Angelo says: For most of its 32 years as a sports facility, Veterans Stadium was reviled and ridiculed as an atrocious place to play or see a game. It didn't even matter if the game was baseball or football; the Vet was an equal-opportunity dump.

My voice was among the loudest in criticism of the place, for all of the obvious reasons. It was cold and dank, the field was too far from the stands, the turf was a green tarmac and the atmosphere was akin to a mausoleum. And, oh yeah, it was riddled with rats, cockroaches and every other appalling, crawling creature known to man.

And yet I'm here now to preach the virtues of the Vet, not the flaws. Veterans Stadium was not just a pit, it was *our* pit. It was not just a pit, it was a *snake*pit—the ultimate weapon against opponents who didn't like vicious fans or decrepit trappings.

Who will ever forget the tableau of Michael Irvin lying on that cratered, unforgiving surface, his career in ruins, as teammate Deion Sanders marched in a ritualistic circle around Irvin's motionless body? Or the time Wendell Davis of Chicago leapt for a pass and managed to blow out both knees when his feet got caught in a pothole?

The end of an athlete's career is never a time for celebration, and yet those mishaps only enhanced the legend of a terrible, yet wonderful place.

Veterans Stadium was home to only one champion, the 1980 Phillies. But it housed its share of stunning moments: Tug McGraw and Pete Rose in 1980, Steve Carlton in '72, Macho Row and the miracle season of '93, Mike Schmidt every year of his amazing career.

And then there were the 1980 Eagles and their unforgettable run to the Super Bowl. In many minds, Wilbert Montgomery will be running forever for the clinching touchdown against the Dallas Cowboys. And don't forget the marauding Eagles of Buddy Ryan—Reggie White, Jerome Brown, Andre Waters, Randall Cunningham, and so many more. A team that won nothing has never been loved more than that eccentric collection.

During the creation of all those great memories, no one was complaining about

Veterans Stadium. In fact, in its own gruff way, the old building made all of it so much better. The mere phrase "700 Level" will embody forever the fervor of the Philadelphia sports fan as no other words ever could.

A walk through the 700 Level was a visit to the inner core of the Philly fan—rough, drunk, hostile or jovial (depending on the score), profane, insane. You didn't like that image? Then bleep you! Why don't you try wearing a Cowboys jacket next time, tough guy?

The Vet was who we were, at a time when Philadelphia wore its reputation on its beer-and-blood-soaked sleeve. Only in its final months did the fans suddenly realize what they were losing. Lincoln Financial Field opened, and fans wondered if they had to remove their shoes before they crossed the threshold. Its inside looks more like a posh hotel than a football stadium.

Yes, the Eagles have a shiny new home now, and so do the Phillies. But those homes represent the dreams of their owners, not their fans. Even the names, sold to the highest bidder, are symbols of a pervasive greed. Veterans Stadium was dedicated to the brave people who defended our country. The namesakes of the two new stadiums offer bridge loans and free checking accounts.

So pardon me if my praise for the new places is muffled. Yes, they are beautiful. Yes, their fields are soft and sweet. Yes, there's more leg room and great scoreboards and you're so close to the field, you can smell the players.

They are a great place to visit.

But for the real Philly fans, Veterans Stadium will always be home, sweet home.

Glen says: You sound like my father, Angelo. That shouldn't be surprising, I suppose, since you're about the same age.

Anyway, my dad was raised in the poorest of tenement neighborhoods, sharing a bed with his grandfather and one bathroom with nine relatives. The roof leaked, the electricity was iffy. When he grew up and earned a few bucks, Marv Macnow bought a house in the suburbs. It wasn't a palace, but we each had our own bedroom. And there were no lines outside the bathrooms.

Still, my father curiously missed the rat-hole he had escaped. Not because it was nice, but because it was where his memories lived.

Veterans Stadium is where our memories live. And that's great.

But don't confuse the place for anything that it wasn't. In the land of stadiums, it's a sixth-floor walkup with leaky pipes.

The Vet—like leisure suits and disco—was part of a misguided 1970s trend of cookie-cutter stadiums. At the time, a concrete bowl housing both football and baseball seemed like a great idea. Turned out, it made as much sense as trying to build one place to house billiards and auto racing.

The big donut (officially, it was termed an octorad) served neither sport well. The 50-yard-line seats for Eagles games seemed as far away as the Jersey Shore. The symmetrical shape took away the quirks that give ballparks their personality. And the size was totally unsuited for baseball. Sure, the 700 Level had fervor during a good Eagles game, but try sitting there during a late-season Phillies contest. You'd have an entire section to yourself.

It wasn't just visitors who hated the place. Mike Schmidt whined of "cat stink" outside the clubhouse (although Schmidt whining about anything is no major revelation). John Gruden, when he was offensive coordinator of the Eagles, heard a strange noise above his head one day while sitting in his office. He looked up, only to see a huge rat come crashing through the drop ceiling onto his desk. As the rat scurried away, a cat tumbled through the hole in quick pursuit.

And then there was the turf. Spread a thin layer of indoor-outdoor across I-95 and dive onto it. That's how the players felt.

The joint was built on the cheap and under scandal. The stadium manager was indicted for taking a $10,000 kickback from a seating contractor. As construction costs skyrocketed, chief architect Hugh Stubbins, Jr. was ordered to eliminate bells and whistles. "Everything was cut to the bone," he complained. Including, eventually, the joints of those playing on it.

Need I go on? The food stunk—and was over-priced to boot. The bathrooms . . . well, let's just say I could have lived without the time I had to explain to my eight-year-old why a grown man was urinating in the sink.

I will not aim to take away your memories, Ange, because they're all of ours. But this ain't Yankee Stadium or Lambeau Field in any historical sense. Hell, it isn't even the Spectrum in that regard. It isn't just that only one title was ever won in the place. Consider that there were just 27 winning seasons by the Eagles and Phillies out of a possible 65.

No argument here that our two new ballparks have a bit of an antiseptic feel. That's just the newness. It's like when you buy a new car—you wash it every week and don't dare leave food wrappers on the seat. Give us a little time, we'll be spilling coffee on the dashboard. We'll make the Linc and Citizens Park our own. Putting us into a palace ain't gonna civilize the great unwashed Philadelphia fans.

By the way, not long ago, my dad went back to the old neighborhood to find his childhood apartment building. He discovered it had been razed, and replaced by a car-crushing yard. Across the street stood a pornographic video store.

Some memories are best just left alone.

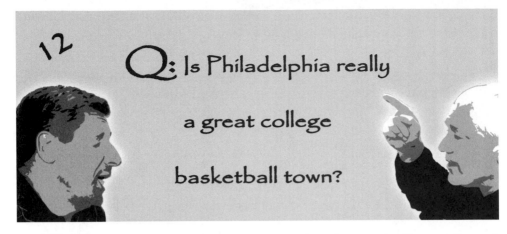

Q: Is Philadelphia really a great college basketball town?

12

Glen says: I'm astounded that you want to debate this, Angelo. If you really need an answer, just wander the halls of the Palestra for a few hours. You know where that building is, don't you? This "part museum, part hall of fame" highlights the greatest moments of Philadelphia basketball. It should convince you that no city in America can boast as rich a history of college hoops.

Take a look at the display cases: Kenny Durrett's tattered old LaSalle jersey. A photo of those great Temple teammates—Eddie Jones and Aaron McKie—smiling after another win. Statistics of the Big Five's great coaches—Jack Ramsey and John Chaney and Chuck Daly (boy, his hair is perfect). And isn't that Yo-Yo in the background?

There are five separate and distinct college basketball communities in our city—six if you include Drexel. Each has its history and its traditions, its heroes and its highlights. There is a passion and hatred among the six (especially, let's be honest, toward Villanova), that sometimes divides the overall fan base into armed camps.

And that's what you fail to recognize, Ange. This isn't like football, where we all root for the Eagles. Nor is it like college basketball in, say, Kansas, where every toddler in the state is taught to chant, "Rock, Chalk, Jayhawk" from the start. It's different here, because there isn't one focal point. So the traditional sports-radio debates we use in other venues don't work for college basketball. No one from LaSalle really wonders whether Phil Martelli should get a hair transplant.

But don't confuse that with not caring about the sport. Mention former Nova coach Rollie Massimino's name to any one of the 230,000 living alumni of Temple University and chances are he or she will spit on the ground in disgust. Or check out any Penn vs. St. Joe's game at the Palestra (33rd and Walnut, Ange, just so you know). From the insulting fratboy rollouts ("Penn grades—More inflated than the basketball"), to the crispness of the dueling bands to the ear-splitting shouts of 8,000 college kids trapped in this glorious oversized garage. This, my friend, is college sports as it should be—not played in a dome, or at Enormous State U., or on prime time network television. But in the city that really understands the game and its history.

Ah, the history. Paul Arizin and Tom Gola. Guy Rodgers and Matt Goukas. Harold Porter and the Villanova scandal of 1971. Eddie Pinckney and the 1985 miracle against Georgetown. Mark Macon and the Elite Eight. Lionel Simmons topping 3,000 points for LaSalle. And be sure to add in the Jameer Nelson-Delonte West St. Joe Hawks of 2004, the scrappy squad from City Avenue that hustled to an undefeated regular season and allowed us to write in a local team at the top of our NCAA office pools without feeling foolish.

Truth be told, none of the local teams will likely win a national championship in this era. Those giant land-grant universities, with zillions of football dollars bolstering the budget, dominate the sport. Every once a decade or so, a Simmons or a Nelson (basically, a homegrown kid overlooked by the Dukes and Kentuckys) will give us a few weeks of hope, but, in reality, just getting to the Final Four alone would be an incredible feat.

That's a shame. But it doesn't lessen Philadelphia as a great college hoops town. If you can't make it to the Palestra, try the Liacouris Center, or the St. Joe's Fieldhouse or even the Ski Lodge out on the Main Line. Try for a night when two Big Five schools are going at it. It doesn't matter who's favored, or who's having a better season. Because records mean nothing in these great rivalries. Passion means everything. That's why this is a great college basketball town.

Oh, and by the way, Angelo: The Hawk will never die.

Angelo says: When I was writing about sports in my hometown of Providence, Rhode Island in 1983, the reason I finally agreed to relocate to Philadelphia was because it was a *pro* sports town, not a *college* town. I hated college sports then, and I still do today.

I was not disappointed once I got here. The first week, I got to see the Phillies fire their manager while the team was in first place. It was love at first sight for me. I felt like I had graduated to the big leagues myself.

And nothing over the past generation has changed my mind. Where I grew up, college sports was the only sports. Unless you witness a real college town, Glen, you cannot see the difference. That's why you're at a big disadvantage in this debate.

You grew up in Buffalo, which is not a college town either. It's minor league, sure, but not college. A college town is about bonfires before the big game, pep rallies, coeds in tight sweaters, keg parties, panty raids, and sis-boom-bah.

Yes, Philadelphia has six great schools, and it does have some impressive history. (How could it not? All of those years, all of those players, you're bound to develop some heroes, no?) The Palestra is a magnificent place. I'll give you that, too.

But a great building and some great teams do not make a college town. It's a state of mind, a perspective based on the unbridled joy of youth, not the edgy cynicism of middle age.

A college town does not boo Santa Claus. It's that simple.

You want it both ways, Glen. You want Philadelphia to be a great pro town and a great college town. There is no such thing. Great college towns are Happy Valley, Pennsylvania, or Ann Arbor, Michigan, or—of course—South Bend, Indiana. They are small, intense pockets of fans who wear the sweatshirts of their local college and count the days till the next game.

The best way for me to explain this, in a way you can relate, is to analyze the 2003-

Try to tell John Chaney this isn't a terrific city for college hoops.

04 miracle season of the Saint Joseph's Hawks. It's hard to imagine a more amazing combination of elements: two memorable players (Jameer Nelson and Delonte West), a compelling, accessible coach (Phil Martelli) and a perfect regular season.

Even their ouster from the NCAA tournament in the Elite Eight was something that will be remembered for many years, losing in the final seconds on a flukey play by Oklahoma State.

As someone who has worked the phone lines at WIP for 15 years, I have been able to gauge the level of interest just by the volume of calls after big games. The Hawks, even at their absolute pinnacle, did not approach the response after an early-season game by the Eagles.

More significant, St. Joe's in 2004, on my radio show, ranked no better than fourth among the teams eliciting fan response—behind the Eagles, the Sixers, and the Phillies, in that order.

And this was after the most amazing season in Hawks history!

As for your invitation to go out to St. Joe's Fieldhouse, I already did, Glen. What I found there was a group of rowdy kids, some happy alumni and a sprinkling of average fans. The people on Hawk Hill loved it. The rest of the city watched on, passively. It was a nice story, sure. Something to do till the Eagles strap on the shoulder pads again.

From those early days back in Providence, I developed a theory about college sports. I think they're a lot like college itself. You should savor every day, every game, while you're in college, and then move on. Graduate. Move up to the pros. Trade in the college sweater for a business suit.

That's the whole point of college, isn't it?

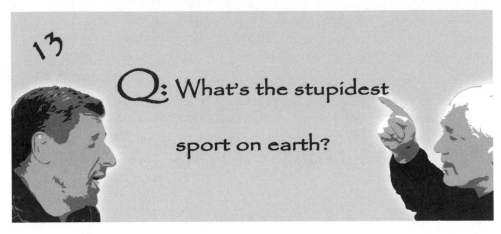

13

Q: What's the stupidest sport on earth?

Angelo says: There's one mystery in sports these days that is driving me absolutely insane, Glen. Every time the national TV ratings come out, I don't just fret that baseball and basketball and even hockey are all losing popularity in America. No, it's much deeper than that.

I worry about the future of our country. I worry about literacy rates. I worry about the IQ of our kids. I worry that the United States of America is becoming the United States of Stupidity.

What other explanation is there for the increasing popularity of NASCAR?

Think about it: People would prefer to watch cars belch exhaust as they careen around and around and around a track for hours than to savor the intricate strategy of a late-inning baseball game. People would rather swelter for hours in the hope that a car will spin out of control instead of indulging in the artistry of a Jason Kidd pass or the brutal force of a Shaquille O'Neal slam-dunk.

As I write this, in spring of 2004, the TV ratings for NASCAR on a typical weekend are twice that of the NBA playoffs, *three times* that of the NHL playoffs, and five times better (or more) than tennis, golf, or Arena Football. And I'm not talking about the Indy 500, Glen. This is just on a typical weekend!

To those of you out there who are watching this junk—if you'll pardon an insult in a book you've so kindly purchased—shame on you. Please seek professional help immediately. You are nuts.

This perspective comes from someone who has covered the Indy 500 (almost), who has been to the track many times and who has met the fine people who populate America's Dumbest Sport.

In fact, I was assigned to cover the Indy 500 for *The Philadelphia Inquirer* back in the mid-1980s. I'll never forget the moment when I got the assignment . . . .

Editor: We're sending you out to the Indy 500 for the next week.

Me: What did I do wrong?

Editor: Nothing. You'll thank me later.

The record will show that I most certainly did NOT thank him later. A week with those hillbillies and morons, and I was on suicide watch. The day of the event, we had to be at the track seven hours before the start of the race to avoid a massive traffic jam. The race was constantly delayed by thunderstorms. In the end, they rescheduled the event for the following weekend. I went home.

Editor: You can go back next weekend if you want.

Me: I'd rather cover a marbles tournament.

Here's the way I analyze auto racing, Glen: Cars go really, really fast. Occasionally, they crash. Huge delays ensue when it rains, a car spins out, or a bird poops on the track. Strategy involves when to take pit stops and when to pass the guy in front of you. Often, the race ends under a "yellow flag," which means someone couldn't hold in all the beer they consumed during the event, or something like that.

I realize there are a lot of bad sports, Glen. Horseracing isn't much better than NASCAR. Boxing is all but dead, and wrestling is for people one intellectual level above livestock (or auto racing fans). Tennis is boring. Swimming, soccer, softball . . . .they're all dreck. It says a lot about sports in the year 2004 that poker is becoming the newest TV craze. Poker!

But auto racing is in a place all its own right now because people are actually watching it. People are sitting down at home, tapping into a keg, firing up some ribs and they're watching cars whir around a track for hours.

The apocalypse must be close now, Glen.

The morons are taking over the world.

Glen says: Here's the good news, Angelo. While too many Americans may have embraced auto racing, they're at least smart enough to reject what is really the world's dumbest sport: Soccer.

NASCAR fans may be hillbillies (Note to readers: That's Ange's description, not mine. Complain to him.). But soccer devotees are something far more insidious. They're proselytizing geeks—like every reformed smoker, low-carb dieter, jogging drip who feels the moral need to sway you to his dreary way of life.

Soccer nerd: "It's really an exciting sport. You've got to try it."

Me: "I'd rather undergo a jalapeno enema."

Soccer is sport's version of the metric system—an archaic European institution that someone keeps trying to shove down American's throats. But just as we're not giving up our yards for meters (or metres, as *they'd* prefer), we're also not giving up our backyards for this garbage. As to the argument that soccer is the world's No. 1 sport, let me say that, (A) That's only because the rest of the world hasn't been exposed to football and basketball long enough, and (B) Just because they consider blood pudding a delicacy in Scotland doesn't mean I have to love that either.

Soccer nerd: "But more American children are playing soccer every year."

Me: "Maybe so. But more American children are also playing tee-ball and they grow out of that too. Soccer's just something kids are forced to play until they can tell Mommy to park the van so they can play something requiring more athletic skill—like bocce."

It makes me proud to be a Philadelphian that the Major Soccer League has never fielded a team here. And while it was a shame to see beauties like Lorrie Fair and Heather Mitts leave town, I sure didn't shed a tear over the demise of the women's professional league.

Soccer nerd: "But it really is a physical sport. Just watch."

Me: "Yeah, here's how physical it is. Every time one of those sissies gets so much as jostled by an opponent, he collapses as if struck by a Sherman tank, flails his arms in agony and twitches on the ground, trying to draw a yellow card (or green card, or whatever gets a penalty). Sure, they're tough guys, all right."

Why has soccer failed to catch on in America? Let me count the ways:

1) NOBODY EVER SCORES! You can't have a sport where the final score is 0-0. That's like calling dinner conversation a sport. I watched a game recently (at least until I could locate my remote) where one team went up 1-0 late in the first half.

Announcer: "That might be an insurmountable lead."

Me (to wife): "Feel free to put on the Home and Garden Network if you like. It's got to be better than this."

2) It's horrible on television. First, there are no TV timeouts, which means someone might actually do something when the game goes to commercial (fat chance). Second, the field is just too large to be translated to TV (this is also hockey's problem). Watching soccer on television feels like watching a bunch of ants attacking a meatball that rolled off the table.

3) There is not a single identifiable American for the audience to bond with. Quick: Name one native-born soccer star. Umm, that bend-it guy. Oh no, he's British. How about that dude with the hair like Sideshow Bob? Or, is Kyle Rote, Jr. still playing? And don't give me 15-year-old Freddy Adu as the future. That's like anointing the sophomore class

president as the next inhabitant of the Oval Office.

4) One thing I've never understood is why soccer refuses to let players carry out the most basic instinct in sports, which is to use your hands. It's like telling a baseball player that he's got to hold the bat between his knees. I've seen John LeClair score a goal off his butt and Shawn Bradley bounce a rebound off his nose into the hoop, but a soccer player can't use his most versatile appendage? Ever wonder how those guys engage in foreplay with their girlfriends?

5) Did I mention that NOBODY EVER SCORES?

Q: Is ESPN bad for sports?

Glen says: Once upon a time, people watched baseball games from the first through the ninth innings. They actually rooted for their hometown squads, as opposed to a fantasy collection of players from around the sport. Pro basketball players knew how to pass, shoot and set up a fast break.

That was way back in 1979. Before ESPN came on the scene. Since then, sports has never been the same—which is to say it's gotten worse. I blame Stuart Scott.

We spend a lot of times as fans these days bemoaning the decline of all the professional leagues. We cite over-expansion and big money and free agency. Valid reasons all, Angelo. But let me throw one more ingredient into this rancid stew. Rather than say it, I'll toss you an audio clue:

"Back, back, back, back . . . Cool as the other side of the pillow . . . Rumblin', bumblin', stumblin' . . . Show me some love . . . Say hello to my little friend . . . Boo-yah!"

Ad nauseum.

Yes Ange, ESPN has turned the object of our devotion into a catch-phrase highlight show. It has stolen from us our sports attention span. Why watch a whole game when the best parts will be featured from 11:06 to 11:08 p.m.? Why invest time in the drama of history when Linda Cohn can sum it up in 22 seconds? I can see every home run in five minutes! Every slam dunk committed on Earth during a single half hour!

And make no mistake: Home runs and slam dunks are exactly what ESPN is about. The most insidious change this network has wrought is creating a mentality among players—professional athletes—that you don't really exist unless you appear on *"Sports Center."* So from the time Little Johnny first stares up at the rim, he knows that the game is not about the fast break or the well-executed bounce pass. It's about woofing your way under the basket, slamming down the ball with authority, and then making gangsta' gestures in your opponent's face. *Da-da-dahhh! Da-da-dahhh!*

The gods of sports should be John Wooden and Cal Ripken and Walter Payton. Instead they're Nike and Scott Boras and ESPN. The Era of Self-Indulgence may not have started in Bristol, Connecticut, but it sure got a 24-hour, wall-to-wall push there.

Truth be told, I watch ESPN more than any other network on television. Its day-to-day coverage of games is incredible. When it aims to air a thought-provoking feature, top-notch journalists like Bob Ley and our friend Sal Paolantonio connect as well as anyone in the business.

But most of my time is spent watching *Baseball Tonight* or *NHL Tonight* or some other quick-hit montage aimed at fantasy sports geeks. Truth is, it's addictive, like fast-food French fries. And just as I curse the calories as I gobble the French fries, I find myself cursing the inane home run calls of some good-hair-good-teeth clone trying to sound a little too cool for the room.

This is what one of them said last night after a Pat Burrell blast: *"Hear the drummer get wicked!"*

Am I supposed to know what that means?

Recently, ESPN has tried to branch out by creating its own dramatic shows. Tell me, Ange, did you enjoy that biopic on Bob Knight? Personally, I found *My Mother the Car* to be more credible. The one-season series *Playmakers* was cheesy and soapy, but also a guilty pleasure (again, like those French fries I ought to avoid). Problem was, the image-conscious NFL leaned on ESPN to can the show and the network—afraid of insulting a partner—caved to the power.

That's a problem. So is ESPN's tendency to blur the line between sports celebrity and entertainment celebrity. So there's been a synergy created in which Jamie Foxx interviews Emmitt Smith and Robin Williams comes on to prattle off some non-sequiter ad libs during highlights. As Stuart Scott said (and doesn't it always seem to get back to Stuart Scott): "Actors want to be athletes, and athletes want to be actors."

At ESPN, everyone—including the athletes—is an actor. I miss my sports.

Angelo says: Many years ago, at the advent of television, Walter O'Malley had a decision to make that would chart the course of his Brooklyn Dodgers. No, it wasn't whether to move the team to Los Angeles. Before that, it was whether to broadcast the Dodgers home games on live TV.

Every law of logic suggested to him that the more accessible something was for free, the less likely people would be to pay money for it. So O'Malley banned all of the games in Brooklyn from this new invention. Meanwhile, the crosstown Giants and Yankees offered their games, home and away, with no qualms.

Do I have to tell you what happened, Glen? Popularity in the Yankees and Giants sky-rocketed, while the Dodgers played their final years in Brooklyn to empty seats and vacant stares.

The moral of the story—like it or not—is that saturation coverage is good for business, good for interest, good for everybody. Yes, even when that saturation coverage is provided by an overly hip and utterly gutless ESPN.

Hey, I'm the last guy to defend the all-sports monster that currently prowls the entertainment landscape in America. I think ESPN stinks. Their supposed superstars are interchangeable jackasses, their preoccupation with player histrionics is juvenile and their spine is made of Jello. (You are totally right about how ESPN buckled under NFL pressure to cancel *Playmakers*.)

But to suggest that ESPN is bad for sports is ridiculous, Glen. Bad for sports? I'm still waiting for you to chart the decline of the individual sports in the quarter-century since the all-sports network came into being.

Let's consider your points one by one:

Attention span. Are you really suggesting that ESPN is responsible for people not being able to sit through a whole game? It seems to me they sit just fine when the sport is football. Could it be that baseball—your example—is slower than ever?

Too many highlights. You claim that you watch ESPN more than any other network, and then you blame them for offering too much! That's like someone suing McDonald's because he's fat. Did you ever consider dropping the French fries for an occasional salad?

Preoccupation with home runs and slam-dunks. If you think the attention span of today's viewer is short now, wait till ESPN starts showing three angles on a beautifully executed bunt.

Bad dramatic shows. I beg to differ here. *Playmakers* was terrific. The ESPN movie called *The Junction Boys* was one of the best made-for-TV films in a decade. Yes, a few of these original dramas were lousy, but so far ESPN's batting average is no worse than the Big Four networks.

No clear distinction between sports and entertainment. Welcome to the 21st century, Glen. You've been to enough games in person to know that smoke and mirrors are the norm now, not the exception. ESPN may have encouraged this trend, but it was coming anyway.

The bottom line is, the games themselves are just not enough for people anymore. They need some razzle and then some dazzle. Like any network hoping to stay in business, ESPN has reflected the changing interests of the American sports fan, not changed them.

And speaking of the bottom line: If all of these influences are so bad, shouldn't the individual sports and ESPN be hurting financially?

Football has never been bigger. Baseball and basketball are doing fine. Hockey is dying, but no one is going to blame ESPN for that. Other sports championed by ESPN—junk like NASCAR and the Extreme Games—are flourishing *because* of their exposure on the network.

As for ESPN itself, during the recent bid by Comcast Corporation to buy Disney, do you have any idea what was cited as the most appealing part of the entire Disney portfolio, Glen?

Yup, ESPN. Those guys are printing money in Bristol, Conn.

My advice to you and all of the ESPN bashers is to stop rumblin', bumblin', and stumblin', because right now you are NOT as cool as the other side of the pillow.

Boo-yah.

15

Q: Was Buddy Ryan a great drafter?

Angelo says: He was a gruff blowhard who tended to choke in the playoffs. He was a defensive innovator who had disdain for offense. He was a man with no social skills, a rotten temper and a stubbornness that often foiled his best game plans.

All in all, Buddy Ryan was a lousy head coach.

But when it came to evaluating talent, there has never been anyone—before or since —who mastered the art of drafting like Mr. Bluster. It would not be pushing a point to call him a true genius once a year, at the college draft.

During his five years as Eagles head coach, Ryan served the role of player personnel director without the title, and he was a virtuoso. Never was that fact more evident than in his very first spin of the player wheel back in 1986.

What a draft that was! Buddy had arrived in town literally a few weeks earlier after celebrating a Super Bowl in Chicago, and he went right to work. In the space of two days, the Eagles were a new team. Ryan chose a starting offensive backfield (Keith Byars and Anthony Toney) and two defensive stars (Seth Joyner and Clyde Simmons), he used one draft pick to obtain a top backup quarterback (Matt Cavanaugh) and he added a half-dozen other special-teams contributors.

Most amazing was *where* Ryan found some of these budding stars. He found Joyner in the eighth round, Simmons in the ninth. That means some 200 players were chosen before Ryan picked them.

In the years that followed, Eagles fans came to expect brilliance from Ryan on draft weekend, if at no other time. Most of the major components of the most fearsome Eagles defense in history were assembled in the five Ryan drafts: Jerome Brown, Byron Evans, Eric Allen, Ben Smith, Reggie Singletary, and the aforementioned Joyner and Simmons.

And though Ryan cared very little about offense, he knew a solid player when he saw one on that side of the ball, too. He drafted Keith Jackson, Cris Carter, Freddie Barnett,

Calvin Williams, Heath Sherman, and David Alexander. Buddy even used the draft to engineer trades for useful additions like Earnest Jackson, Ron Solt, and Jimmie Giles.

The naysayers in the crowd are just looking for something to complain about when it comes to Buddy Ryan's draft. Sure, Glen, he blew it with Alonzo Johnson, Jesse Small, Robert Drummond, yada, yada, yada.

Stop the presses. Ryan wasn't perfect.

Well, the truth is, nobody's perfect in the college draft. It is the most inexact of all sciences. My best argument is a simple one, Glen: If Ryan was overrated as a drafter, name someone who brought more talent to his team in five years than Buddy did. I need one name. Just one.

During my years covering Ryan's Eagles for the *Inquirer*, I often asked Buddy if there was a secret to finding great players in the draft. In his usual condescending manner, he would dismiss the question with a wave of the hand, as if to say that I would never understand.

But years later, when he had mellowed a little, he explained the method. He said you had to keep looking at the tape after a big play. Did the kid revel in his moment, or did he shrink from the spotlight? Did he really, truly like to hit people? Was he trying to stake a claim to his territory on the field?

Buddy said that those tapes were like an x-ray. They showed you what was inside the kid. You just had to know how to read them.

And nobody knew how to read them any better than Buddy Ryan.

Glen says: One name? You just need one? How about Chuck Noll, who drafted four future Hall of Famers for the Pittsburgh Steelers in one single year? How about the late Jim Finks, who picked eight Super Bowl starters for the Chicago Bears in 1983? Buddy, who served as defensive coordinator for the 1985 Bears sure was thankful for Finks' 8th-round selection of Richard Dent, don't you think? How about Bill Walsh, who engineered all those great drafts for the 49ers? Or, I hate to say it, Jimmy Johnson in Dallas?

Fact is, Buddy was a decent drafter. But he falls far short of great.

We tend to remember the hits more than the misses. So late-rounders Joyner and Simmons are held up as testament to Buddy's genius. That's fair enough. But don't just slough off Alonzo Johnson, Jesse Small and Mike Bellamy—all second-round duds. The second round is where you should be finding foundation players, not guys who lacked heart (Bellamy), lacked brains (Small) or lacked the courage to stay off drugs (Johnson).

Like you, I once talked to Buddy about his late-round drafting prowess. He told me about studying the films, but also conceded that once you get past the fifth round, there's a whole lot of luck involved. Let's call Joyner and Simmons good hunches and leave it at that.

Not so good were his hunches at several other positions. In five years, he drafted 10 running backs. Not one of them ever even rushed for 700 yards in a season. And it's not like talent wasn't there to be picked. In 1990, for example, he chose defensive back Ben Smith in the first round. We'll never know what Smith might have done if injuries hadn't ended his career. But we do know how the run- ner Buddy passed up—Rodney Hampton —went on to succeed for the Giants.

Similarly, Buddy couldn't spot a talented offensive lineman if one pan- caked Norman Braman in the locker room. Of the nine blockers he draft- ed, only David Alexander became a full-time starter. Remember Matt Darwin? Ben Tamburello? Matt Patchan? All early-to-mid-round picks. That's more busts than a full episode of *Baywatch*.

I'll say this for Buddy: He draft- ed better than he traded. You describe Cavanaugh as a "top backup quarter- back." Based on what? His paltry 55.2 passer rating as an Eagle? The Eagles sacrificed a second and third-round pick for that lusty performance.

"I knew how to draft 'em Rich. You just didn't know how to play 'em."

And then, Angelo, you define Ron Solt as a "useful addition." You're like a slick lawyer, figuring that if you slip in enough lies nobody will notice them. Well, I recall Ron Solt as a chemically enhanced freakazoid who lost 50 pounds and his career when the NFL began testing for steroids. Buddy paid a first and fourth-rounder to Indianapolis for that Michelin Man. The first-rounder became Andre Rison, who caught 743 passes in his career—more than the combined sum of the six wide receivers Buddy ever drafted.

The bottom line, Angelo, is that I like Buddy Ryan. I think he did a hell of a lot to resuscitate a moribund franchise. Gave the Eagles an attitude. Beat up the Cowboys on a regular basis. I'll always appreciate him for that.

But he falls a bit short of the words you use: "True genius." A true genius wouldn't have projected Alonzo Johnson as the best second-round linebacker in 1986. Hell, he wasn't even the best linebacker named Johnson. That would have been the great Pepper Johnson, who went to the Giants three picks later.

Buddy may be the best Eagles drafter in recent history, but that's like being the tallest midget in the circus. Talk about damning with faint praise. So at least I'll give him this: It wasn't Buddy who invested two first-rounders in the disastrous Antone Davis. That was the year after he left. And that was our pal Richie Kotite.

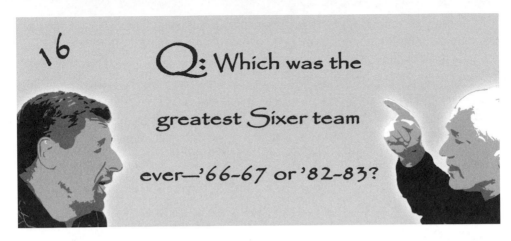

16

Q: Which was the greatest Sixer team ever—'66-67 or '82-83?

Glen says: Whew, this is a close one. Both teams boasted Hall of Fame players and coaches. Both teams knocked off the previous season's champion on their way to a title. The final records, including playoffs, are nearly identical—79-17 for Wilt's Sixers versus 77-18 for Doc's.

And, for what it's worth, neither team repeated as champions. So much for dynasties.

But if I'm forced to choose between the two greatest Sixers teams ever, I'm going with the more recent one. I've got several reasons why.

First, a little background on my choice. The team that general manager Pat Williams put together was already superb when he added Moses Malone just before the season opened. As Julius Erving said, "We knew, right at that moment, that our time had come."

Moses was the missing piece, the inside force who could intimidate the other team's big man into playing a bit further away from the basket. He also remains the greatest offensive rebounder in NBA history.

Go through the rest of the lineup. Andrew Toney was the league's preeminent two-guard until his feet betrayed him and some guy named Jordan showed up. In his day, Toney could break guys down better than Allen Iverson. A tiny flinch of the head and shoulder, and defenders backed away in fear and respect. Oh, and don't forget the jumper that earned him the nickname, "The Boston Strangler."

Bobby Jones, the sixth man, was a superb defensive stopper. On offense, when others were doubled, he'd stick a jump shot or drive to the basket. And no one played the pick-and-roll better.

Mo Cheeks was his usual superb self in '82-83. Magic Johnson may have been flashier, but Mo topped any point guard in terms of getting his teammates into position to make shots. My favorite Cheeks moment? How about when he punctuated that final victory over the Lakers with a last-second breakaway dunk? Teammates insist it was the only dunk of Mo's career.

The Sixers went four deep on the bench with guys who could have started on almost any other team. Oh, and they had some guy named Doc who, I'm told, contributed a little bit, too.

Moses' pre-playoff prediction of "Fo'-Fo'-Fo'" was seen as foolish bravado, what with the Celtics and Lakers in their 1980s primes. He had to amend it to "Fo'-Fi'-Fo'," when the Bucks snuck in one lucky win, but how do you quarrel with that degree of greatness? Just one other team, the 2000-01 Lakers, won the title with just a single playoff loss (to AI's Sixers, if you recall). Your '66-67 squad lost *four* post-season games along the way.

In sweeping the Lakers, Moses averaged 26 points and 18 rebounds per game, bullying Kareem Abdul-Jabbar into surrender. This was not some feeble Los Angeles team, this was "Showtime" in the making.

But you want to know, Angelo, how my squad would beat yours? Not easy, I'll grant you. But I'm working on the fact that your squad didn't play much defense (they gave up 116 points per game!) and that Wilt more than occasionally showed up disinterested.

I won't attempt to argue that Moses would shut down Wilt, but his size and physical play would give the Stilt his biggest test this side of Bill Russell. I've also got Mark Iavaroni and Earl Cureton each ready to take six fouls on Chamberlain. And we know how well your guy does at the foul line. You've heard of "Hack-a-Shaq?" This will be "Clip-a-Dip."

I'm going to put Bobby Jones on Chet Walker, and let Toney handle Hal Greer. See, my team is taller, faster and more athletic than yours. That's where 16 years of basketball evolution plays in my favor.

Now, how are you gonna handle my offensive weapons? Who's guarding Toney? You've got no one with that kind of quicks. And how are you presuming to cover Erving? Luke Jackson may try roughing him up a bit, but eventually, Doc's going to fly right over him. I may need every game of a best-of-seven series, but eventually, my guys will prevail. The highlight will be Dr. J flying past a baffled Chamberlain for a reverse stuffer. The hard slam beats the finger-roll every time.

I've got one other thing in my favor. One secret weapon. Your sixth man—Billy Cunningham—happens to be my coach. If anyone knows how to stop the Kangaroo Kid and his cohorts, it's the genius himself.

Angelo says: This is a close one? What are you smoking, Glen?

The real argument here should be: Were the '66-67 Sixers the greatest team in NBA history? And the answer to that question is yes. But we'll save that argument for our sequel.

The '66-67 Sixers were a perfect team in every way. They had a starting five that complemented each other, they had an unstoppable force in the middle, they had one of the

The Kangaroo Kid starred for one great Sixer team and coached another.

best sixth men ever, they had a fantastic (and underrated) coach, and they even had an ideal rival to bring out their best.

In the history of the NBA, no one comes close to Wilt Chamberlain—not the one-dimensional Bill Russell, not the over-marketed Michael Jordan, and not Magic or Larry or Oscar. You can look it up. Wilt owns the record books. Heck, he averaged 50 points per game in one season!

The backcourt featured arguably the best point guard in team history, Hal Greer, and one of the franchise's best shooters, Wali Jones. Up front were steady role-playing pros Chet Walker and Luke Jackson. Coming off the bench was a fireplug named Billy Cunningham, who was already learning how to be a great coach from the guy sitting next to him, Alex Hannum.

Wow! Do we really need to argue about this any further? The best asset on that '82-83 team—other than Julius Erving, of course—was Cunningham himself, who was basically a hand-me-down from the better '66-67 team.

You make a noble attempt here to state your case, Glen, but the logic is lacking:

• Moses was the best offensive rebounder in NBA history? Puhleeze. Wilt Chamberlain was the best rebounder—offensive and defensive—by far. (And second was Russell, not Malone.) Chamberlain averaged 28 rebounds one season. Moses never got a sniff of that number.

• You extol the virtues of your starting six, sure, but mine is as good as, or better, at every position but one. Wilt smokes Moses. Greer is better than Cheeks. Wali Jones and Toney are a wash. Cunningham stops Bobby Jones. Dr. J crushes Walker, I acknowledge, but when he gets near the basket, he'll have a problem with that reverse stuffer if Wilt is waiting for him there. (Your insertion of the names Earl Cureton and Marc Iavaroni gave us all a good chuckle, Glen. Thanks.)

• The sweep of the Lakers by the '82-83 team was impressive, but not as impressive as you make it sound. Jabbar was well past his prime by then. Meanwhile, the Sixers only had to beat the biggest dynasty in NBA history to secure their championship. It took the Sixers five games to obliterate that Celtic dynasty in '66-67. The '82-83 Sixers lost only one game in the playoffs because there was no Boston behemoth to face that year. Enough said.

• Yes, opponents of the '66-67 team averaged 116 points, but not because of a porous defense. Back then, before the decline of the NBA, everybody shot better, handled the ball better, rebounded better. They had mastered the fundamentals back then. I won't even concede the athleticism point you make because in that regard the '66-67 team was ahead of its time. There was never—NEVER!—a better athlete in pro sports than Wilt.

You made one brilliant argument, Glen, and I will concede it wholeheartedly. Cunningham was a genius. He had a good teacher, but he was truly the smartest coach in

Sixer history.

That's why I defer to his judgment on this issue. And make no mistake, I have asked him, more than once, which was the better team. Do I really have to tell you what he always says?

OK, I will.

You lose this one, Glen.

17

Q: Did we treat Mike Schmidt unfairly?

Angelo says: Mike Schmidt isn't just one of the greatest baseball players in history, he's also one of the smartest. In fact, it's a pretty safe bet that he is the single most intelligent athlete ever to wear a Philadelphia pro sports uniform.

And that's why it's so amazing that Schmidt never figured out why the fans didn't really like him when he played, and still don't like him now. The solution is as obvious as the omnipresent scowl on his weather-beaten face.

There is no joy in Mikeville. The Mighty Schmidt has struck out—at least with the fans.

I'll never forget the day I was assigned to write a newspaper article on Schmidt in the very first week I had arrived in Philadelphia after living 32 years in my hometown of Providence, Rhode Island. To say I was frightened was an understatement. I was *terrified*.

Schmidt's reputation as a miserable, temperamental superstar had traveled the 250 miles between Philadelphia and Providence with many miles to spare. I knew I was in trouble when I spotted him scowling at his locker a couple of hours before the game. I approached with all of the sophistication of a teenager propositioning a hooker. Somehow, I stammered out an introduction.

"You work for the *Inquirer*?" he snarled. "Oh, good. Somebody new who can rip me in the papers."

I turned away in humiliation, and then was startled to hear that same voice invite me to grab a seat. For the next 20 minutes, he filled up my notebook with observations and insights that I had no right to expect. By the end, he had morphed into a gracious and cordial man.

In succeeding years, I would interview him maybe five or six more times. In each case, the first few moments would be tense and uncertain, followed by a thawing that would usually end with wisdom and maybe even a little humor.

The fact is, the fans of Philadelphia rarely, if ever, got to see the real Mike Schmidt. He wouldn't allow it. He was never really secure when he didn't have a bat or a glove in his hands.

The greatest Phillie of them all had one enemy he could never overcome—himself.

People who argue that the real Mike Schmidt did surface near the end of his career are kidding themselves. Yes, he did wear a wig one day when he threw the ball around the infield. And yes, the day he retired, the emotion poured out of him so ferociously that it changed the fans' reaction from sadness to discomfort.

The wig incident was nothing more than a hollow gesture designed to mollify the media after one of Schmidt's trademark rants against Philadelphia. If Schmidt indeed was trying to win back the city, he would have followed it up with a more accessible attitude. He did not.

As for the retirement announcement, I'll leave it to the psychologists to explain why a man as outwardly unemotional as Schmidt would erupt in tears the way he did. Maybe he finally regretted his detachment from the fans. Maybe the dike finally burst, and two decades of repressed emotion burst through. Or maybe he was just sad that it was all over.

By then, it really didn't matter anyway. Schmidt was never going to be the kind of player Philadelphia loves. On the field, it was all just too easy for him—the majestic home-run swing, the wizardry at third base, the grace and honor of pure talent. Philly will take a guy with a dirty uniform, a Lenny Dykstra or a Pete Rose, any day.

Off the field, it was just too hard. The burden of revealing himself—even if what he was revealing would have only enhanced his image—was more than he could handle.

And that's why, to the fans, Mike Schmidt will always be a puzzle with no solution.

How could a guy that smart be so dumb?

Glen says: Let's see if I've got this right. Mike Schmidt was a private man in a public business. A bit of a sourpuss. A poor communicator.

He also happens to be the greatest player at his position in baseball history.

Yeah, let's boo him!

You're going to defend this, Angelo?

For the most part, Philadelphia fans get it right. We can spot when a guy is a first-round fraud (Mike Mamula), a lazy thief (Shawn Bradley) or a self-centered jackass (Scott Rolen). The rest of the world may have thought we were unfair to Rich Kotite, but we warned those New York Jets fans what a bumbling incompetent they were getting.

With Schmidt, however, we hit the wrong target.

Mike Schmidt's biggest sin in life was that he could never be one of the guys. In a clubhouse with raucous personalities like Bowa, Rose, and McGraw, he was the withdrawn intellectual who never learned how to give a teammate a hotfoot. Never really cared to. No doubt he was ultra-sensitive, but how would any of us have reacted if work mates referred to us as "Titleist Head" for having as many pockmarks as a golf ball?

He was not a drunk driver, a spouse abuser or a coach killer. He always showed up at practice, never demanded a trade and didn't balloon up by using steroids. He wasn't thrown out of his sport for gambling, although he has stood up for a former teammate who was.

Should it really have mattered that he could be a bit temperamental?

Just look at the résumé. Schmidt played 18 seasons in Philadelphia—more than any pro athlete in our history. He hit 548 home runs—ninth all-time in the majors. He captured ten Gold Gloves and three Most Valuable Player awards. He holds nearly every offensive record that the team keeps.

Go to Cooperstown and search for the Hall of Fame plaques featuring players sporting the Phillies "P." I'll tell you this, it's a small club—just seven guys. But while Robin Roberts and Richie Ashburn became truly beloveds, while Steve Carlton and Jim Bunning are lauded for their work ethics, Mike Schmidt was the guy we hounded for close to two decades.

I know the two main raps on Schmidt and they're both unfair. First one is that he was a terrible clutch hitter. Grounded into too many double-plays with the bases loaded. But when it really counted, he delivered. Consider that towering blast he clubbed against the Expos to clinch the division in 1980. Then he hit .381 with two home runs against the Royals to lead this sorry franchise to its first and only world title. He was the MVP of that World Series. Doesn't that count as clutch?

The other rap is that the guy never dived in the dirt. Played entire weeks without muddying his uniform. True enough, but shouldn't we give him credit for not having to hit the ground? The bottom line is that Schmidt dived so rarely because he was so great at defending his position. He knew where to station himself for each hitter, anticipated where the ball was going and got there with ease after the crack of the bat. Mike Schmidt didn't dive, but he sure did glide.

So what's left to criticize? The guy had a prickly personality. Too often, he said the wrong thing—mostly about the fans. Eighteen years here and we never felt that he opened up the door enough to really let us know him.

That's unfortunate. But I'll take that tradeoff for the hundreds of amazing moments he provided.

Mike Schmidt remains today the most under-appreciated athlete ever to come through our city.

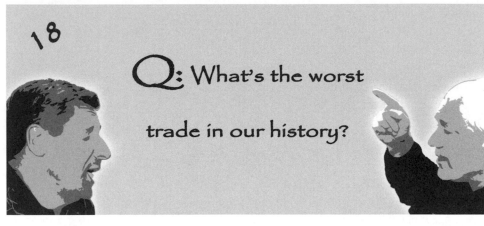

18

Q: What's the worst trade in our history?

Glen says: You want to know why the Phillies have captured just one title in 120 years, Angelo? Consider these deals:

• Richie Allen to St. Louis in 1969 for Tim McCarver and Curt Flood. Allen is the all-time "what-could-have-been" player in franchise history. Flood took the W.C. Fields approach to Philadelphia and launched the court case that forever changed sports.

• Larry Bowa for Ivan DeJesus in a 1982 swap of shortstops with Chicago. The Phils also tossed the Cubs minor-league prospect Ryne Sandberg, who became a ten-time all-star.

• Curt Schilling to Arizona in 2000 for Travis Lee, Omar Daal, Nelson Figueroa and Vicente Padilla. The first three stiffs are gone and hopefully forgotten. Padilla is a decent third starter. Schilling, meanwhile, went on to win a World Series MVP award and twice finish in the money in Cy Young voting.

But the single worst trade in the Phillies'—and our city's—history was the 1966 deal that sent young right-hander Ferguson Jenkins to the Cubs for pitchers Larry Jackson and Bob Buhl, also known as "Who?" and "What?"

Phils manager Gene Mauch thought he could contend that year with the two veteran starters (combined age: 68). Wrong again, Gene. The Phils finished fourth, and didn't sniff first place again for a full decade. Buhl was out of baseball in one year; Jackson hung around for three.

Jenkins, meanwhile, went on to a Hall of Fame career. He won 284 games and a Cy Young Award. During a six-year stretch with the Cubs, he *averaged* 21 wins, 23 complete games, 306 innings and 253 strikeouts. He was every bit the workhorse that Steve Carlton turned out to be for the Phillies. Imagine what this franchise could have won with the lefty Carlton *and* the righty Jenkins starting every fourth game through the 1970s.

Giving away Fergy is especially galling because it accentuates two of the franchise's biggest failings over the years: Its inability to develop pitchers and its failure to hang on to talented black players.

Let's examine this closely, Ange. We'll take the period from 1963 to 2003. We'll look at players who came out of the Phils' farm system, so that transplants like Carlton don't count here. And we'll define a "front-line" player as anyone who made at least two All-Star Games as a Phillie. Sounds pretty modest, eh?

Here is a list of every black player meeting that criteria over more than 40 years: Richie Allen, Jimmy Rollins.

And here is the list of every pitcher: Chris Short.

Oh, one more list. Here is every African-American starting pitcher—home-grown or import—who made even *one* All-Star Game as a Phillie:

Pretty sad, eh?

Jenkins would have made each of those lists one name longer. Instead, the lily-white Phils stumbled around for decades with a roster that only David Duke could love. Fergy is part of the franchise's legacy of shame as much as its decision to pass on trying out a young outfielder named Willie Mays in 1950. The Phils were the last National League franchise to sign a black player, and the biggest plus on that guy's scouting report was that he was said to be "no trouble." You mean you don't remember John Kennedy, Angelo?

To be honest, not until recent years have the Phillies successfully developed black players like Rollins and Marlon Byrd. And that's stretching it.

They've had just as much trouble developing pitchers—regardless of hue. This doesn't make them unique. In fact, I've always disagreed with the axiom that hitting a baseball is the toughest thing in sports. I say it's tougher finding someone who can consistently shut down the hitters.

Ferguson Jenkins was that guy. He did it for nineteen seasons and, though he shuffled around late in his career, he wound up winning more games than any pitcher—including Carlton—ever did as a Phillie.

Imagine, Angelo, if he had stayed here.

Angelo says: I'll never forget the reaction when the news came over the wire services, a gnawing tension that starts in the gut and works its way up the esophagus. The

Sixers had made a trade. No, wait a minute. Two trades.

The date was June 16, 1986, and no team in the history of sports was dumber or more illogical than the Sixers were that day. As the trades were announced, people all over Philadelphia were rendered speechless.

Sixers trade Moses Malone, Terry Catledge and two first-round picks for Cliff Robinson and Jeff Ruland.

Sixers trade the No. 1 pick in the draft, Brad Daugherty, to Cleveland for Roy Hinson.

Huh? How is this possible? The Sixers traded one of the top fifty players of all time, the same Moses Malone who had led the team to an NBA championship three years earlier, for a journeyman guard and an injury-prone center. And they gave up Catledge to boot?

PLUS TWO NO. 1 PICKS!

Impossible.

If you'll only count one trade in this debate, Glen, I'll take that one. But if you want to consider both draft-day deals in 1986 as one, then I'll add the similarly illogical swap of the top pick in the entire draft for a nondescript forward. Since when does a scrub like Roy Hinson merit the No. 1 pick in the draft. That's like trading Allen Iverson for Monte Williams.

Please keep in mind that the Sixers are notorious for making insanely stupid trades. This is the same organization that gave away Charles Barkley for dreck named Jeff Hornacek, Andrew Lang, and Tim Perry; the same organization that gift-wrapped the greatest player ever, Wilt Chamberlain, for Darrall Imhoff, Archie Clark, and Jerry Chambers.

And still, June 16, 1986 tops them all. After the cloud of stupidity had cleared on that fatal day, the story behind the deals was almost as outrageous as the deals themselves. Years later, I remember asking the general manager of the Sixers, Pat Williams, how he could have made such an absurd pair of trades. He was one of the best GMs in the league. What the heck was he thinking?

To the surprise of no one, Williams said he had very little to do with the decisions. (As if he would ever admit that he did.) He said they were the brain cramp of owner Harold Katz himself, who didn't want to pay Malone top dollar for declining skills. In effect, the first deal was a salary dump. The second maneuver was a product of the sheer brilliance of the owner.

The story Williams has never told—but has not denied either—is that he was actually thrilled at the deals because Williams was about to be named president of an expansion franchise in Orlando. From the perspective of an opponent, the trades were a going-away gift.

So Katz was left minding the store that day. The store got robbed. People who defend Harold Katz should have the date *June 16, 1986* tattooed on their foreheads. It was really the only time when Katz was his own GM, and somehow he managed to irreparably destroy his franchise.

The team has never recovered from those trades. The Sixers have gone a generation now without another NBA title, and there are no signs of one in the immediate future. Malone went on to play nine more largely productive seasons with Washington, Atlanta, Milwaukee, and—yes—Philadelphia. Daugherty was a star for Cleveland before injuries cut short his career. Jeff Ruland, Cliff Robinson and Roy Hinson became very close friends —on the bench, nursing injuries. The Sixers had a terrific injured-reserve list in that 1986- '87 season.

If anything good came out of that dark day, it was the permanent scars it left on the image of a horrible owner, Harold Katz. Even though he had brought a title to the city, the fans despised him from that day forward. He sold the team a grim, tedious decade later because he no longer felt welcome in his own city. He should have left sooner.

Your choice of the Ferguson Jenkins trade is OK, Glen, but I think your social conscience is getting in the way of your judgment. Yes, Jenkins became a sensational pitcher, and yes, it was contemptible how the Phillies failed to develop black players. But at least Jackson and Buhl didn't spend the rest of their careers in the hospital after the deal. And the Phillies didn't give away two top draft picks, too.

To be honest, I don't really care who wins this debate, Glen. After talking about all of these horrible trades, I think I'll just go shoot myself.

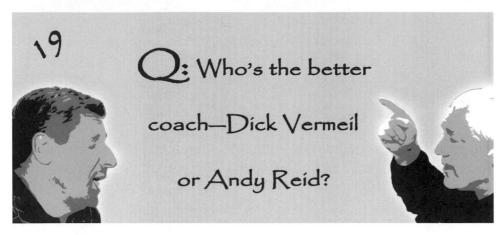

19

Q: Who's the better coach—Dick Vermeil or Andy Reid?

Angelo says: It's hard to imagine two more different men than Dick Vermeil and Andy Reid. Vermeil is intense. Reid is stoic. Vermeil is emotional. Reid is measured. Vermeil is trim. Reid is not.

The only thing that these two coaches have in common is that, over the past quarter-century, they have been the very best at leading the Eagles.

So who's better?

That's easy. Dick Vermeil, by a landslide.

Vermeil is a coach who starts with a team and ends up with a family. He is loyal to the extreme, inviting players to visit his home, sample his dinner, sleep on his couch. Dick Vermeil doesn't believe that pro football is a cold business that has legislated away the bond between men working toward a common goal.

When Vermeil coached the Eagles in the late 1970s and early 1980s, he built relationships that prevail to this day. His Eagle players speak of him reverentially, even now. Ron Jaworski sees him as a role model. Bill Bergey calls Vermeil a father figure. Wilbert Montgomery says he'd take a bullet for the man.

Vermeil was beloved in Philadelphia—heck, he still endorses products here, a generation after he quit the Eagles—because he is a perfect reflection of what Philadelphia values most. The fans love a competitor, a man who'll literally risk his life out on the field and then cry after the game either in joy or sorrow. Philadelphia loves Bobby Clarke (the player), Dave Schultz, Tug McGraw, Larry Bowa (the player), and Chuck Bednarik—guys who'll not just try to beat you, they'll spit in your face, too.

And that's why Vermeil, who won no Super Bowls in Philadelphia, is still the most popular coach or manager who ever worked in the city. He was no phony. He was no loser, either, even when he did lose. Vermeil wanted to win so badly, he slept for weeks in his office at the Vet. He wanted to win *too* badly, in the end. He tightened the reins on his team so much before the Super Bowl in 1981 that he strangled the life right out of them.

But the fans forgave him for that miscalculation because he was Dick Vermeil, the one coach who cared about the Eagles as much as they did. When he went on to win a Super Bowl in his second life in the NFL, Philadelphia cheered for his triumph. There were no grumbles that he did for St. Louis what he couldn't do for Philadelphia. In fact, Vermeil held the trophy aloft that day and said he only wished he could share it with Philadelphia, too.

Andy Reid doesn't have a Super Bowl trophy, and he will probably never get one. He is the anti-Vermeil. He pretends to build a family, but then he places some of his offspring up for adoption at the end of every season. He screams for loyalty in the locker room even while he's plotting the dismissal of some of his best players because they no longer fit his subjective and cold calculation of value to the team.

The only loyalty Andy Reid has is to his own philosophy. Ask Hugh Douglas about Reid. Ask Troy Vincent, or Bobby Taylor, or even Jeremiah Trotter. Reid dumped all of them, with no apparent remorse. He booted them because they didn't fit inside his narrow definition of usefulness. He booted them because room under the salary cap is more important to him than honor and loyalty.

How ironic is it that Reid preaches every year about the sad realities of the sports business while Dick Vermeil openly weeps over his love for his players. The sports world is only ruled by the bottom line if you're ruled by it yourself.

And the bottom line for Vermeil and Reid is very simple: Vermeil has two Super Bowl teams, one Super Bowl ring and hundreds of former players who are friends for life.

Reid has money under the cap.

The time is yours.

Glen says: I'm sorry, Angelo. I thought we were debating who was the superior coach between Dick Vermeil and Andy Reid. I didn't know this was a popularity contest. I didn't know we were voting for Mr. Congeniality.

Yes, Dick Vermeil is one of the truly beloveds in Philadelphia sports history. And deservedly so. But just because Reid is dull, dismissive and arrogant, that doesn't mean he isn't the better man with the clipboard.

You talk about loyalty. Well, that was easier in the Vermeil Era, when a couple thousand of Leonard Tose's bucks could settle any contract dispute. That was before the salary cap and multi-year, mega-dollar deals. The NFL plays a different game now. These days, loyalty means paying $1 million-plus to an aging kick returner because he's good in the locker room. So you say goodbye.

Vermeil's team was a family. Reid's is a corporate entity. Mom 'n Pop vs. Team Microsoft. But cold-hearted works in the NFL today.

Need proof? Let's look at the records. Both coaches inherited horrible teams when they came to Philadelphia—Vermeil succeeding Mike McCormack and Reid taking over for Ray Rhodes. In seven years here, Vermeil went 54-47. Take away his first year, when he really didn't have his own players, and Vermeil's a more-impressive 50-37. That's a .575 winning percentage. Not bad.

Reid, by contrast, rang up a 51-29 record during his first five seasons. Again, subtract the first year, and he's 46-18. And that, my friend, translates to a .719 winning percentage. It is, quite simply, the franchise's best four-year run since 1946-49. Now, if you want to argue that Greasy Neale was a better coach than Andy Reid, you might have me there.

You note, Angelo, that Vermeil went to the Super Bowl while Reid didn't. True enough. Vermeil didn't win that game, but give him credit for going one step further than Reid's three losing trips to the NFC title game. If, however, you go beyond that one trip to New Orleans, you'll see that your guy won just three playoff games during his tenure with the Eagles, while Reid won five through 2003.

In fact, here's the all-time list of post-season wins by Eagles coaches:

Reid 5

Vermeil. 3

Neale 3

Buck Shaw 1

Rich Kotite. 1

Rhodes 1

Not exactly the Green Bay Packers, eh? Seventy-plus years and just 14 playoff victories. And people wonder why Eagles fans boo so much.

But I digress. So I'll ask you this: What great talent has pushed Reid to his terrific record? Seriously, unless Donovan McNabb starts channeling Johnny Unitas' psyche, it's safe to say that Big Red hasn't coached any Hall of Famers during his years here. He won 12 games in 2003 with defensive ends who combined for eight sacks all season. He won 11 games in 2000 with Torrance Small and Charles Johnson as his wideouts and Darnell Autry as his primary running back. Incredible.

Fact is, Vermeil was helped along the way by a cagey general manager. Carl Peterson traded for Bill Bergey and Ron Jaworski, and snagged stars like Wilbert Montgomery and Carl Hairston with late-round draft picks. Peterson bought the groceries, Vermeil cooked the meal.

Reid never got that kind of help from his general manager. Most years, Reid's general manager was, well, Andy Reid.

Reid the GM could never deliver like Reid the coach. Remember, the question here is who was the better *coach*. It's not who was the better procurer of talent.

When it comes down to it, Andy Reid is a top coach for the very same reason that he infuriates us so much. He just keeps winning with mediocre talent.

20

Q: What's the best Philadelphia team not to win a title?

Glen says: If we know about anything in this town, it's the big tease. Since our last parade down Broad Street in 1983, we've watched our teams go to the championship series five times—only to die each time. And that doesn't even count the Eagles' three straight losses in NFC title games.

We know about close.

We know about heartbreak.

Looking back, most of those teams were somewhat of an illusion—maybe not frauds, but certainly a bit lucky. Each got hot, went on a run, collapsed in the end and never came close again. What does it say that the Phillies followed up their 1993 World Series appearance by finishing seven games under .500 the next year?

But one of our also-rans really was a team for the ages, Angelo. And that was the 1986-87 Flyers.

To truly assess how terrific those Flyers were, put them in context of the team that eventually beat them. The Edmonton Oilers of that era may be the most dominant club in hockey's history. They boasted not just the sport's God in Wayne Gretzky (he racked up 183 points that season), but another immortal in Mark Messier. Add to that Hall of Famers Grant Fuhr and Jari Kurri, two-time 50-goal scorer Glenn Anderson and the most-prolific scoring defenseman ever in Paul Coffey.

Those Oilers won five Stanley Cups between 1984 and 1990. Only one team stretched them to seven games in the finals. That was Mike Keenan's Flyers.

Do you remember the history? The Flyers entered that season still recovering from the tragic death of goaltender Pelle Lindbergh the previous year. Ron Hextall was all of 22 when he was handed the starting job. He responded by winning the Vezina Trophy as the league's top goalie and winning local fans' hearts by hatcheting any opponent wandering near his crease.

This was an inexperienced team, with ten regulars aged 24 or younger. Posters featuring baby-faced stars Rick Tocchet and Peter Zezel hung above the beds of thousands of local teenyboppers. Just one team member, Mark Howe, was older than 30—assuming, of course, you trust Kjell Samuelsson's dubious birth certificate.

Keenan ran his charges like a Marine drill sergeant. The players hated him, feared him, complained to ownership about him—but played brilliantly for him.

They beat up the Rangers, Islanders and Canadiens (all strong teams then) to get to the finals. Along the way they lost Tim Kerr, who scored fifty-eight regular-season goals, with his annual shoulder injury. Howe, the greatest defenseman in Flyers history, was hampered by a charley horse going up against the Oilers.

No one gave them a chance. And when they lost the first two games in Edmonton, newspapers there published the Oilers' championship parade route.

The start of Game Three at the Spectrum seemed to affirm that sentiment. The Oilers went up 3-0 after two periods. And then . . .

"And then," Hextall told me recently, "we said to ourselves, 'What the hell, these guys ain't Superman.' We decided to stop being intimidated."

The Flyers rallied to tie the score before winning on a late goal by Brad McCrimmon, of all people. It was the first time since 1944 that a Cup finalist had overcome a three-goal third-period deficit. More remembered than that bit of trivia was Hextall's vicious slash across Kent Nilsson's leg after the Oiler crowded him a bit too much.

The Oilers bounced back to win Game Four, 4-1. As the Flyers skated off the ice, home fans gave them a standing ovation, appreciative for a great season that seemed about to end.

But Keenan wasn't ready to quit. Before Game Five, the coach purloined the Stanley Cup and placed it on a folding chair in the middle of the Flyers locker room. Whether his players needed that motivation is unclear, but they beat the Oilers, 4-3, with Brian Propp getting assists on all four goals. Hextall—taunted as "Hackstall" by the angry crowd—stoned Gretzky and Coffey on breakaways.

Even the Flyers' staunchest loyalists hadn't expected them back in town for a Game Six. The crowd, says Hextall, "was the loudest I ever heard the old Spectrum, from the start of the game to the finish." It exploded when J.J. Daigneault scored to break a 2-2 tie with 5:32 to go.

And suddenly, the team that had been left for dead had a chance to win. They headed back to Edmonton for their 26th game in 54 days.

Of course, this being Philadelphia, the fairy tale wasn't going to end happily ever after. The Flyers played heroically in Game Seven, but lost, 3-1. Hextall won the award as the playoffs' most valuable player as well as praise from Gretzky, who called him, "The best goalie I ever played against." Nilsson had no such kind words.

In our town, Ange, we know about losing in the end. Going out to the 1993 Toronto Blue Jays or the 2003 Carolina Panthers is no grand moment. But pushing the greatest team in hockey history to seven tough games, that's something worth remembering.

Angelo says: The fans who believe there is some kind of supernatural hex against Philadelphia sports teams offer many examples of promise unfulfilled. You're right, Glen. We know heartbreak. But you're wrong about the best example of this close-but-no-cigar syndrome.

If you want real sports injustice, consider the improbable fate of the 1991 Eagles. Now *that* was a team that knew how to trample the emotions. Of all of the Eagles pretenders over the past 15 years, this was the one that people will never forget. Without question, it was the most talented group of players in Eagles history.

Today, the epitaph of that football team reads like a trivia question: What team won seven of its last eight games, had the top-rated defense in the NFL, *and failed to make the playoffs*?

Of course, it had to be a Philadelphia team. No other city could ever be that unlucky.

The 1991 Eagles began the season with the greatest defensive player in their history, Reggie White, in his absolute prime. They ended the season with four other Pro Bowlers on that defense: Jerome Brown, Clyde Simmons, Eric Allen and Seth Joyner—not to mention two other elite players, Wes Hopkins and William Thomas.

How good was that 1991 defense? It is the only unit in Eagles history that finished the season ranked number one in both run and pass defense. In ten of the 16 games, that smothering defense held the opposing team to two touchdowns or less.

If talent were the only barometer, the offense was almost as good as the defense. The most explosive player in the NFL was at quarterback, Randall Cunningham. Behind him in the backfield was one of the most versatile players in the game, Keith Byars. Fred Barnett, Roy Green, Calvin Williams, and Kenny Jackson provided a deep receiving corps. Tight end Keith Jackson was emerging as a huge threat that season.

So what's wrong with this picture?

Well, I gave you a clue earlier in this essay when I used the phrase "without question." That's right. This Rolls Royce was being driven by Mr. Magoo.

The coach was a dimwit named Rich Kotite.

Buddy Ryan, who had assembled this amazing collection of football skill, often said in the years after his abrupt departure that the 1991 team was "The One." When owner Norman Braman had decided to fire Ryan after another quick playoff exit in 1990, Ryan pleaded for one more year. He knew how close they were. But Braman had another plan.

If you really want to torture yourself, consider that the baguette-eating owner even had an option that could have led these Eagles to the Super Bowl without Ryan. He had a young defensive genius named Jeff Fisher as a candidate for the head job. But Braman picked the dumbest coach in the history of the NFL instead.

And what Kotite couldn't accomplish with his own stupidity, he achieved with incredibly bad luck. Cunningham went down with a season-ending injury in the first week, but even that was not a fatal blow. The backup was Jim McMahon, a swaggering swashbuckler who had led the 1985 Chicago Bears to a Super Bowl. Then McMahon got hurt, too.

Enter the NFL's version of the Three Stooges: Brad Goebel, Pat Ryan, and Jeff Kemp. All three were hand-picked by Kotite. All three were as inept as the coach himself.

By the time McMahon had recovered, the most talented Eagles team ever was 3-5. And then—even with Kotite calling the shots—they went on a tear. Their only loss in the ensuing half-season was to a team that would soon dominate the league, the hated Dallas Cowboys.

But it was too late. Despite a 10-6 record, the Eagles were denied a berth in the play-offs by the tiebreaker. They were never that talented again. Soon, White would leave for Green Bay. Brown would die in a tragic car accident. Cunningham would never be the same after the injury.

Glen, I will concede that the '86-'87 Flyers were heartbreakers, too. And they came a lot closer to the big prize than the 1991 Eagles. I actually spent three weeks in Edmonton covering that seven-game Final. To come so close against a dynasty like the Oilers was downright cruel.

That is our fate as Philadelphia sports fans, I guess.

We lead the league in pain.

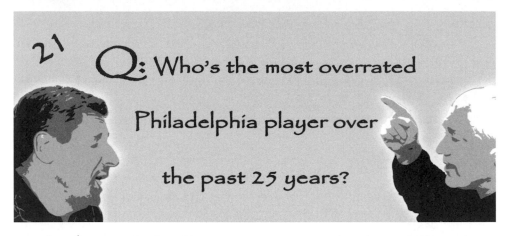

Q: Who's the most overrated Philadelphia player over the past 25 years?

Angelo says: The day of his appearance on my TV show late in the 2003 season, Troy Vincent called with some bad news. He would *not* be appearing on Comcast Sportsnet because he saw a commercial on the station that didn't reflect his wholesome image.

I was incredulous. Troy Vincent had been portrayed for eight blissful seasons as *the* role model of Philadelphia athletes, if not the entire country. Troy Vincent would not leave me hanging a few hours before an important show because of a TV commercial, would he?

Oh, yes. He would, and he did.

I never saw Vincent the same way after that. So please understand if I'm carrying a little baggage as I proclaim him the most overrated player in Philadelphia sports history. From the day he arrived in 1996, I was not impressed with him as a football player. By the time he left, I didn't think much of him as a person, either.

And not just because he stood me up that night on live TV. In the days following the end of the 2003 season, I began to monitor his comments as he toured NFL teams in search of a new home. It became clear pretty quickly that he was vastly overrated as a role model.

Can you spell P-H-O-N-Y?

First, at the Pro Bowl, he professed his love for Carolina—the very team that had ended his career in Philadelphia with a devastating loss in the NFC championship game—and said he would like nothing more than to return "home" in 2004.

Wasn't Philadelphia supposed to be home? Didn't he grow up in Trenton, New Jersey and dedicate years of his life trying to rebuild that downtrodden city?

That was then. This was Carolina.

His next audition was in Denver, where—yup, he did it again—he regaled reporters with stories of his close bond with the Mile High City. (I think one of his second cousins spent a night in Boulder back in the late 1980s.) The media ate it up.

Then he signed a contract to play in Buffalo.

OK, so maybe Vincent wasn't everything he tried to be off the field. Surely, he was a terrific player on it, no?

Uh, no. He was a good player, sure. He did make the Pro Bowl five times in his 12-year career. But he was hardly the impenetrable force that he would have people believe.

In his last three years, he averaged less than three interceptions a season, and was nowhere to be found in the biggest games of his career, the NFL title contests. In fact, big plays—a true measuring stick of a cornerback—have been rare throughout his career.

I challenge you, Glen, to name the game-saving tackles or the drive-ending interceptions that marked Troy Vincent's eight seasons in Philadelphia. Even with forced fumbles, he was responsible for less than five turnovers a season—way below contemporaries like Darrell Green or Aeneas Williams, to name just two.

What Vincent did better than anyone was sell himself. He won the support of fellow players and fans in the Pro Bowl voting by flashing that radiant smile until he started to resemble a Miss America candidate. And he courted the media at every turn, ready with a quote that always showed himself in the best possible light—often to the point of absurdity.

At the end of his tenure with the Eagles, he even tried to write the postscript of his partnership with fellow cornerback Bobby Taylor. Vincent said: "For the last eight years, we've been the cornerstone. We believe that we're going to go down as one of the best duos in the history of the game."

It sounds like Vincent is already rehearsing his Hall of Fame speech. And if he does, we can all look forward to him telling us how great it is to be back home in Canton, Ohio.

Glen says: Take the career statistics, divide them by the 12 years this player spent in as a Phillie, and here's what you get: An average season of 11 home runs, 47 runs batted in and a .245 batting average.

Sounds like Marlon Anderson, doesn't it? Or Travis Lee. Or some other mediocrity that management brought in over the years. But it isn't. Those numbers belong to a guy whom many will tell you—straight-faced—was the greatest catcher in franchise history.

I come here not to bury Darren Daulton, but to put his career in perspective. Sure, he was the clubhouse captain of that thrilling 1993 World Series team, finishing seventh in the voting for National League MVP (teammate Lenny Dykstra finished second). He was also solid the year before that, leading the league with 109 RBIs. (Boy, hasn't baseball changed? These days, 109 RBIs doesn't land you on the top ten.)

But that's about it. The rest of Daulton's lengthy career was spent either on the disabled list or battling the Mendoza Line. Five separate seasons he hit under .210. Two of those years—1987 and 1991—he couldn't reach .200. And, other than 1992 and 1993, he never topped 57 RBIs in a season with the Phillies.

Still, when Phils fans voted their all-time Veterans Stadium team in 2003, the winner at catcher was Dutch Daulton. What? Over Bob Boone? How could that be? Boonie was about as good a hitter as Daulton, albeit without the power, and as reliable a backstop as you'll ever find. You don't want to debate me about the fielding. Boone won seven Gold Gloves to Daulton's, uh, zero.

The baseball stats guru (read: nerd) Bill James devised a formula for comparing player's careers. Known as "similarity scores," it tells you what player's numbers most resemble another's. Boone's "similars" are five-time all-star Tony Pena and Hall of Famer Al Lopez. Daulton's are Ernie Whitt and Mike Macfarlane. I wonder if fans in Kansas City voted to put the anonymous Macfarlane on their all-time Royals Stadium team.

How does this happen? Well, I've got a theory. Actually, it comes from noted philosopher Jules Winnfield (played by Samuel L. Jackson) in Pulp Fiction. Explaining why people eat pigs but not dogs, Winnfield said, "Dog's got personality. And personality goes a long way."

Dutch Daulton was neither a pig nor a dog, but he did have a ton of personality. Guys wanted to be with him. Women wanted to, umm, be with him. Personality goes a long way. He also had that million-dollar smile and flowing light-brown hair that made him look like a winner. For the very same reasons we believe that Keanu Reeves can act or that Dan Quayle was actually a competent leader, we choose to believe that Daulton was a star player.

He had his moments, for sure. Hell, Reeves pulled off "The Matrix," as well. But for most of his career, Daulton was disappointing or unreliable. Nine knee surgeries didn't help, but the debate here isn't health, it's reputation. When he finally got to the big stage of post-season in 1993, Dutch was under-whelming. He hit .238 with two homers in 12 games.

Daulton's two good seasons came after seven which could generously be termed mediocre. Phils management then fell into the trap of believing that the exception was the rule. Ignoring history—and all those knee operations—they awarded him a three-year, $15.4 million contract extension. For all that money, they got a lusty 20 homers and 97 RBIs before finally trading him to the Florida Marlins in 1997 for the forgettable Billy McMillon.

All-time Vet team? I sure don't get it.

By the way, I picked Darren Daulton for this honor by the narrowest of margins over Darryl Dawkins, the backboard-shattering heartbreaker. The lesson here, Angelo: Never trust those Double-Ds.

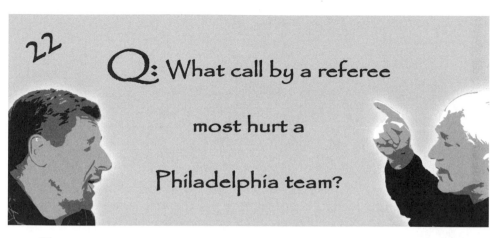

Q: What call by a referee most hurt a Philadelphia team?

Glen says: Actually, I'll cite a non-call here. And I'll tell you that it was so outrageous that it may have cost this city a championship.

Go back to May 24, 1980. The Flyers trailed the Islanders, three games to two, in the Stanley Cup Finals. But Philadelphia had won Game 5 and had momentum going into the Nassau Coliseum that Saturday afternoon. The Islanders, back then, had a reputation for choking.

The good guys got an early lead on a Reggie Leach power-play slapper. Then, the Islanders' Denis Potvin batted a rebound out of the air to tie the game. Potvin's stick was above his shoulder, and the goal should not have counted.

But that's not the blown call I'm talking about, Angelo.

No, the real cause for outrage came later in the first period.

New York winger Clark Gillies skated down the left boards, crossed the Flyers' blue line and dropped the puck to trailing center Butch Goring. The puck clearly passed back across the blue line and into the center-ice zone before Goring collected it and carried it over the line himself.

Veteran linesman Leon Stickle was in perfect position to see the offsides, which would have blown the play dead. The infraction was so evident that back-checking Flyers winger Brian Propp eased up, a decision he has regretted for a quarter century. Also, Flyers defenseman Moose Dupont pointed his stick at the blue line, signaling for a whistle.

The whistle didn't come. Stickle instead gave a "safe" sign and play continued. Goring flipped a pass to right winger Duane Sutter—Propp's man—who lifted the puck over goalie Pete Peeters to give the Islanders the lead.

The Flyers went berserk, but what good would that do? Television replays showed an obvious blown call, but the referees were having none of it.

Stickle saw those replays—much later—and admitted his mistake. "I guess I blew it," he said. "The puck came back across the line. Maybe there was black tape on Goring's stick and it confused me. Or maybe I was too close to the play."

Or maybe you're just an incompetent idiot.

Regardless, the Flyers fought both the Islanders and the officials to tie the game at 4-4. Seven minutes into overtime, Islander Bobby Nystrom broke toward the Flyers' goal, took a pass on his backhand and thrust it past Peeters.

Season over. The Flyers' chance for their third Stanley Cup was gone. The Islanders, previously known as "Team Choke," won their first of four straight titles.

Afterward, Ed Snider addressed reporters in his usual understated style. "It was an absolute, total, bleeping mistake," the Flyers owner opined. "Anybody who's impartial knows we took a screwing today. The officials who come out of Toronto and Montreal don't want us to win . . . . The problem with this league is (referee-in-chief) Scotty Morrison. He should be shot."

Truth be told, the Flyers had plenty of chances to come back and win that game. But Stickle's call was so contemptuously inept that few fans would fault Snider for his anger at the time. Stickle hailed from suburban Toronto, which on Flyer maps was located just a few miles from Moscow.

This game should not have been played!

History records that the Flyers had the NHL's best regular-season record during the 1979-80 season. They set a league mark by going thirty-five games without a defeat. But, as Bobby Clarke said at the time, "The only thing people will ever remember is who won the Stanley Cup."

In this town, what people remember is Leon "Bleeping" Stickle. To the credit of our fans, he was booed every single time he stepped on the ice in Philadelphia for the rest of his 27-year career.

We could go another 27 years booing him and we still wouldn't be even.

Angelo says: Leon Stickle will live forever as a nemesis of Philadelphia, as well he should. In fact, whenever this topic arises, Stickle's name is sure to follow—like Christmas with the Grinch.

But is he the biggest villain wearing stripes in our history? No, he is not. There was a far bigger miscarriage of justice than a missed call by a sight-impaired linesman, Glen. What if I told you a ref ruined an entire season, and maybe an era, for the most beloved of all our teams?

It happened on December 31, 1988, at a time when the Eagles were poised to fulfill the bold promises of coach Buddy Ryan that were three seasons in the making. Randall Cunningham was the MVP of the NFL that year, Reggie White was terrorizing quarterbacks at a historic pace, and the Eagles were favored—no, they were *expected*—to bury an aging and deteriorating Chicago Bears team.

Ever the agitator, Ryan celebrated the Eagles' first playoff appearance in seven years by holding an impromptu parade, horns blaring, around Soldier Field upon the arrival of his team the day before the game. Back then, Ryan was a hero in Chicago for leading the Bears defense to their Super Bowl in 1986, but he was already more beloved and admired (and sometimes hated) by his new Philadelphia fans.

When the contest started at 11:30 a.m. central time, conditions were playable, and there was no inkling that a cold-air mass was filtering into the warm air over Soldier Field. There had been no predictions of fog that day. Rain, maybe. Snow flurries, possibly. But no fog.

Early in the second quarter, with the Bears holding a tenuous 7-6 lead, the fog began to roll over the field so quickly and so completely that play was halted several times while the refs tried to decide what to do. Head official Jim Tunney, aware that the NFL was broadcasting another playoff game three-and-a-half hours later, refused to halt the game and wait until conditions improved.

How bad was it, Glen? The NFL agreed to allow the media to watch the second half from the sidelines because no one could see the field! But the commissioner's office never seriously considered a delay that would have been the only fair resolution to an impossible situation.

The rest of the story is a bit of a blur, Glen. Because no one really knows exactly how it all played out. The final score was Chicago 20, Philadelphia 12. The stat sheet showed Cunningham with an amazing 407 yards passing in the fog, but it didn't show the dropped touchdown pass by Keith Jackson or the motion penalty by Anthony Toney that nullified a TD pass to Mike Quick. Both Jackson and Toney attributed the miscues to the fog.

Even more sobering is what happened in the ensuing years of Buddy Ryan's reign. The Eagles would be back to the playoffs in the succeeding two seasons, but they would never win a playoff game under Ryan. Ask Ryan today what his biggest regret was in his five years in Philadelphia, and he'll tell you it was the Fog Bowl.

If the Eagles had won that contest, what would have happened the next week in the

NFC championship game? The Bears got crushed by San Francisco, 28-3. Would the Eagles have beaten the eventual Super Bowl champs? Probably not. But would the fate of Ryan in Philadelphia have taken a different course? Without question.

And all because of one irresponsible, absurd decision by a group of officials on the foggiest day in football history.

There's an amazing postscript to this story, too. Jim Tunney, the man who didn't have the wisdom or the guts to wait out the weather, now lists the Fog Bowl on his résumé for speaking engagements. He's trying to make money from the worst miscarriage of justice in Philadelphia sports history.

That's something even Leon Stickle would never try.

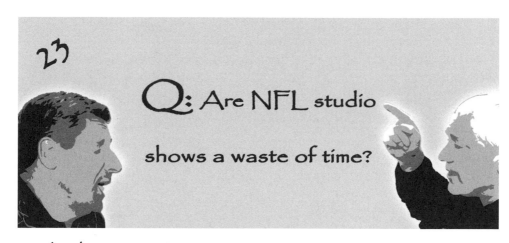

Q: Are NFL studio shows a waste of time?

Angelo says: Not so long ago, every Sunday football started at precisely 12:30 p.m., when Brent, Irv, Phyllis, and Jimmy would pop up on the screen for a 30-minute precursor to six magical hours of sports entertainment.

Back then, the hosts of *The NFL Today* on CBS didn't even need their last names. They were that popular. Brent Musberger was the energy behind the show, Irv Cross was the amiable expert, Phyllis George was the eye candy and Jimmy "The Greek" Snyder provided the essential information—namely, who to bet on.

It was never really considered a great show back in its 1980s heyday, but it sure seems terrific today, compared to the forced, phony and irrelevant presentations on Fox, CBS and ESPN. For me—and many others, I assume—football Sundays start at the one o'clock first-game kickoff now. I cannot stomach one minute of these nauseating pre-game shows.

Fox is the leader in the ratings. It would need a major upgrade to become terrible. James Brown is OK as the host, but Terry Bradshaw is like a weekly flare-up of prickly heat. He radiates so much energy, so much fake hilarity, that you want to restrain him and jam valium down his throat. Howie Long is an intellectual by comparison, filled with a smug coolness based on absolutely nothing. Jimmy Johnson's hair remains the only noteworthy aspect of his TV persona.

Once every year, I force myself to sit through an entire 60-minute pre-game show on Fox, just to see what improvements they've made. (OK, so maybe I also do it to have more ammunition for my radio rants.) The fact is, the show just keeps getting worse.

Jillian Barberie with the weather? If Jillian Barberie actually knew anything about the weather, she wouldn't bare her midriff and upper thighs every winter. (Not that I'm complaining.) Frank Caliendo with impressions? Well, at least he finally made people appreciate Jimmy Kimmel.

It's all so much baloney. And the irony is, the one thing they might actually have to offer—opinion—has been sold a long time ago to the highest bidder: the NFL, of course. If anybody knows the NFL, they would no more allow strong criticism on these shows than they'd permit Al Davis to sing the National Anthem at the next Super Bowl.

The sad part is, the Fox show may be the best of the bunch. CBS, which owned the franchise with Brent, Irv, Phyllis, and Jimmy a generation ago, actually thought so highly of the Fox program that the network made a carbon-copy, right down to the fake football field where the fellas can map out a play together. (Has anyone ever actually learned anything in this segment, except that these old guys are out of shape?)

Like Fox, the quarterback is fine. Jim Nantz is a pro. But Dan Marino? He's as entertaining as a ruptured tendon. Boomer Esiason is the only TV studio host willing to actually state an opinion, but it is invariably shouted down by the dopes surrounding him. A case in point is Deion Sanders, who dressed with so much flair, he should have been working the streets with Jillian Barberie. Sanders left after the 2003 season when CBS offered him only a cool million a year for his TV bling-bling. How dare they.

ESPN is the worst of the lot because they have a full *two hours* to fill each Sunday, and they don't even have a decent quarterback. Someday, someone is going to explain to me the appeal of Chris Berman. He's not particularly knowledgeable. He's not a good interviewer. He's not funny. His clothes look like he raided the bin at the Salvation Army. And he lives in the back pocket of just about every NFL team in the league.

The rest of the crew is pathetic. Steve Young is to sports entertainment what saltpeter is to topless bars. Sterling Sharpe is the biggest fraud in broadcasting, a self-obsessed jerk who never spoke to the media until he was a member of the media. And his interview style is reminiscent of Barbara Walters—only it's the viewer who's crying at the end, not the subject.

Of course, I wouldn't embark on an essay like this, Glen, without some of my own ideas on how to present a good pre-game show. This is not just what I want. This is what the fans want.

• Go back to the 30-minute format. The day is long enough without all of that blabber before the first kickoff.

• Hire funny people, not people who just laugh all the time. My choice would be someone like Philadelphia's own Dom Irrera, who is hilarious and knows more sports than the athletes doing these shows.

• Clean out all of the good-old-boys. Hasn't anyone come along since Terry Bradshaw and Howie Long who would be more current and have more to offer?

• Bring back the tout. Gambling has been the 800-pound gorilla in the pre-game studio ever since Jimmy The Greek was dumped. People would still love to know what an expert thinks. And he should use the spread when he makes his picks. It's much harder that way.

There is no better day in the year than a Sunday in the fall, Glen. Football Sundays are precious to lazy old bums like us. I just wish they had a proper introduction.

Glen says: Boy, you gripe a lot, Angelo. And for a guy who thinks these pre-game shows are such a waste of time, you sure spend a lot of hours watching them.

Look, I'm not going to argue here that this is Masterpiece Theater (although I'd enjoy seeing Terry Bradshaw cast as Willy Loman, and Howie Long as Biff). What I'll say is that the shows do a good job of setting the stage for a full day of gridiron mania.

An hour is too long for you? How can you call yourself a fan? Considering there are nine full hours of games every Sunday, I've got no problem setting up my day with a 60-minute brunch with former players and analysts. Those guys are my companions as I brew up a big pot of coffee, scour through the Sunday paper and get my bookie on the cell phone. It's part of the ritual. I wouldn't have it any other way.

Certainly, some are better than others. Yes, we could drop Deion Sanders, Michael Irvin, Jillian Barberie, and Jimmy Kimmel down a deep well and the world would be a better place (Kimmel was hysterical on "The Man Show," but he's been unable to transfer that humor anywhere else).

But I'll stick up for Dan Marino and Steve Young here. In fact, I've found that most former quarterbacks (notable exceptions: Joe Montana and Randall Cunningham), do a terrific job of interpreting the game and explaining it to the viewer. Esiason is the best, because he's the most critical and does it from a position of knowledge.

Speaking of knowledge, you left out an entire group of experts here, Angelo. Fox's John Czarnecki and ESPN's Chris Mortenson and John Clayton make my Sunday mornings that much more enjoyable (read: profitable) by providing up-to-the-minute factoids on player's health, field conditions, and which coach is going through a mid-life crisis. Mortenson is so connected that, if he says Clinton Portis is out for a game, I see the line move a half-point between the time I dial the phone and my bookie answers.

You bemoan the loss of Jimmy the Greek, Ange. Trust me, Greek's opinions on the line were about as accurate as his scientific observations on race and biology. The guy was as credible on football as Martha Stewart and Sunday afternoon investors knew it.

The great thing about these shows is that they take you through every game on the schedule. You don't have to watch every minute. If, for example, you don't care about Cincinnati at San Diego, Angelo, you can always force yourself out of the La-Z-Boy and reintroduce yourself to family members. Don't take too long, however, because Terry Bradshaw's soon going to take another swipe at Donovan McNabb. You don't want to miss that.

In an era of bland, Bradshaw, Howie Young, Jimmy Johnson, and a few others are unafraid to give strong views. Yep, their comments sometimes get swallowed up by the good-ol'-boy histrionics, but at least they have opinions. And they really know the game.

The amazing thing about football, above all other sports, is that fans can't get enough. Tens of millions of people who never actually attended an NFL game in person still plan their entire Sundays—from September through January—around watching every televised morsel they can (okay, maybe not the "Andy Reid Show"). Imagine if they mapped out the rest of their lives so meticulously.

The pre-game shows give those people (and by "those people," I mean me and everyone I know), a chance to slide into a full day of couch potato action. From Chris Berman's 11 a.m. sign-on, through Howie and Terry's yukfest, through the inside info that Kurt Warner is battling a carbuncle, I can't get enough.

So make my eggs over-easy. Freshen up the coffee. And get "my man" on the phone. Another glorious Sunday is just beginning.

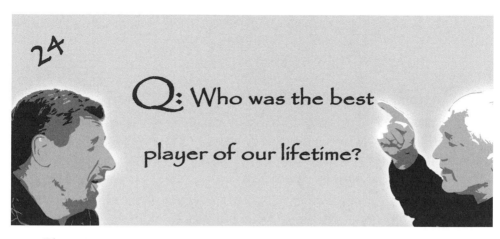

24

Q: Who was the best player of our lifetime?

Glen says: Well, to start, Angelo, he's a guy I always rooted against. You did too, as I recall. He was a Grade A phony and a guy who never took a stand for anything more than making a buck.

So, imagine how great Michael Jordan had to be for me to get past all that and cite him as the top player of our lifetime (which, in your case, goes back a little further than mine). But, really, there's no other choice than this compulsive-gambling, endorsement-grabbing, recidivist-retiring money machine. For years I argued that Wilt was basketball's best-ever player, until Jordan's accomplishments forced me to give up that ghost.

After that, who's left? Joe Montana? Jim Brown? Actually, I think Jerry Rice is the best football player of our lifetime, and I can't take him over Jordan.

Nor can I take Barry Bonds, because the greatest baseball player we've seen came up light in the post-season and heavy in the cheating department. And I'll stay away from Wayne Gretzky and Bobby Orr largely because, even though I'm a proud hockey geek, I recognize that hoops is played on a larger stage.

So it's gotta be, like, Mike.

Where do I start here? I could give you the numbers. He's the NBA's all-time leading scorer. His 30.1 points per game over fifteen seasons rank about one finger-roll above Chamberlain. He led the league in scoring ten times. Plus, he was a great stopper, placing second all-time in steals and making the league's all-defensive team nine separate seasons.

He collected more hardware than Tim the Toolman. Five MVP awards, 10 All-NBA first team citations and, most importantly, five MVP awards from the NBA finals. Because, as much as squeezing out a buck, Jordan was about winning. He led the Bulls to three championships, retired to play baseball (what the hell was that about, anyway?), and came back to lead them to three more titles.

He had a flair for the dramatic. Remember 1998, when, as a 35-year-old, he swept the three MVP honors (regular season, All-Star Game and NBA Finals) and capped it off by hitting that title-winning jumper against the Utah Jazz with 5.2 seconds left in Game 6? I still think he pushed off Bryon Russell, by the way, but it doesn't matter. What a perfect way to end a career.

Oh, he came back again, you say?

Regardless. Go through the entire history of the NBA. Who would you rather have take the final shot with the game on the line? Not Bird, not Oscar, not West. Nobody, really. Everyone always knew Jordan would get that "look." The other team's top defender was always in his face. And still he always made it.

Jordan's 1995-96 Bulls went 72-10, the best record in league history. I won't insult you by saying they were the best team ever because, after Jordan and the overrated Scottie Pippen, they were just a bunch of guys. And, yes, it's a watered-down league. Still, give Jordan credit for establishing that season-win mark almost single-handedly.

One more point: Jordan was more popular than any team athlete in the past 50 years. Like Ali, he was bigger than his sport. How many millions of kids had that tongue-wagging, high-flying "Air Jordan" poster on their walls over the years? How many zillions of pairs of sneakers did he sell? How many jerseys—with two different numbers?

It's a shame that we must value our jocks by how many boxes of Wheaties or gallons of Gatorade they can move, but that's what sports has become. Jordan did that better than anyone in history.

And the fact remains that since his last retirement (at least I pray it's his last), pro basketball has gotten boring. Am I supposed to get charged up about an NBA Conference Final pitting Ben Wallace vs. Reggie Miller?

Please, wake me when that's over.

Angelo says: Let me start this discussion with a disclaimer, Glen: I have excluded Wilt Chamberlain as the greatest player of our lifetime because we are restricting this distinction to mere humans. As I point out elsewhere in this book, Wilt redefined greatness. In addition to his many fine literary efforts, you might want to pick up his best one. It's called *The NBA Record Book*.

Likewise, Wayne Gretzky has authored so many astonishing milestones in his career that he could make the same claim in hockey. In a sport with names like Orr and Hull and Lemieux and Howe, Gretzky redefined greatness. He was so much better than anybody else, there is no reasonable debate about who was the best ever.

But was Gretzky better in his sport than Michael Jordan was in his?

Absolutely, Glen. It's really not even close.

Setting aside for a moment the character issue—remember, I said *for a moment*—just consider the issue of dominance. At last count, Gretzky held or shared 61 individual scoring records, including most points (2,856), most goals (895), most assists (1,962), most 50-goal seasons (9), most 100-point seasons (15) and every imaginable post-season landmark in the sport.

And it's not just that Gretzky holds these marks; he *owns* them. His most-points total is 1,001 better than the runner-up, teammate Mark Messier. His most-assists mark is nearly 800 ahead of Messier. If Messier keeps playing into his 90s, he might actually challenge Gretzky's records.

Yes, Jordan holds the career-scoring mark in the NBA, by "about one finger-roll above Chamberlain." Those are your words, Glen. I won't even discuss Wilt's change of emphasis late in his career from offense to defense. Let's just say their career numbers in scoring are very close. No one is in the same area code with Gretzky. Wayne Gretzky dominated his sport as no one did—maybe not even (gulp) Wilt himself.

You also accurately point out the flair for the dramatic that became Jordan's trademark, especially in amassing six NBA championships. Well, I don't think you'd disagree that Gretzky's four Stanley Cups in Edmonton come close to matching that accomplishment, especially since the second half of his career was dedicated to reviving bad franchises (Los Angeles, New York) and trying to save his dying sport.

And this is where Jordan really loses the battle, Glen. Do you believe for a second that Jordan ever could have set aside his own personal interest for the sake of his sport the way Gretzky did in the final years? Not a chance. In fact, Jordan abandoned his sport for a year to pursue his half-cocked dream of playing baseball. With Jordan, it was always just about MJ. He was the most selfish player in the history of sports.

Gretzky was the most generous. To know this man was to revere him. In my experience, he was the most accommodating, most accessible superstar ever. He was everything that the marketers tried—and failed miserably—to create for Jordan.

Michael Jordan was a jerk. Wayne Gretzky was a gem. Enough said.

And there is one final reason why Gretzky is the greatest human athlete of our lifetime, Glen. You see, he's at the top of just about every individual record in NHL history. Jordan is not. Jordan never scored 100 points. He never grabbed 55 rebounds. He never so dominated his sport that the league had to change the rules to give opponents a chance to compete.

Wayne Gretzky was the greatest hockey player ever, Glen. By far.

Michael Jordan was the second-best basketball player. Wilt was the best. By far.

In the words of Casey Stengel, you could look it up.

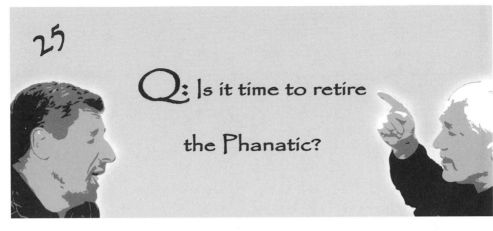

25

Q: Is it time to retire the Phanatic?

Angelo says: We may not have the best teams or the best coaches or the best players, but Philadelphia has one thing that no other sports city in America can match.

We have the Philly Phanatic—the best mascot in the history of sports.

When the Phillies made the switch from Veterans Stadium to Citizens Bank Park, there were a few murmurs that the Phanatic should stay behind. The sadists in the crowd even suggested that the furry one park himself right under the 700 Level when the building was imploded.

These people, of course, are humorless jerks who never had kids and who have forever lost the child in themselves.

One of my best memories of being a dad was back in the 1980s when my daughter was about five or six and my son two years younger. It was the Phanatic's birthday, and he had decided to career down a tightrope from the top of the left-field foul pole all the way to home plate.

I can remember having to explain that there was no chance that the Phanatic would plunge to a fur-filled death in front of 60,000 fans on his birthday. The Phanatic will never die, I told them that day. Like so many other children, my kids cheered the big guy when he was safely back on the ground. Today, my grandkids are cheering him.

The biggest complaint about the Phanatic is that he never changes his act. Why should he? Has anyone ever really tired of the green man's lascivious hug of some beautiful woman in the stands? Has anyone ever *not* looked forward to the Phanatic jumping up on the dugout and boogie-ing his way through the seventh-inning stretch at every game? Who doesn't love the mocking of opponents, the feuds with the Tommy Lasordas, that patented hip-thrust of utter disdain?

I honestly didn't realize how important the Phanatic was to the culture of Philadelphia until his head went missing in the winter of 2004. For two sad weeks, the city mourned the loss of those devilish eyes and that darting tongue. Kids were crying in the streets.

Rewards in the thousands of dollars were offered. A furhunt was launched by Philly's finest.

The Phanatic's first appearance at a game after his head was found told the whole story. He was at the new spring-training home of the Phillies in Clearwater, Florida, harassing an opponent that rarely had seen his act, the despised New York Yankees. Instead of watching the Phanatic go through his antics, I focused that day on the multi-million-aires in the visitor's dugout. To a man, they were laughing uproariously as the Phanatic went through a new routine as a bank teller.

Look around the league at all of the dumb, tired mascots who are designed to look like the Phanatic but could never hope to fill his floppy size-36 sneakers. It's not even close. I actually applauded Randall Simon last year when he clobbered that kielbasa in Milwaukee. That dopey mascot deserved it.

It's no coincidence that, in all his years of poking fun at players and managers, not one of them has ever tried to retaliate against the Phanatic.

You know why?

Because the Phanatic would have kicked their ass, that's why!

And he'll kick yours, too, Glen, if you don't watch what you say about him.

Glen says: You're right about one thing Ange—once upon a time, the Phanatic was a fun and innovative act. Of course, once upon a time, my friend, those leisure suits and wide lapels you still wear were considered high fashion.

Times change. Smart entertainers re-invent themselves periodically to keep up. But the Phanatic's act has gone as moth-bitten as the ratty suit he wears day in and day out. Let's see now . . . push your belly out at the pregnant woman . . . shine the bald guy's head (and, yes, I've received the chamois treatment myself a few times) . . . cast the evil spell on opponents' bats. With apologies to Henny Youngman, jokes tend to lose their edge when you've known the punch line for twenty years.

This is not meant to be an attack on either Dave Raymond or Tom Burgoyne, the athletic and talented men who have served as "the Phanatic's best friend" over the years. But the Phillies have changed managers, uniforms, logos, stadiums, and even their attitude over the years. What's so sacrosanct about a green hair ball?

I realize I'm taking the curmudgeon side of this argument. But I cringe at every cutesy-pie, big-snouted, bug-eyed pile of fluff that stalks our nation's sidelines these days. The Phanatic is to blame for this population explosion of adorable animals, vegetables and, yes, even processed-meat products. And, besides, he's not even a true mascot. The Saint Joe's Hawk is a breathing, flapping representative of that fine university's team nickname. The Phanatic is a . . . well, what is he anyway?

We know that the Phanatic was the brainchild of Phillies executive Bill Giles, who decided somewhere along the line that actual baseball wasn't sufficient to entertain fans at a baseball game. We needed freak shows. Giles wasn't alone among baseball people in this line of thinking. So, New York got a snorting, steaming big apple, Milwaukee got a guy in lederhosen who slides into a beer stein and we got a fat man in a shag carpet.

This philosophy invaded most sports arenas in recent years. The Flyers and Sixers constantly bombard their fans with video messages, movie clips and trivia games during every time out. Some folks gripe that Flyers fans have become too passive in recent years, blaming the lack of passion on the move from the Spectrum to the Big House. I'll tell you where the hush comes from: We spend so much time gazing at the overhead scoreboard wondering which puck the cell phone is hidden under that we've forgotten how to start up a rowdy "Let's Go Flyers" chant.

But I digress. The best argument for the Phanatic is that he's able to entertain little kids at the Phillies games and that, somehow, that will transform them into future devotees of the sport. I don't know. To me, he's really more of a babysitter, a side show to keep the tykes distracted for five or six innings so that dad can actually enjoy a three-hour game. But a distraction should not be the attraction.

If you want to make a child into a baseball aficionado, try to sell them on the magnificence of a Billy Wagner fastball or a Jim Thome upper-decker. Yes, baseball moves slowly, but that's the beauty of the sport. Spend some time in actual conversation with your youngster, explaining how to keep score or why the infield shifts on a particular play. If the sport really isn't dead, that should be enough to entertain everyone for an afternoon.

26

Q: Did booing McNabb embarrass the city?

Glen says: Gee, I don't know. Did dropping a bomb on Osage Avenue hurt Mayor Goode's image? Did presenting Mike Quick with an empty golf bag make Norman Braman look like a cheapskate?

Sorry, Angelo, but the heckling of McNabb on Draft Day 1999 ranks among our lowest moments as a sports town. I understand all the extenuating circumstances. I understand that the anger was aimed more at *not picking* Ricky Williams than actually *picking* McNabb. But the bottom line is the bottom line—it made our city look like a barn full of jackasses.

The Booing of McNabb has replaced Snowballs at Santa as the collective albatross slung around our necks. In fact, it's worse, because no one has tape of Kris Kringle dodging the ice bombs back in 1968. But we all know that every time the Eagles are on Monday Night Football, here comes that infernal video clip: Thirty of our most ardent fans, faces painted green-and-silver, sputtering in anger and shaking their fists as Commissioner Paul Tagliabue announces the pick. The camera cuts to a mortified McNabb, searching the crowd for his tormentors as Tagliabue tries to soothe the frazzled kid.

There ought to be a statute of limitations on this, but there isn't. So whenever I'm out of town and tell people where I work, they always hit me with, "Aren't you the guys who killed that quarterback when he got drafted?"

"Well, yeah," I stammer, "but, you see, we weren't really booing *him*. We were actually booing the circumstances . . . ."

There's really no good way of explaining it.

But I'll try.

With the sad-sack Birds owning the second pick in the draft, fans wanted them to pick a player who could have an immediate impact. Most of us favored Ricky Williams, the monstrous University of Texas running back. So, we campaigned for Ricky. Loudly.

The Eagles weren't listening. Newly hired architect Andy Reid had blueprints to build around a quarterback. And McNabb, the star from Syracuse, was his guy.

You organized the brilliant radio stunt, Ange, of chartering a bus to New York City so that fans could watch the draft in person. Problem is, the folks on that Greyhound fueled up with beer and, as they rolled up the Jersey Turnpike, foolishly convinced themselves that the Eagles would ultimately see it their way and select Williams.

So when Tagliabue announced the pick, the knuckleheads were flabbergasted. They reacted with shock and awe. They didn't mean to be rude, but neither does the wedding guest who barfs in the punch bowl.

Be honest, Ange. We ruined McNabb's day. Despite all the apologies, I'm not sure he's ever gotten over it. Certainly his mother still holds a grudge. And, fair or not, the pompous windbags who look for any excuse to knock the Philadelphia fan base now use this episode as Exhibit A of our boorishness.

In hindsight, McNabb turned out to be a pretty good pick, don't you think? Reid made a fine choice picking him over Williams.

What we didn't know at the time was that Williams had all the talent—but not the mindset—to become an NFL superstar. He showed that after escaping the purgatory of New Orleans. During his two seasons as a Miami Dolphin, he averaged more than 1,600 rushing yards and 14 touchdowns. The problem was, he apparently enjoyed smoking pot more than playing football, retiring in 2004 after flunking three drug tests and saying he wanted to spend more time with his friends in Jamaica.

It's a shame, really. I had these visions of McNabb and Williams going into the Hall of Fame together. They'd be up on the podium in Canton, making their speeches and sharing a laugh. And I guarantee that ESPN would cut to that old tape. We may have booed McNabb for 10 seconds, but the embarrassment will last a lifetime.

Angelo says: Thank you for making my case for me, Glen. The booing of Donovan McNabb will indeed outlive us all. It will be shown on film clips decades from now. No doubt, if McNabb ever wins a Super Bowl, one of the first questions will be about how he started his pro career with a cascade of boos. If he makes the Hall of Fame, everyone will refer to the boos in their speeches.

All of which make it the single greatest radio promotion in Philadelphia history.

Now don't get me wrong. I have apologized profusely for the booing because it was—and will always be—misunderstood, and that's my fault. It was never the intention of our band of thirty idiots to screw up the greatest day in the young life of Donovan McNabb.

But it is not the criminal act you and your legion of hyperbolists claim it to be.

Let me tell you the whole story, Glen, and then you can decide just how terrible it was.

Then-Mayor Ed Rendell called my show one day and said we should organize a campaign to convince the Eagles to draft the big running back from Texas, Ricky Williams. The mayor said he'd throw all of the power of his office behind our effort.

At the time, I will now admit, I didn't really have a strong opinion about what the Eagles should do in the 1999 draft. But I had a very strong opinion about overseeing a radio promotion endorsed by the mayor himself.

In the weeks leading up to the draft, the movement took on a life of its own. We had no trouble getting thirty tickets for the draft in New York, nor did I have any difficulty at all forming a collection of "real Eagles fans" to fill those seats. We even gave them a name, The Dirty Thirty.

On the day before the draft, Mayor Rendell suddenly realized the one weakness in our campaign: What if the Eagles picked someone other than Williams? At the time, it was beginning to look like Andy Reid was leaning toward McNabb.

"Whatever you do," Rendell warned, "don't boo McNabb if he ends up being the guy. We don't want to ruin it for him."

Unfortunately, at that point it was way too late. I knew we were in trouble when the thirty drunk zealots broke a window in our bus on the way up to New York. A 400-pounder named Dough Boy thought it would be a great idea to moon a bus filled with senior citizens while we were side by side at a tollbooth. When his cheeks pressed too hard against the glass, the entire pane gave way.

I was praying that the Eagles would pick Williams and avoid the inevitable, but no such luck. I can say this: No one ever planned to boo. It was strictly a spontaneous reaction to the announcement by the commissioner.

As McNabb gazed into the gallery with an embarrassed grin on his face, I felt a pang of shame, yes. He deserved better.

Still, it was also very funny. You cannot deny that, Glen. The ESPN announcers were in a state of shock at the response. The New York fans were so impressed with the volume of the boo that they felt compelled to join in. Within hours, WIP and its band of morons were the talk of the country.

I don't have to explain radio to you, Glen. You've been doing it nearly as long as I have. A radio promotion is something designed to get attention, to spread the call letters far and wide. Have you ever heard of a more effective promotion than the booing of Donovan McNabb? Did you not benefit from the publicity we generated that day?

In the years since the incident, I'd like to believe that the entire McNabb family has forgiven us, though it's pretty clear they'll never forget the boos. I have personally talked

There was no doubt about who the fans wanted in the 1999 NFL draft.

to Donovan, his mom and dad, and his wife about what we did, groveling as best I could at every opportunity. They all took it in surprisingly good humor. They are really terrific people.

Since then, McNabb has emerged as one of the best quarterbacks in the NFL, he's signed a contract that will pay him well over $100 million and he has impressed everyone with the classy way he responded to the first adversity in his pro career.

If McNabb has gotten over it, Glen, why can't you?

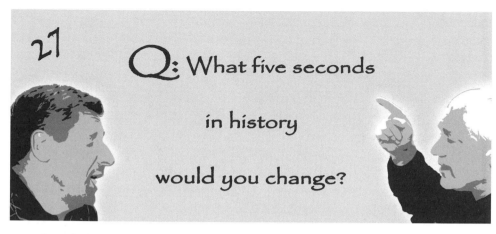

27

Q: What five seconds in history would you change?

Angelo says: Of all the topics in this book, the idea of changing five seconds in time is the most intriguing to me, and the most haunting. I actually can picture myself stepping into the fancy sports car that served as a time machine in my all-time favorite movie, *Back to the Future.*

Hmmmm. . . . This is a big responsibility. Where do I go? What do I change?

My first instinct is to prevent a tragedy, intervene in the horrific car crashes that prematurely ended the lives of two extraordinary young athletes, Pelle Lindbergh and Jerome Brown. If we could actually go back in time, Glen, obviously we all would love to change the fate of those two beloved sports heroes.

But I don't think that's the point of this exercise, nor is it proper to undo a trade or to change a draft choice. Those mistakes took way more than five seconds to make. And who's to say, with morons like Dr. Jack Ramsey or Harold Katz making the decisions, that they wouldn't do something just as stupid as trading Wilt Chamberlain or Moses Malone anyway?

Finally, I have settled on going back into a game, and doing something that would not just alter the outcome of that contest, but maybe of Philadelphia sports history itself. I've gone through dozens of moments—the Chico Ruiz steal of home that triggered the collapse of the 1964 Phillies, the infamous Leon Stickle call in the 1980 Stanley Cup Finals that ruined a season for the Flyers, the Mitch Williams pitch that ended the 1993 World Series, Ron Jaworski's errant pass early in the 1981 Super Bowl that started the downfall of the heavily-favored Eagles . . . .

In the end, though, I'm going with my gut, Glen. The play that I'd most want to change is a far more recent one, and one that will live forever in the mind of every Eagles fan.

The date is January 19, 2003, the final football game in the history of Veterans Stadium. When Brian Mitchell takes the opening kickoff back 70 yards against a cold and befuddled Tampa Bay team, the crowd is as loud as any in the history of that decrepit old building. Minutes later, the favored Eagles are already ahead, 7-0, and a trip to the Super Bowl seems inevitable.

Even when the Buccaneers answer with a field goal, no one is the least bit worried. The Eagles have already beaten the Bucs four straight times, and the temperature is in the mid-30s. Tampa has won one game in 22 tries with the temperature under 40 degrees.

With 50 seconds to go in the first quarter and the Bucs backed up on their own 29, third down and two, the moment of truth arrives. Brad Johnson drops back and flips an innocuous-looking pass into the hands of Joe Jurevicius. A possession receiver with modest speed, Jurevicius collects the ball and slinks through the middle of the Eagles secondary until he reaches the opposite sideline.

In my mind, Jurevicius is still running right now, and he will always be running. The stat sheet shows he stopped after 71 yards, getting pushed out at the Eagles' 5. But I doubt it.

Of course, the Eagles never recover. Their spell over the Bucs is broken with that one terrible play. The weather instantly warms to the low 80s. The crowd stops screaming. The Vet says goodbye to football with tears in its eyes.

The years since then have provided no relief. In fact, more information on that play has only made the moment more painful. Blaine Bishop, the strong safety responsible for Jurevicius on the play, later admitted he could barely walk when the ball was snapped. He was playing despite a serious leg injury that day, even though a terrific young rookie named Michael Lewis was ready and able on the sidelines.

I would give anything to change that play. So now I will . . . .

I step into the DeLorean, set the clock for 4:47 p.m. EST, January 19, 2003.

I've got five seconds to change fate.

I'm Andy Reid.

"Get in there for Bishop," I screech to Lewis. "And watch the crossing pattern!"

Lewis breaks up the pass. Fourth down. The Bucs punt. The Eagles have the lead now, great field position, the crowd whooping louder than ever. The temperature is dropping, and so are the chins of the Tampa players.

The Eagles win. Then they easily avenge their only other Super Bowl appearance by beating Oakland for Philadelphia's first NFL championship in 42 years. The parade is like none in sports history. Four million people clog Broad Street for hours and hours. Veterans Stadium is preserved forever as a historic monument.

And everybody lives happily ever after.

Glen says: Fine choice, Angelo. But my time machine would go back a few years further—all the way to the last five seconds of Game 7 of the 1965 NBA Eastern Conference Finals between the Sixers and those damned Boston Celtics.

I'm sure you remember the history, Ange. The Celtics had won six straight NBA titles going into the season, and no one predicted the Sixers would challenge that streak. As expected, the Sixers languished below .500 at mid-season.

But on All-Star Game day in January, the Sixers pulled off the best trade in their history, bringing home native son Wilt Chamberlain from San Francisco in return, I recall, for Manny, Moe and Jack. It took a while for Wilt to blend with his new teammates, but the Sixers snuck into the playoffs and then polished off Oscar Robertson's Cincinnati Royals in four games.

That set up the conference finals against Boston. Even in those prehistoric days of the NBA, the rivalry was intense. Dating back to the Sixers' days in Syracuse, the Celts had knocked them out of the playoffs three times in a row. And with a final record twenty-two games better than the Sixers in this season, the Celts were prohibitive favorites again.

But this time, things were different. Led by the undefendable Chamberlain, the Sixers won games 2, 4 and 6. That set up a Game 7 showdown at the Boston Garden.

The contest was close, but the Celtics pulled into a 110-103 lead with two minutes to go. Then, Wilt scored six straight points over Bill Russell and, with exactly five seconds to play, the Sixers trailed by just one.

Boston began to panic. A nervous Russell tried to throw an inbounds pass over Wilt, but the ball hit a guy-wire supporting the basket. The Sixers got possession, and a chance to win it.

Hall of Fame guard Hal Greer prepared to toss the ball inbounds under his own basket. The logical target was Chamberlain, but Russell fronted him. Greer spotted forward Chet Walker, seemingly open beyond the key. Boston's John Havlicek was lurking several feet off the direct line between Greer and Walker, making it look like Walker was open when he really wasn't.

Havlicek sneaked a peek over his shoulder at Greer just as he prepared to release the ball. He moved into the passing lane, and . . .

The infamous call comes from Beantown homer Johnny Most:

"Greer is putting the ball into play. He gets it out deep. But Havlicek steals it! Over to Sam Jones. Havlicek stole the ball! Havlicek stole the ball! It's all over! It's all over! It's allllll over!"

I'm told that some treasonous Philadelphia talk-meister ended his morning show for years with part of that call, but that's an argument for another time.

The Celtics had the win, and would go on to take their seventh straight championship. Philadelphia fans, not for the last time, had their hearts torn out and stomped.

113

So I'm changing those five seconds. Screw Johnny Most and the Celtics. I'm going to let the last word belong to our former colleague Steve Fredericks, who was calling the game that day for the good guys. Here's how history should have sounded, out of Steve's mouth:

"How do! And now Greer looks to toss it in. He throws it to Wilt, who easily flicks Russell aside. The Dipper passes it to Chet Walker, who lines up a 15-footer . . . bang! It's good! And the Sixers win! Sixers win!

"The Sixers have just ended the Boston streak, the Boston curse. The spoiled-brat fans here in the Garden are devastated! The Sixers will go on to take the NBA title and begin their own streak of six straight championships. And this will open the gates for great things to happen for the Phillies, the Eagles and some new hockey team I hear they're thinking about bringing to town. I'm Steve Fredericks. See ya'."

Well, what the hell, it's my time machine.

28

Q: Who was our most beloved sports figure?

Glen says: This one's not even close. Richie Ashburn didn't just wear No. 1. He was No. 1.

For close to 50 years, "Whitey" meant baseball in this town. He meant summer vacation, and sunny afternoons, and a bottle of beer or lemonade, take your choice. He meant listening to the radio—on the stoop in South Philly, the playground in Ardmore or the beach in Wildwood—to hear him tell Harry Kalas those same old stories. Like your two favorite uncles, chatting on the porch.

Harry and Whitey weren't just voices. They were friends. They were *our* friends. Players came and went. Managers, too, even owners. The broadcasters—like the fans—were the constant. You'd tune in the station driving late at night, just in time to hear him snicker, "Hard to believe, Harry," and you knew you were close to home.

Only the old heads remember him as a player anymore. He came here from Nebraska in 1948, fast as a deer, to patrol centerfield at what was then Shibe Park. He always hit .300, stole bases when no one else did and saved the 1950 National League pennant by making the perfect throw home to nail Cal Abrams in the season's final game. There was no finer leadoff hitter.

He had the bad luck to play in the shadow of the New York centerfield troika of Willie, Mickey and the Duke. That kept him from the Hall of Fame until 1995. When he finally got to Cooperstown, with the more-talented but less-adored Mike Schmidt, more than 15,000 locals made the drive north to share in the moment. It was, Hall officials said, the biggest turnout ever.

Ashburn played 12 years here before he was treasonously traded to the Cubs. Three years later, he came back to broadcast the games, first with Byrum Saam, then Bill Campbell and finally, in 1971, with Kalas. Unlike most former players, he was candid and critical. You'd hear him let out an exasperated, "Oh, brother," and you knew one of the Phils hadn't played up to Whitey's standards. He was going to let you know about it. But he never ridiculed anyone. He respected the game too much.

He was honest and he was homespun and he was economical. Let the others overanalyze, Whitey could sum it all up with, "He looks runnerish." Sometimes, the game would go two or three batters between Ashburn's comments. That was okay. You'd picture him there, with his pipe and his professorial cap, and you'd wait for his golden words.

The stories were uncomplicated and familiar. Could you ever tire of hearing about the day in 1957 when Ashburn hit a fan named Alice Roth with two foul balls in the same at-bat? You'd be driving in your car, laughing at the tale, and you'd wonder, "How many other people are laughing with me right now?"

Chances are there were thousands. I never met a person who didn't like Richie Ashburn. In this town, where familiarity too often breeds contempt, that's an amazing feat. He was our version of Will Rogers—opinionated and self-deprecating, with a humor that alternated between corny and as dry as the Sahara.

When he died in 1997, it was like a relative had passed. Older folks who had watched him play cried unashamedly at losing the first great Phillie they could remember. All of us under 50 wondered how we might get by without the favorite voice that soothed us nearly every day for six months out of the year. And who was left to thank Gladys from Glenolden for those oatmeal cookies?

You remember, Angelo, what it was like on WIP after he passed away that Monday night in New York? We opened the phone lines the next morning to allow people to call in their tributes.

Six days later, Whitey was still the only topic on the station.

Angelo says: I can see Richie Ashburn reacting to your nomination of him as Philadelphia's most beloved sports figure, Glen. He would crinkle his weather-beaten nose, shake his head and utter that same trademark phrase you so admire: "Hard to believe, Harry."

Richie Ashburn was an excellent baseball player and an enjoyable announcer. He was also a fine man, admired by many and disliked by no one.

Your problem is, Glen, you defeat your own argument with one simple phrase. You write: "Only the old heads remember him as a player any more." And, of course, you are right about that.

How can a man be called most beloved sports figure when his exploits on the field have no meaning to people? Did he ever win a championship for his city? If he did, would anyone be able to remember that far back? Are you actually saying that Ashburn's announcing alone was enough to raise him to "most beloved" status?

Hard to believe, indeed.

I'm not sure Ashburn deserves to be in the top five. Is he more beloved than his partner, Harry Kalas? I'm not sure. More beloved than Muhammad Ali or Joe Frazier, both of whom have Philadelphia ties? More beloved than Bernie Parent and Bobby Clarke? More beloved than Dr. J or Wilt Chamberlain or even Mo Cheeks? Too close to call, I say.

You cite the reaction in Philadelphia to Ashburn's shocking and sudden death, Glen. Yes, it was extraordinary, but doesn't that often happen when an icon dies so unexpectedly?

Ironically, another death convinced me of who truly was the most beloved Philly sports figure. The reaction to his illness was even more devastating. I can still see the news and sports anchors on WPVI-TV breaking down on camera as they reported the sad news. I can still hear the cries of anguish for weeks on our WIP phone lines after his brain tumor became public knowledge.

There should be no doubt that the most beloved sports figure in Philadelphia history is Tug McGraw.

Like Ashburn, McGraw amassed a following from activities outside of the ballfield—as an incurable prankster, a quirky TV reporter and the father of a famous country singer. His final months were an inspiration to everyone who knew him or followed him as he fought the disease with the same determination that he displayed on the field.

I will not lie to you, Glen. Tug McGraw hated me and everything I do on the radio. He never appeared on our show, balking at every invitation — often with disdain. He didn't think there was a place for public criticism of Philadelphia athletes. I returned fire more than once in his direction, I admit.

But when he died, I could no longer deny the obvious. Tug McGraw was beloved in a way that is unique to Philadelphia. His personality lit up a room. His joy at living was unrivaled. You gotta believe. Tug sure did. Right to the end.

Oh, I almost forgot. Tug McGraw did one other thing to endear himself forever to Philadelphia. He threw a fastball past Willie Wilson in Game 6 of the 1980 World Series that gave his city its only baseball title in history.

Do you remember that leap after the last pitch, Glen? Remember the celebration that followed? Remember that precious championship?

Richie Ashburn described it.

Tug McGraw won it.

29

Q: Is hockey dying in Philadelphia?

Angelo says: The year was 1997, and I was sitting on a narrow perch atop City Hall watching a crew of crackpots try to squeeze a Flyers jersey onto the rusting body of William Penn. The city's proud hockey franchise was going to the Stanley Cup Finals, four victories away from a championship.

We took the temperature of the city that spring, and we all had the same diagnosis: Flyers Fever!

I don't have to tell you, Glen, that radio people like us lust after playoff runs like the one in 1997 because it translates into big ratings. And big ratings mean bonus money and contract extensions. The only scoreboard that counts for radio people is their bankroll.

But when the ratings finally came out that summer, we were all devastated. This alleged surge in interest translated into absolutely nothing for our show. The ratings, in the parlance of our industry, were flat. No change.

That was when I first began to wonder just how big a deal hockey was in Philadelphia. Now I know the answer. Hockey is no big deal at all. Hockey is not totally dead in our city, but that's only because the doctors won't unplug the resuscitator.

Please understand that this proclamation comes with no joy. Hockey is a fabulous sport, especially for those who can witness the speed and physicality in the arena. It will never be a good TV sport for many reasons, but there is nothing more breathtaking than a playoff overtime in the NHL.

The problem is, fewer and fewer fans can afford the price to sit in that arena, and the already-small base of support has eroded to dust. On top of that, the changes in the game have whittled away whatever appeal the sport once offered to Philadelphia.

I don't have to tell you why our city fell in love with hockey in the early 1970s, Glen. Ed Snider tells us every time someone asks him if interest is waning, he looks back to the amazing championship parade in 1974, when two million fans turned out to embrace a team that reflected the personality of its fans like no other. Snider acts as if nothing has changed in the past three decades.

But it has—more than any other sport, really. The game of hockey played today in almost no way resembles the sport of 30 years ago. Today, finesse and speed are the priorities, not physical intimidation. I know, I know. The checks are still punishing, the players still get hurt, yada, yada, yada.

Phooey. Philadelphia loved hockey because our players dropped their gloves and kicked the crap out of the other guys. It's that simple. The Broad Street Bullies played the game well, yes, but they won over the fans with their fists, not their sticks.

As the fighting slowly ebbed from the game, so too, did interest in Philadelphia. The Flyers were able to fill their building because there's always been a core of zealots, but the TV ratings have been in the dumper for decades—here and across the nation—and hockey is now such a distant fourth among the major sports that it is in danger of dropping right off the list.

I made a decision in 1997 that has served me well, Glen. I decided never again to turn over my entire show to the sport of hockey, regardless of the situation. I have two co-hosts (Al Morganti and Keith Jones) who are recognized as authorities, but I have never—not once—spent an entire show discussing only hockey. I'm not even sure I'll do it on the day after the Flyers win a Stanley Cup, if that ever happens. I'm serious. There are just too many people who don't give a damn.

I know it hurts to admit the truth, Glen. You love hockey. I really like it, too. But it's dying a slow and painful death in Philadelphia.

Get out the black suit. Call the florist. Unplug the machine.

It's over.

Glen says: Never let the facts stand in the way of a good argument, right Angelo? And the facts say that hockey is not just surviving in Philadelphia, it's thriving. That patient you're about to administer the paddles to just went out for a five-mile run.

Now I'm not going to sell you on the notion that hockey is flourishing nationwide, because it isn't. There are too many NHL teams in bad markets, the ticket prices are outrageous, and, yes, the game itself is not as exciting as it once was (although I'll blame that on the old clutch-and-grab, rather than speed and finesse).

But in our good city? Well, here's everything you need to know:

• The Flyers averaged 19,376 fans per game in 2003-04, more than 99 percent of capacity at the Core-Union-First-Wachovia Center, or whatever they call that place these days. I realize that all those fans in orange T-shirts during last season's playoffs created the illusion of empty seats on television, but surely your old eyes are still strong enough to see past that.

• The club's television ratings are solid. On local outlets, the Flyers consistently draw higher numbers than the Sixers and often pull more viewers than the Phillies. Now, it's true that the Sixers are in a down period. And I'll confess to comparing Flyers playoff ratings to Phillies early regular-season ratings, but the numbers are what they are. And they show that the only thing that was dead about the Flyers during their 2004 Stanley Cup run was their power play.

• In a league of haves and have-nots, the Flyers reside between Park Place and The Boardwalk. They are in the top five in every category—ticket income, broadcast revenue, merchandise sales, you name it. Ed Snider's protests that the franchise is losing money to the contrary (and get me a lie detector for that one); if every NHL club had the Flyers' means, the league wouldn't be approaching financial ruin.

But it goes beyond the Flyers, Ange. Hockey is a growth sport in this area. Youth leagues and high school programs are growing exponentially. New rinks are being built every year. Kids are playing street hockey . . . Wait a second, I'm starting to sound like one of those annoying soccer zealots. So I'll let that argument go and just focus on the big boys.

Yes, I remember 1997, Angelo. And our ratings at WIP were flat during the Flyers' run. But you, more than anyone, must know what we've all learned about this market— if it ain't about the Eagles, it ain't mass appeal. The Flyers are no different than the Sixers or Phillies in that their quest for a title still wouldn't draw as much interest as the Birds' fourth-round draft pick.

We live in a niche-market society. But that doesn't mean that the interest isn't there. The Flyers' Game 7 against Tampa Bay wasn't just the highest-ranked program in Philadelphia that Saturday night last May. In fact, it drew as many viewers as the next six TV stations *combined* over the prime time hours. And the competition included a Phils game, a Dick Van Dyke Show reunion and a re-airing of "Scarface." In other words, Dorny's, "Stop it right there," trounced Tony Montana's, "Say hello to my little friend."

My point is this: The Flyers may never again approach the popularity they received during the Broad Street Bully days. That was a special team that captured the city's heart and, even today, remains the most beloved in Philadelphia history.

But don't confuse the natural cycle of things with the death of a sport locally. The rest of the NHL may be in trouble, but the Flyers are popular, profitable and healthy—well, except for their octogenarian lineup.

You might want to listen to Jonesy and Morganti a little more, Angelo.

30

Q: Should Philadelphia host a Super Bowl?

Glen says: Try to recall the greatest football games ever played. The 1958 NFL Championship—damp and gray in New York as Alan Ameche falls into the frozen end zone to give the Colts an overtime win over the Giants. Or maybe the 1967 Ice Bowl in Green Bay. Bart Starr blows into his hands to fight the minus-13 temperature before that famous game-winning plunge.

Hell, the most memorable game ever played in this town was the 1981 NFC Championship against the Cowboys in a numbing wind chill of minus-17. Go back and look at the television footage. You'll see 70,000 fans huddled under blankets, fortified by their mackinaws and their flasks. Their frozen breath steams out as they chant: "E-A-G-L-E-S–EAGLES!"

See, that's football, Angelo. The way it was meant to be played. In real elements. Under a real sky. When it's really cold. Without a single bottle of sun block.

Somewhere along the way, the NFL forgot that notion. Because somewhere along the way, the league's pooh-bahs changed the Super Bowl from being the "ultimate game," as our friend Tom Brookshier called it, into a giant corporate junket. The Super Bowl isn't played before true fans. It's played before sponsors and CEOs whose weekend would be ruined if a little slush landed on their $160 Ermenegildo Zegna neckties. The kind of people who know more about Vuitton than Vinatieri.

The current Super Bowl is about yacht parties and Cristal and Hollywood starlets. About five-hour pre-game spectacles and MTV-produced, mammary-popping halftime shows (not that there's anything wrong with that). Every once in a while a good game sneaks in, but that's purely coincidental. Because the Super Bowl isn't about the game, it's about the expense account. And no Fortune 500 muckety-muck wants to spend his weekend in mukluks.

So the North (i.e. us) is screwed.

As I write this, Paul Tagliabue has just announced that the 2008 game will be played in Phoenix. Excuse me? What did Phoenix do to deserve a Super Bowl beyond being located south of 35 degrees longitude? Is there a worse football city than Phoenix?

Here's a list of America's greatest football towns: Kansas City, Pittsburgh, Cleveland, Buffalo, Denver, Green Bay. And, of course, Philadelphia. You know what they all have in common? None has any shot at all of ever hosting the game.

Instead, it's played in non-football cities like Atlanta, Houston, New Orleans, and San Diego. Oh, and once a decade or so, the league goes north, only to stick the game in a dome.

Perhaps if the game were played in real elements, we'd learn who the true fans are. The hoards of socialites and pseudo-celebrities would give way to the diehard fans. People who know how to dress for warmth and not just fashion.

So why not Philadelphia? Hell, we paid 10 gazillion dollars for that new stadium, couldn't we use it just one more weekend? Our city certainly has the first-class hotels, fine restaurants and premier attractions to entertain a few thousand visitors. January or not, don't you think we have more to offer than Houston?

And if it snows, we'll all handle it. The players, too. Maybe we'll even get a repeat of the 1948 championship, played here in a driving snowstorm. Players on the Eagles and Chicago Cardinals pitched in to roll the tarp off the field before the game and again after halftime. Hey, c'mon, Donovan, lend us a hand, eh?

I'm not even going to delve into the economic arguments because, quite frankly, I don't believe them. But even if a Super Bowl doesn't provide a financial shot in the arm, wouldn't it be great to bask in all that positive national attention? Put us on the cover of Conde-Nast Traveler. We promise to behave.

Of course, if I were king of the NFL, I would make sure that the Super Bowl was played each year in the home stadium of the finalist with the best regular-season record.

And I guess, that being the case, Ange, we'd never get to host it anyway.

Angelo says: The Super Bowl should be played in Philadelphia?

Great idea, Glen. And let's hold the Winter Olympics in Florida sometime, too. Maybe the NBA Finals should be played outdoors, since lots of the players developed their love for the game on playgrounds. And let's move the Masters to the moon, where the craters alone would add tons of drama to the event.

The purpose of holding a championship game in any sport is to determine the best team. The idea of putting two great teams into the icebox that is Philadelphia in late-January is ridiculous, for more reasons than I can name here.

Let's start with the obvious problems. Philadelphia may be the worst place in football to play a game involving two teams that are not named the Eagles. Is there a more provincial place than our own city? How often have you tried to bring up an issue on the air involving a team outside of Philadelphia, only to learn that no one cares?

And with all of the corporate sponsors, the fans from the two teams, the friends of the NFL and the many other glad-handers associated with the Super Bowl, exactly how many Philadelphians do you think would actually be going to this game? When fans find out that maybe a couple of thousand tickets are being made available to the host city, how do you think they'll react to that?

In the history of the Super Bowl, the NFL has gone to a cold-weather city just twice. The first time, when they tried it in Detroit in 1982, it was an unmitigated disaster even with a domed stadium. What you fail to acknowledge is that the Super Bowl is more than a game. It is a weeklong celebration of the sport featuring dozens of parties and events throughout the city. One snowstorm could wipe out a year of planning and anticipation. Half the events were blown away in 1982 by a Great Lakes blizzard.

Now I realize that the 2006 Super Bowl is headed back to Detroit, but that has nothing to do with its suitability as a site. The NFL bartered a new stadium for Detroit by dangling that carrot. The fact that 24 years intervened between visits to Detroit domes should tell you all you need to know. And that's with a posh indoor stadium to play in!

I acknowledge your point about the great games being waged in the elements. There would be no NFL today without the magic of the dank 1958 setting in New York, and the Ice Bowl nine years later was a huge building block for the league. But that's where your argument runs out of steam.

The great 1981 Eagles victory in the championship game would still be played in Philadelphia today. In fact, conference title games *were* played in Philadelphia both in 2003 and 2004. The playoff games will never be moved to a warm-weather city. And that's the whole point here. There are plenty of opportunities for these "weather games" throughout the NFL schedule.

Can we please protect one game a year from the elements? Can we please allow the two best teams each year to go to a neutral site, play in pristine conditions and determine which is the best team? Is that asking too much?

And there's one other thing you haven't considered, Glen.

Imagine for a second if the NFL tried to hold a halftime show like the one staged during Super Bowl XXXVII. There's Janet Jackson gyrating on the stage. Along comes Justin Timberlake.

Riiiiiiipppppppppp!

Do you have any idea how bad frostbite is?

31

Q: Who was better— Ali or Frazier?

Angelo says: From the moment he appeared, the crowd was mesmerized. Women in short skirts and men with wide grins waited like kids standing in line to visit Santa Claus as the greatest athlete of our lifetime, Muhammad Ali, worked his way through the crowd.

I have never been more impressed in my life by anyone. And I will never forget that night for as long as I live. I spent close to an hour one-on-one with the great Ali in the coffee shop of the Sheraton Biltmore Hotel in Providence, Rhode Island on a cold winter night in 1981. At one point he even took my reporter's notebook and drew a design for me.

Charisma? Well, let me put it this way. I met Reggie Jackson, Billie Jean King, and Marvin Hagler all that same year, and Ali had more charisma in his left ear than the three of those sports immortals put together.

I love Muhammad Ali—always have, always will. And that's why it pains me to say that he was not the greatest boxer ever. He wasn't even the greatest boxer of his generation.

Joe Frazier was.

I know, I know. Ali beat Frazier two of the three times they faced each other, not to mention every time they met at a news conference or out on the streets. Ali was an orator, a wordsmith who captivated and entertained. Meanwhile, Frazier mumbled out cliché after cliché through a menacing glare and clenched teeth.

But the truth is not always popular. The good guy doesn't always win. If you strip away all of the Ali bluster, if you put on dark shades and keep your eyes away from the Ali sparkle, the truth is obvious. Frazier was better.

Just look at the three classic fights between these two legendary heavyweights:

Fight one, March 8, 1971. With the world rooting against him, Frazier burst the bubble of Ali's invincibility by outboxing and outpointing the former champ. There was no doubt who the better fighter was that night.

Fight two, January 28, 1974. Ali returned the favor in this least interesting of the three great bouts. Two things to keep in mind: Frazier had been touring with his singing group rather than training, so he wasn't in top shape for the fight. And Ali didn't win the title from Frazier that night. Smokin' Joe had already lost the crown to George Foreman a year earlier.

Fight three, October 1, 1975. The Thrilla in Manila is the greatest fight I've ever witnessed, a war of wills won by Ali only after both men collapsed before the 15th round. Since Joe surrendered first, Ali won. But the truth is, Frazier got the better of Ali through most of that bout. Ali spent a week in the hospital after the battle. It is foolish to say Ali was the better fighter because he didn't give up first in the greatest fight in boxing history.

What this debate comes down to is pretty simple, really. Ali was the better entertainer, but Frazier was the better fighter. Ali was a technician in the ring, but Frazier was lethal. (Frazier knocked out 27 of 37 opponents, Ali only 37 of 61.) The whole point of Ali's style —in and out of the ring—was deception. Frazier had all the finesse of a sledgehammer.

If you perceive a slight lack of conviction in my defense of Frazier here, Glen, please understand why. I love Ali. I can barely stand Frazier, who has become an even bigger boob in retirement than he was during his boxing career.

Everyone is rooting for you to win this argument, Glen.

Even me.

Glen says: Funny thing, Angelo. I've never had the pleasure of meeting Ali, my all-time hero in sports. I have met Joe Frazier a few times. Boob, you say? Well, he doesn't have the charisma of Ali (of course, *Elvis* didn't have the charisma of Ali), but I've seen Frazier charm the room.

Regardless, Ali was unquestionably the better fighter. Ali lacked Smokin' Joe's devastating power, but his overall body motion, leg movement, head and neck control were better than any big man ever. "I never saw a fighter—in any weight class—with quicker hands," marveled Rocky Marciano, who knew a thing or two about boxing.

Usually, Ali would outrun his opponent, pepper him with jabs and combinations, and when his enemy tired, move in for the kill. Against bigger, stronger fighters, he would back-pedal, taunt, and wait for the enraged foe to take the bait. When the fool charged, Ali greeted him with a straight right that could stagger an ox. You remember? "Float like a butterfly, sting like a bee."

As a young man, he avoided punishment by dancing out of harm's way. As he slowed, he could take a blow better than anyone. He was 215 pounds, and whatever of that was not mouth was surely heart.

You argue, Angelo, that Frazier "got the better" of Ali in Manila, but surrendered first to the punishment. But isn't the ability to take and ignore pain one way in which we judge the greatness of fighters? The two men exchanged bombs for 14 rounds, until one of them —Frazier—had absorbed enough.

"I hit him with punches that would bring down the walls of a city," Frazier said afterward. "Lordy, he's a great champion."

Ali described the fight as, "the closest thing to dying that I know of. Joe took me to hell and back." No doubt, many of Ali's debilitating illnesses stem from that night in the Philippines.

Shame is, the two men never met during Ali's prime, which was 1964-68. His battle with the government over his military draft status stole more than three years from his brilliant career. When he came back to fight Frazier in 1971 he was covered in rust. When he beat Joe twice, he was older, smarter and relying more on tact and less on talent.

Imagine if they had met a few years earlier.

Actually, it almost happened when they were both living in Philadelphia in 1969, which gives us the basis to write this chapter. Ali first lived near City Avenue and later moved to Barbara Drive in Cherry Hill.

As the story goes—at least from Ali's side—both fighters used to run through Fairmount Park. One day they nearly ran into each other.

Two old champions, who fought bitter wars, share an uneasy peace.

"You really think you can whup me?" Ali challenged.

"You're doggone right I do," replied Frazier.

"Then let's get it on right here." Ali started flicking jabs, but Frazier, who had nothing to gain as champion, backed away. He stammered that he would meet Ali in a local Police Athletic League gym.

Ali readily agreed. Their handlers set up a time for the "private championship fight."

Of course, Ali couldn't keep anything private. Word began to spread on the appointed day of the fight and the once-and-future champ arrived with a parade of about 1,000 fans plus a few confused policemen. Frazier, for his part, never showed.

"He wants to show he can whup me," Ali shouted. "He says he's the champ. Well, here I am. I haven't had a fight in three years, I'm 25 pounds overweight, and Joe Frazier won't show up."

We'll never know, Ange, but my money says Ali would have won the fight at the PAL gym that day. Would have whupped him in Fairmount Park as well.

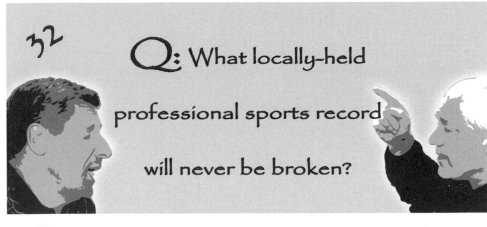

32

Q: What locally-held professional sports record will never be broken?

Glen says: I know where you're going with this, Angelo. So I'll ignore the obvious and just say that if you must cite the Dipper, I'm more impressed with his records of 55 rebounds in one game, 4,029 points in one season, and 20,000 women in one career.

Something special certainly happened in Hershey that night, but I've got five records that will be tougher to beat. Let's rank them in degree of difficulty:

5) Dave Schultz's 472 penalty minutes in 1974-75. That's basically one fighting major and one roughing minor per game. It won't be touched until the NHL brings back the bench-clearing brawl or accepts Glen Cochrane's petition to get back into the league.

4) Andy Reid coaching three straight Pro Bowl teams. You've got to lose three straight NFC championship games to get to Honolulu and who else will ever do that?

3) The 1979-80 Flyers 35-game unbeaten streak. In this age of numbing parity, can you imagine any team going nearly a half-season without a loss?

2) Connie Mack managing a major league team for 50 seasons. Well, maybe Terry Francona has a shot with the Red Sox.

And the record that will NEVER be broken is . . . .

1) The 1972-73 Sixers going 9-73.

Before the season opened, coach Roy Rubin declared, "I don't think Boston will be that tough." His team finished 59 games behind the Celtics.

And what a squad it was. The 76ers opened the year with 15 straight losses. They tossed in losing streaks of 20, 14 and finally 13 to end the season. Rubin—who had been a moderately successful coach at that hoops hotbed of Long Island University—was canned at 4-47, leaving player-coach Kevin Loughery to finish up the disaster.

Ownership should have known better from the start. At Rubin's introductory news conference, he admitted that he had never heard of guard Hal Greer, a Hall of Famer in his fifteenth season. Philadelphia hoops guru Sonny Hill describes Rubin as being "like a teenager put in charge of a Fortune 500 company. He had no idea what to do and he had no control over his employees."

Need an example? During a game against the Detroit Pistons, Rubin tried to pull forward John Q. Trapp, who refused to come out and signaled Rubin to look behind him. A friend of Trapp's, standing near the bench, opened his jacket to reveal a gun. Trapp stayed in, and the team lost by 28.

Nineteen players shuttled through the lineup that season, including nonentities like Dale Schlueter, Freddie Boyd and a center whose entrance into the game always inspired PA announcer Dave Zinkoff to bellow, "Manny Leaks on the floor!" The biggest shame was that Greer's brilliant career ended with him surrounded by this collection of slop.

Fred Carter, who would later coach another bad Sixers squad, was the top scorer and most valuable player. "I don't know if I got that award for leading the team to nine wins or leading it to 73 losses," Carter later mused.

The good news is that the team used the first pick in the 1973 draft to pick Doug Collins. Three years later, they were in the playoffs.

But the 9-73 record—a .111 winning percentage—is not just the worst in team history. It still stands as the worst-ever record in the NBA. Only two franchises since then—the 1992-93 Dallas Mavericks and the 1997-98 Denver Nuggets—have even made a run at the record. Both of those teams went 11-71.

This is one mark that will never be broken. Hey, if we can hang our hats on anything in this town, it's a record for futility.

Angelo says: It is now official: Glen Macnow has been living in Philadelphia for too long. How else to explain that he chooses a mark of utter futility as the one record that will never be broken?

Come on, Glen. We've had some of the greatest players and teams in the history of sports in our town, and you choose 9-73 as our best stab at immortality?

Assuming you're serious, your choice is the wrong one for two reasons: First, that record *will* be broken. Heck, it was almost broken a couple of times around the turn of the millennium by those awful post-Michael Jordan Chicago Bulls teams. And the Los Angeles Clippers have been, and always will be, a threat, too.

More importantly, though, that 9-73 mark is a record that anyone could beat anytime they want. In a day and age when clubs often tank games late in seasons to improve their position in the draft lottery, it is pointless to consider the final record of any terrible team.

Finally, who cares? What's the difference if a team finishes at 10-72 or 8-74?

(If you'll allow one brief digression here, however, I do wholeheartedly endorse the use of a gunman behind the coach in times of extreme duress. Philadelphia might have had several more championship parades if that John Q. Trapp thug were perched behind Andy Reid or Jim Fregosi when they bungled key decisions with the season on the line.)

The mere fact that you correctly predict my choice for the best record ever proves that it is, Glen. Wilt's 100-point game has survived 40 years without serious challenge. It has weathered not just the test of time but also the test of talent. If the supposed greatest player of all time, the superhuman Jordan himself, could only score 69 points in his best game ever, what chance do the Kobe Bryants or the LeBron Jameses have?

In those four decades, no one has gotten any closer than David Thompson's 73 points in a meaningless end-of-season game in 1978. And here's the best stat of them all: Of the top 20 single-game scorers of all time, 15 of them have the same name: Wilt Chamberlain. The Big Dipper also holds the second-highest total ever (78), and had two other 73-point efforts to match Thompson.

But numbers are not the only story behind the single greatest achievement in sports history. There is so much more. I can confirm what I am about to tell you because Wilt himself told the story on my radio show in 1991.

At the time of that game on March 2, 1964, Chamberlain was living in New York City, presumably because he had run out of Philadelphia women to sleep with. The night before the game, he had been busy adding to another number that you refer to Glen: 20,000 women. In fact, as the limo proceeded from New York to Hershey, Pennsylvania, where this historic game would be played, Wilt was accompanied by lots of wine, women, and song. By his account, he did not sleep one minute the night before the game!

As game time approached, he was understandably hung over and exhausted. He even considered not suiting up because he felt so terrible. But a charity basketball game between the NFL's Philadelphia Eagles and the Baltimore Colts that served as a preliminary to the main event gave him just enough time to recover. He decided at the last minute to play.

And play he did, before a paltry crowd of 4,124 in the dreary Hershey Sports Arena. By the fourth quarter, the New York Knicks had decided to defend only Chamberlain in an effort to thwart his effort to reach 100. The Knicks even resorted to fouling the other Warrior players as soon as they touched the ball. Nothing worked. Wilt would not be stopped that night.

At game's end, the box score told the whole story. Wilt was 38 for 63 from the field and—most amazing of all for a poor free-throw shooter like Chamberlain—he was 28 for 32 from the line.

The performance at the time was heralded as the single greatest achievement in the history of sports.

Forty years later, it still is.

One final postscript to this amazing night: Wilt cruised in his limo back up to Madison Square Garden for a game the very next night against the Knicks. By then, he was near complete exhaustion. (After all, the girls were still with him, and so was the booze.)

Twenty-four hours after his 100-point performance, Wilt Chamberlain was held by his opposing center, Darrell Imhoff, to a mere 54 points. The New York crowd that night rose to its feet and gave an ovation like no other that season.

To Darrell Imhoff. Not Wilt Chamberlain.

That's how great Wilt was, Glen. He was the best basketball player who ever lived, and March 2, 1964 was the night that made him an immortal.

33

Q: Who's our best broadcaster ever?

Angelo says: I'm always amazed when people talk about Philadelphia broadcasters because they invariably leave out a name that belongs at the very top of the list.

Think about it for a second, Glen. Which names come up right away?

- Harry Kalas (member of the Baseball Hall of Fame)
- Gene Hart (member of the Hockey Hall of Fame)
- Merrill Reese (longtime voice of the Eagles).

Don't get me wrong. Philadelphia is incredibly lucky to have such accomplished play-by-play talents working our games. I'd even add Tom McGinnis to that list for his spectacular work describing the Sixers games.

But one velvet voice drowns out all of the others, by far.

The best Philadelphia broadcaster in the past 50 years, if not forever, is Bill Campbell.

Compared to Bill, those other fellows are all one-trick ponies. Bill Campbell is the essence of great broadcasting, a wordsmith who can call any sport at any time, then he can talk about it for hours on the air, and finally he can craft an eloquent postscript to the game.

Which broadcaster in Philadelphia was the chief play-by-play man for three professional teams in three different sports?

Bill Campbell, of course. He preceded Reese in the Eagles booth from 1952 to 1966, and he did so with great distinction. In fact, Campbell was so good, the Phillies hired him in 1962 to do their games, too, thus making him the play-by-play man for two major sports at the same time, a dual distinction he held for four years.

In 1962, Bill also did the play-by-play for the most amazing single-game performance in sports history, the 100-point game by Wilt Chamberlain. Later, he did a nine-year stint as chief play-by-play announcer for the Sixers from 1972 to 1981.

But that's not where the story ends. Oh, no. Bill also did a phenomenal job as a talk-show host at WIP for a few years in the infancy of the sports-talk format, and now, in his late 70s, still performs regularly as a commentator on KYW radio.

I cannot even begin to tell you how much Bill has impacted my own career, and that of many others in Philadelphia. Bill was there when I started at WIP in 1990, and he had every right to show disdain at my sudden appearance within his domain. I had been a writer all my life, and I was presented with a full-time radio job in a plum time slot with almost no experience. On top of that, I was definitely not doing radio in Bill's style. I was shrill, caustic, often downright outrageous. Bill has never been any of those things.

Instead of shunning me, however, Bill helped me. He answered every question with patience and class. He did for you, too, Glen. And for all of us at WIP. He could have tried to intimidate us with his incredible résumé, but instead he took on the role of mentor and teacher. His very presence at WIP in those early days gave all of us more credibility than we deserved.

Even more amazing to me was the way he handled our daily impersonations of him in the years when Joe Conklin worked on the WIP Morning Show. There was no voice Joe had mastered more—or used more—than Bill's. Sometimes the characterizations pushed boundaries of good taste that the real Bill would never have ventured near.

I can't tell you how many times after a show we'd brace ourselves for a call from Bill blasting us for disrespecting him. I *can* tell you how many times he actually made that call: none. In fact, Bill often told Joe that he had become more famous through Joe's imper-sonations than he had ever been during his long and varied career.

He may have been right about that, and it's a shame. Bill Campbell is more than the dean of broadcasters in Philadelphia. He is the paragon. He is the standard against which we should all be measured.

As long as Bill is still around, Glen, the only hope for the rest of the broadcasters in Philadelphia is a distant second place.

Glen says: In a city where the broadcasters usually outshine the teams, you cited a great one Angelo. Bill Campbell, along with Steve Fredericks, built sports-talk radio in Philadelphia. And I'd also cite Harry Kalas as an all-time, all-timer, and Tom McGinnis as the next great hope.

But, if I've got to single out one, I'll take Gene Hart, the voice of the Flyers for their first 28 years. The sport that came here in 1967 was as foreign to Philadelphia as quoits. So this jolly, articulate professor didn't just announce hockey, he taught it. It was Gene who explained to everyone what off-sides was, who Bernie Parent was, where Flin Flon was.

We listened. And by the umpteenth time he told us that, "The Flyers are skating from right to left on your radio dial," we had fallen in love—with the man and the sport. For decades, every neighborhood kid who poked one in during a street hockey game gleefully shouted, as Gene would, "He scores for a case of Tastykakes!"

Gene (nobody called him by his last name) painted word pictures. An out-of-position goalie wasn't just scrambling, he was "dancing like the first man on the sun." A push-and-shove match became a "rugby scrum." And yapping players "weren't just exchanging their how-do-you-dos."

Of course, his most-famous words, on May 19, 1974, sent two million Flyer fans parading onto Broad Street:

"Ladies and gentlemen, the Flyers are going to win the Stanley Cup. The Flyers will win the Stanley Cup. The Flyers have won the Stanley Cup."

Is there a better call in our history? In any sport? For Philadelphia fans, this is our version of Russ Hodges' "The Giants win the pennant." Or maybe Al Michaels' "Do you believe in miracles?" It still brings chills.

Hockey might be the toughest sport for a play-by-play man. Possession goes back and forth, the pace can be frantic, the names, especially since the European invasion, are often unpronounceable. Gene was always on top of the action. His words machine-gunned out at the rate of 300 per minute, without even stumbling over Reijo Ruotsalainen. And when the pitch went higher, almost to a falsetto, you knew that Propp was feeding Kerr in front of the net.

For sure, he was a homer. The Flyers were his favorites, and he wouldn't insult you by pretending otherwise. In Gene's mind, the refs never gave the orange-and-black a fair shake, an institutional mindset that continues to this day. But, unlike his successors, Gene wasn't beyond telling you when the boys were playing poorly. Usually it would come out in one sentence: "The Flyers have stopped skating." That's all it took for you to sense his disappointment.

But most often, he was joyous. He addressed listeners as "my friends," and you knew he meant it, even if you'd never met him. You also knew by listening that he could be a bit of a showoff, and that he loved telling you everything he knew—about hockey, about opera, about food. Gene had a lot of passions.

They phased Gene out in the 1990s, first taking him off television, and then off the radio broadcasts altogether. Sure, he had slipped a little, but most fans still considered his ouster treasonous. For his part, Gene never showed bitterness. He still considered himself a company man and showed up for every game.

The last time I saw Gene Hart was in early 1999 in the press box that now bears his name. I sat next to him for three periods and got an education in Bizet, stir-fry cooking and the left-wing lock. In fact, over close to three hours, Gene stopped talking for just two minutes. That was when his beautiful daughter, Lauren, sang the National Anthem. Oh, he beamed with pride.

If ever a man was perfect for a job, it had to be Gene Hart for calling hockey games.

Q: What's the best seat in the house?

Glen says: So many great options here. Which one to choose? A ticket on the 50-yard line at the Linc? Behind the goal judge at a Flyers game? Near the home bench for the Sixers? How about among the rowdy students during a Big Five death match at the Palestra?

For my money (and the price is hefty), I'll take two on the aisle behind first base at the beautifully designed—but horribly named—Citizens Bank Ballpark. You want specific? Okay, give me Section 116, seats 1 and 2, about 15 rows behind the Phillies dugout.

That, my friend, is perfection at the ballyard. From there I've got a perfect angle for plays at first base and home plate. I can watch Larry Bowa coming out of the dugout snarling, and Bobby Abreu passively strolling back after another strikeout. I've got a great view of the big scoreboard and the city skyline as the sun sets over leftfield. And I'm close to the off-field action along Ashburn Alley.

There's nothing like enjoying a game among your 40,000 best friends. The collective anticipation when Jim Thome approaches the plate, and the chance to high-five strangers when he hits one out. The seventh-inning stretch on one of those July nights when the girls are all in halter tops. The chance to say "I was there" when something spectacular occurs.

The cavernous Vet had its moments, but never brought that sense of baseball community. Now, at the new park (I will not repeat its name), fans can share in the collective joy of real grass, impeccable sight lines, a quirky asymmetrical field, and double-wide concourses.

This park invites you to wander. Start outside, by admiring the statues of our Four Horsemen—Schmidt, Carlton, Ashburn and Roberts. Grab a beer at McFadden's before finding your seat. Lean on the railing above the visitors' bullpen, heckling Armando Benitez before he shuts down the Phils yet again. You're no more than 15 feet away, close enough to see the dust-smoke when the ball hits the catcher's glove. It's like standing on your porch and watching the Phils play.

Keep wandering. Baseball is, above anything, about food, and there are concession kiosks everywhere. At the Vet, you could buy a hot dog. Here, you can get the best from Philadelphia institutions like Geno's Steaks and Tony Luke's. My favorite is the Original Schmitter from McNally's Tavern in Chestnut Hill. It's steak on a Kaiser roll with melted cheese, tomato, fried onions, salami and a secret sauce. It's a heart attack on a plate, but if you wash it down with Flying Fish Ale, it's the most fun you can have with your clothes on. And, hey, they even built a cup-holder into each seat so your hands are free to catch a foul ball.

A day at the ballpark is something special. I learned that from my dad 40 years ago. Now, I go there to bond with my kids. It's a day out with no Internet, no remote control. Hell, we even turn off our cell phones for a few hours. Baseball, more than the other sports, offers a chance to actually hold a conversation with your kids. And if they yawn at my hundredth retelling of the story about Curt Schilling striking out five straight Braves, well, that's okay, too.

If you keep wandering, you'll find some beautiful murals, and a Hall of Fame and all sorts of interactive doodads. The video board is wide enough that they can split the screen in half to show replays from several angles simultaneously. Very cool.

You know who I envy, Ange? All those kids who are about eight years old and just discovering baseball. All of their memories will be formed at this ballfield.

Angelo says: I went to see a baseball game recently, under perfect conditions.

The temperature was 68 degrees, and the view was so great, I could actually see the ball curve on its way to the plate. The food was fantastic, too—and cheap! The seats were soft and perfectly contoured to my body. The bathroom facilities were clean and always available.

I had all the comforts of home.

Because I was home.

Isn't it ironic that Philadelphia has helped to foot a $500 million bill for two spectacular new stadiums, but there's still no place like home to see a sports event?

Please spare me the roar of the crowd or the smell of the peanuts, Glen. It's all hogwash. If you really want to experience a sports event, I strongly urge you to park in your own driveway, turn on your own TV and reach for the trusty old remote control.

If the new stadiums have proved anything to Philadelphia sports fans, it's that you have to see a game on TV to really understand what's happening. I can prove this argument in any of the four major sports.

Baseball is a no-brainer. Most of the action takes place between the pitcher and the batter. Thanks to the centerfield camera, home viewers can see what kind of pitch is thrown, the location of the pitch, and anything that might be hanging from the batter's nose. At the game, it's all just a rumor.

Football is a sport whose popularity didn't take hold until TV claimed it. You know why? Because it is designed for TV, governed by TV and performed primarily for a TV audience. Anyone who has attended an NFL game—and twiddled his thumbs during the frequent delays for commercials—knows exactly what I'm saying. Plus, if there's a really close officiating call, guess how they determine it. Yup. By watching it on TV.

Basketball at the arena is laughable. Unless you're related to Jack Nicholson and can sit courtside, the players are little blips on a huge radar screen. Sit in the upper reaches of the Wachovia Center sometime, Glen, then tell me about the joy of experiencing a Sixers game in person.

The one sport I might have conceded is better in the building is hockey, but that was only until I watched a game on high-definition television. The one problem with televised hockey has always been trying to follow the puck. With the new TV technology, that drawback is gone. High-definition TV allows you to see the puck, admire the artwork on the goalies' masks, and count the number of stitches on Jeremy Roenick's face.

It is so easy to preach the euphoria of live sports, Glen, until reality hits you in the face like a snowball. Basically, live sports is cold, loud, uncomfortable, and irritating. How many times have people missed the big play because a drunk was ordering his 19th beer from the vendor camped right in your line of vision?

The first time I ever took my son to a football game, he missed half of it watching a drunk fan get his head bandaged after a brawl in the 700 Level. The first time I took my daughter to a baseball game, she asked when it was going to start—and that was in the fourth inning!

I could easily anticipate your wrong-headedness on this one, Glen. You want to hug the stranger next to you when Tiki Barber is stuffed on fourth-and-one with the game on the line. You want to dance in the aisles after Billy Wagner throws the last pitch of the game past Barry Bonds.

Good. Have a great time, Glen. I'll be watching, too, from the comfort of my Barcalounger.

Give me a call when you get home.

In a couple of hours.

Q: Why does this town never win a title?

Angelo says: Since the last championship parade in Philadelphia, the Berlin Wall has tumbled, the Communist government in the Soviet Union has fallen, Iraq has lost two wars with the United States and there have been six presidential elections. No other major city in America has languished through a drought as long or as puzzling as this one.

A great sports town like Philly deserves one great team every generation, doesn't it? Is one parade every 20 years asking too much? Apparently it is, at least to the owners who are responsible for this embarrassing streak of failure. And make no mistake: The owners are the one and only reason for this debacle.

Here's a list of the men who have owned and operated sports franchises in Philadelphia over the past generation: Leonard Tose, Norman Braman, Jeffrey Lurie, Bill Giles, Dave Montgomery, Harold Katz, and Ed Snider (Flyers and Sixers).

With the exceptions of Tose and Snider, these owners all had one thing in common. They cared more about making money than winning championships.

Braman was the all-time bloodsucker in Philadelphia, a businessman who screwed over a desperate (and no doubt tipsy) Leonard Tose when he bought the team, milked every dollar he could out of the franchise for seven years, and then found another sucker in Lurie. Speaking of Lurie, he wins a title every year—The Most Money under the Cap championship. The parade for that title is a small one. Lurie and Joe Banner march alone to the bank every year with gobs of the fans' money.

Giles and Montgomery are even more maddening because they shafted the fans for about 15 years and then suddenly changed the rules. Year after year, these disingenuous ingrates pinched pennies and treated Philadelphia like a small-market team. Then, suddenly, they opened up their wallets and sprung for Jim Thome because they had a new ballpark to fill. Now the city is warming up to the Phillies again. Great. And how about all those years when we were treated like Podunk, Illinois?

Katz won the most recent title in 1983 and then lost his mind. The man won a championship by spending the money for the final missing piece, Moses Malone, and then he must have undergone a radical lobotomy. How else can you explain the trade of Malone? The almost-trade of Julius Erving? The hiring of Doug Moe? By the end, this man who loved basketball found an even greater love: money. Pat Croce waved some green in front of Katz's face, and poof! He was finally gone.

Of course, Croce—who actually had a vision for winning it all—was denied the privilege of finishing the job by the one man most responsible for the drought, Ed Snider. First, Snider forced Croce out after Pat had maneuvered and exhorted the Sixers all the way to the NBA Finals, and then Ed Snider presided over the same kind of futility that he has perfected over three decades with the Flyers.

Snider is a relic of a distant past, a man so far behind the times that he can't see, after years and years of failure, that his GM is not the same Bobby Clarke who won him his only two titles in 1974 and '75. Unlike his counterparts, Snider *does* spend lots of money, but almost never wisely. He is loyal to the extreme—far more loyal, in fact, to his old buddies from the 1970s than he is to a fan base that only lately has been eroding.

There are thousands of theories about why Philadelphia has waited so long for a pro team to win a championship. Yes, the injuries have been prolific. Sure, the fates have not always been kind (Joe Carter, Leon Stickle, Jerome Brown). And OK, the fans themselves have been maybe a bit too quick to boo and then bail on their teams.

But none of that matters if George Steinbrenner is an owner here. Who's complaining here if Jerry Buss owns one of our franchises? Nowadays, it all begins with ownership in sports.

And for the past generation in Philadelphia, that's why it always ends in failure.

Glen says: I don't believe in omens or fates. Sure, like all Philadelphians I have heard of the Curse of Billy Penn, as well as the Massamimo Malocchio. I don't buy either of them.

Nor do I think that propping a Phillies hat or a Flyers jersey atop City Hall really causes our teams to collapse in the end. How would a bad aesthetic move lead to Mitch Williams throwing that damned pitch anyway?

Oh, and I agree with you, Angelo, that our owners have often seemed a collection of scoundrels who lacked either the interest or the intellect to bring us a parade down Broad Street.

But we're here to argue, so I'll take another route. Perhaps the fault, as that noted Sixers fan Billy Shakespeare once wrote, "lay not in the stars, but in ourselves."

Maybe the fans are to blame.

Don't get me wrong. I don't agree with those pompous windbags who insist that we never win because we're too tough, too mean, too unforgiving. You know the argument: We heckle our quarterback so we're doomed to a lifetime of disappointment. We bring failure upon ourselves with our negativity. As if Donovan's just too frail to survive a boo or two.

No, that's just the bleating of the uninformed. Ignore such rampant stupidity.

My argument is the flipside of that coin. I'd say that one big reason our teams never take a title is that we're just too damned supportive.

Consider this: What's the real incentive for Jeff Lurie's Eagles to win a Super Bowl anyway? Psychic glory? Bragging rights among the mossbacks who run other football franchises? Sure, that might be nice for Lurie, but at what cost?

If Lurie's a cheapskate, as you allege, it's because we let him get away with it. Eagles fans are the most loyal and passionate in the country. We invest in the personal seat licenses for his new palace. We buy jerseys featuring the team's latest star—only to know we'll have to replace the shirts once that guy reaches age 30 and gets pushed out the door.

Other NFL cities have their games blacked out because of unsold seats. Not here. Season after season, Eagles fans fill the stadium to support their team—whether it be good or bad. Hell, in 1998, the final year of Ray (Dead Coach Walking) Rhodes, the Vet averaged 66,002 fans for a team that went 3-13.

We'll always be there. The owner knows that. So why should Lurie dig deep into his pocket to overpay the mega-stud free agent who might push the team over the top but could put a few dents in his salary cap championship trophy? What's the incentive for pulling out all the stops when you know the paying customers will be there tomorrow and the next year and the year after that?

Your diatribe against Phillies ownership, Angelo, half makes my point. Give our baseball fans some credit, in that they stopped buying tickets for the inferior product that Giles and Montgomery fielded for a full decade. Only when the Phils were poised to move into their new stadium and saw visions of empty seats, did ownership decide to invest in high-priced talent. If baseball fans were as plentiful as football fans at the Vet all those years, do you think for a second that the club would have acquired Jim Thome, Kevin Millwood and Billy Wagner.

Flyers fans, like Eagles fans, will always fill the building. But I can't accuse Flyers management of cheapness—just of taking too many years to figure out that it helps to have a European or two in your lineup. Sixers fans are more like Phils fans. Give them a good show and they'll be there. If not, well, the Big House can be pretty cavernous.

The trick, I think, is to make Eagles fans a little more like Phils fans. A bit more discriminating. A bit less blindly supportive.

But we can't. It's in our blood. And as long as the fans keep going, the owners know they don't have to push it to the next level.

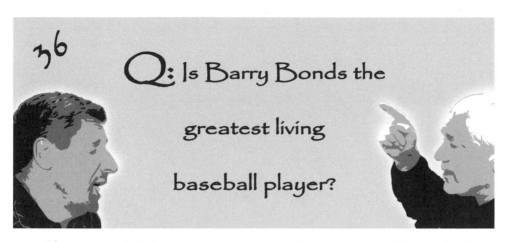

Q: Is Barry Bonds the greatest living baseball player?

Glen says: I feel like I'm nominating Hannibal Lector as world's top chef here, Angelo. Because, frankly, I can't stand Bonds. In many ways, he's everything that's wrong with baseball—surly, standoffish, self-congratulatory. And I have no doubt that he cheated the aging process with magic and illegal potions.

That said, he is the greatest baseball player alive—unless and until someone opens the freezer and thaws out Ted "Popsicle" Williams.

Now, I'm not a stats geek. But baseball is the only sport where you can actually compare players using the numbers. And when you do, Bonds comes up second to none . . . well, maybe second to Babe.

He is the only player in history with 600 homers and 500 steals. Hell, he's the only player with 500 homers and 400 steals. He holds the single-season records for homers (73), walks (198), slugging percentage (.863) and on-base percentage (.572).

He's won six National League MVP Awards, plus a batting crown at age 37. He also won eight Gold Gloves and is considered one of the greatest defensive left fielders ever.

Comparing players from different eras is tough, because the game changes. No doubt, today's offensive numbers are inflated by juiced balls, juiced bats, juiced biceps. But numbers from the Williams-DiMaggio era have to be looked at skeptically because of the exclusion of black players. And stats from the Mays-Aaron-Mantle era are diminished because they came before the great influx of Latinos into the game. Plus, how often did those guys approach the plate in the ninth inning with someone like Eric Gagne or Billy Wagner staring down from the mound?

You can, however, compare players to their own time to see how far they excel above the norm. That's what our friend Jayson Stark did on ESPN.com, attempting to measure Bonds against Willie Mays, who is often cited as the greatest living player. Stark looked at both men's OPS (on-base percentage plus slugging percentage) and the amount they exceeded the league average. He found that Mays' career OPS (.941) was 29 percent higher than the players of his era. Meanwhile, Bonds' OPS (1.003) was 36 percent higher than the players of his. And that comparison came before Barry's eye-popping seasons of 2002 and 2003.

That's the amazing thing about this guy. The older he gets, the better he gets. Again, while I acknowledge that he may not be doing this by strictly following a low-carb, high-protein diet, you've got to be impressed. No one else ever marked his 35th birthday by averaging 55 homers and 112 RBIs over the next three seasons. And he did it playing in a home ballpark where no one else can clear the fences.

When he's all done, Bonds will likely break Hank Aaron's all-time home run mark. He'll also hold the record for walks and, perhaps, extra-base hits.

Is there a hole in this case?

Yep, there is. The knock on Bonds is that he's come through small in the post-season. How can a guy be termed the all-timer if he shrinks when the spotlight is at its largest?

That's fair. But if we're going to criticize Bonds here, we also have to look at Mays. In 151 post-season at-bats, Bonds hit just .245 with nine homers and 24 RBIs. Mays, meanwhile, had 89 post-season at-bats. He hit .247 with one homer and 10 RBIs. So if you disqualify Bonds from the title of best-ever for his poor post-seasons, you've also got to disqualify Mays—regardless of any legendary catch against Vic Wertz.

The other knock is his personality, which is a mouthful of sour milk. But Ty Cobb wasn't exactly Miss Manners either. And no one ever disqualified the Georgia Peach from contention for that. In this debate, charisma is not a prerequisite for greatness.

I love baseball, Angelo. But one of its biggest problems has always been the mindset that everyone who played the sport in an earlier era was superior to anyone playing today. I can only imagine what it was like seeing guys like Ruth, Williams, Mays and Mantle in their primes. But I have watched Bonds' entire career. And I believe he has dominated the game as much as any great star from the past.

Angelo says: High school debate coaches would never endorse this tactic, Glen, but I'm going to start my rebuttal to the Barry Bonds issue by agreeing with absolutely everything you wrote. You are right on all points.

Bonds is not just an astonishing player, he is also a physical marvel. To be doing what he's doing as he approaches his 40s is unprecedented.

Still, I will not concede the bigger question: Is Barry Bonds the greatest living player? I still vote no. An emphatic no, in fact.

I define the term *greatness* differently from you, Glen. Yes, greatness encompasses exploits on the field of play. Greatness is measured by the respect other players give to the superstar; those walk totals are an irrefutable testament to the fear other teams have for Bonds.

But doesn't true greatness extend beyond all of those numbers and those signs of respect? Doesn't it also require a contribution to the game that gave the superstar a forum for his heroics? Doesn't he have to give something back?

The best point you make, Glen, is the initial one: Bonds is everything that's wrong with baseball. He is a miserable jerk who probably took steroids, in other words, cheated, to get where he is today. How can you reward someone like that with this title as greatest living player?

Let's just say that there was an awards ceremony for this honor, Glen. And let's say you were the one presenting a towering, glittering trophy to this incorrigible ass? Could you do it? Could you smile pleasantly when he didn't show up and announce to the crowd: "Mr. Bonds could not be here tonight. He thanks the Academy for this honor."

If it were me, I'd puke right on the dais. Then I'd say: "Mr. Bonds *could* be here tonight but he chooses not to be. He doesn't give a damn about you or this award. Thank you."

In the big picture, Glen, you are an enabler. You grimace when a player acts poorly but you continue to honor him. I don't. If a player wants a permanent place in history, my first requirement is that he respect the people who gave him this chance. Bonds respects no one.

This is a man who in May, 2004—with a federal steroid investigation swirling around him—visited New York for the only time all season. He begged off the first two games of a three-game series with *a cold!* While waiting for his sinuses to clear, he did grant the voracious New York media a rare insight into his character. Here are some excerpts from that session, minus the many, many expletives:

Q. Can you hit .400 this season?

A. It's May, dude. You think anyone's going to hit .400 in October? Hell, no. Not even me.

Q. Why are you considering retirement after 2005?

A. Because I want to leave. I want to do something else, that's why.

Q. What?

A. None of your business.

Q. Will you be the home-run champ by then?

A. Probably not . . . I want to beat (Babe) Ruth's (714), . . . then you won't talk about him no more.

Q. Are you bothered by the steroid investigation?

A. Does it look like it?

Q. Is there any chance they'll get you?

A. (Snort) Get me? You couldn't get me if you tried.

Greatness, Glen? The greatest living player? Please.

Now I realize that I can't take this position without offering my own choice for the honor. No problem. I will not pick the most popular other candidate, Willie Mays, because he's got some ghosts in his own closet. The end of his career was an embarrassment, and his actions since retirement—casino affiliations, fan altercations—disqualify him, too.

So I'll go with another obvious choice: Hank Aaron. The last time I looked, he was still the all-time homer champ, he was truly great at the plate and in the field, and he has conducted himself with class and distinction his entire life.

Someday, Barry Bonds might pass Hank Aaron in home runs, but he'll never catch him as a human being.

In the game of life, Barry Bonds is a .200 hitter.

Q: Who's the best college coach in town?

Angelo says: Phil Martelli is a bald, rumpled man who could just as easily be your corner grocer or your tax accountant. He has no aura of brilliance, no posse of boot-lickers, no fancy cars or flashy jewelry. There is no neon sign that says this man is great.

But he is great. In fact, Phil Martelli is the best college coach in the Philadelphia area —better than John Chaney at Temple, better than Fran Dunphy at Penn, and far better than the aging and crotchety Joe Paterno at Penn State.

The only reason Martelli doesn't get the same gushing tributes as those other coaches is because he doesn't campaign for adulation. When he smiles for the cameras—which he does tirelessly—it is always to promote his kids or his school, not himself.

In my 30 years covering and talking sports, Phil Martelli is the most unselfish, most honorable coach I have ever encountered.

I already know what you're going to say, Glen. I have a friendship with Martelli that is affecting my judgment. Yes, I will concede that I have violated my self-imposed rule not to associate with the people I talk about, but that's the whole point here. Martelli is such a terrific guy that he completely belies the notion that a coach has to be a jerk. Hey, even I couldn't resist getting to know him better.

The story of how Martelli became the head basketball coach at St. Joseph's University is a classic example of the fickle fortunes of sports. Martelli had functioned as an assistant with the Hawks for 10 years and had already been passed over a couple of times when John Griffin abruptly resigned in 1995 to return to Wall Street. Martelli had decided to leave St. Joe's if he was rejected again. Then the call came in. The job was his.

What took so long? After a decade at the school, the Hawks still weren't sure he could do the job. He just didn't have that slick, pressed, hungry look of the prototypical college coach.

Well, the Hawks are sure now—and so is everybody else. Martelli has made it to the

Sweet Sixteen twice in the past seven years, with two entirely different teams. He plays in a rinky-dink league (the Atlantic Ten), is restricted in recruiting by the tough academic standards at St. Joe's and he plays in a fieldhouse that could also double as a landfill.

And still he prospers. Against all odds, he manages to recruit players like Jameer Nelson, Delonte West and Marvin O'Connor. You know how, Glen? By using the same honest, down-to-earth approach that he uses with everyone. Ask people in the sports community whom they root for most. Phil Martelli will win your poll by a wide margin.

Once in a great while, good guys actually do finish first.

And that's just the beginning of the story with Martelli. Along with his amazing success on the court, he is even better off it. I spent a few days on campus during his undefeated regular season in 2003-04, Glen. I never saw anything like it. Beloved? The man would have to be St. Joseph himself to receive more worship.

His kids go to school, they graduate, they conduct themselves with class at all times, they are great to the media and fans, they stay out of jail, and they seem to be having the time of their lives in the process. Coaches are not supposed to be able to develop this kind of discipline in the 21st century. Martelli does it effortlessly.

Meanwhile, he is also the funniest person in Philadelphia sports, and has been for years. On his own coach's TV show, he does Carnac impersonations, grills his wife on their private life, and cavorts with mascots and cheerleaders. In good times and bad, Martelli knows how to smile—and how to make other people smile, too.

For many, many years, I have said that if my son were an elite athlete, I'd want him to play for Joe Paterno. No more. Paterno has lost it, and John Chaney isn't far behind. But Martelli is in his prime right now, doing it as well as it can be done. Martelli is the coach I'd pick above all others.

Those who have listened to my radio show know that Phil Martelli is a pretty terrific football prognosticator, too. One year, he went twelve weeks into the season before he missed predicting correctly the outcome of an Eagles game. Well, I'd like to turn the tables now and offer a prediction of my own, Glen.

I predict that Martelli someday will be considered the best college coach ever in Philadelphia.

Glen says: Your last words say it all, Angelo. *Someday* Phil Martelli may be known as our best-ever college coach. But he's got a long way to go.

Martelli is a master strategist and a terrific guy (although I've lost a few shekels betting his football picks). I've had the privilege of hearing him speak to my journalism students at St. Joe's and I recognize what an amazing resource he is to the university.

I have no such relationship with Temple's John Chaney. In fact, the last time I spoke with Chaney he accused me of knowing nothing about barbecuing ribs—my epicurean specialty. So this statement comes with no bias: John Chaney is the best college coach in Philadelphia.

We could start with the mind-boggling numbers. After his first year at Temple, Chaney rattled off 21 winning seasons in a row. His .681 winning percentage at the school (483-224) is among the top 10 in Division 1 over that period. Temple has won 23 NCAA Tournament games under the Old Man, and been to five Elite Eights.

He does this while playing what is perennially the toughest schedule in the nation. Chaney believes that to flourish in the spring, you've got to suffer in December, so he punishes his team with a brutal tour of the Top 25 to initiate every season.

Under his tutelage, Temple has won or shared 13 Big Five championships, and captured eight titles in the Atlantic Ten. You know, Ange, that "rinky-dink league." Throw in his ten seasons at Cheney State, and Chaney becomes one of a handful of coaches ever to reach 700 wins. And he's one of just three active college coaches (along with Mike Krzyzewski and Bob Knight) in the Basketball Hall of Fame. Hell of a résumé, eh?

Now, the knock on Chaney is that he never got to a Final Four, and that's true. But let's be honest, Angelo. While perennial powers like Duke, Kentucky and Arizona can attract McDonalds All-Americans just by letting them glimpse the campus, what's John got to sell? North Broad Street and the 5 a.m. wake-up call?

No one has ever done more with less than the guy who not only stands for Temple U, but actually has come to uncannily resemble the school's owl mascot over the years.

The stats don't even begin to tell the story. What Chaney represents is opportunity. As a young man, he emerged from a neighborhood of broken houses and broken dreams. Now he sees as his life's mission offering that same chance to others. So he takes kids who might be troubled or underprivileged and teaches them lessons—about commitment, about passion, about discipline, about team. Sometimes basketball even fits into the equation.

Now all of that may be as anachronistic as Chaney's defense-first, low-risk style of hoops. But my grumpy old man doesn't succumb to demands to change. The youngsters who come to play for him know what that entails: Be at practice at 5:30 a.m. No woofing or posing for the cameras. No high-fives, no chest bumps. You want glamour, go play for North Carolina. Temple is a place for drudging, aesthetically ugly, fundamental basketball. It usually wins.

And his players usually earn degrees. They stay in touch, too. Aaron McKie says a day rarely goes by that he doesn't talk to "Coach" at least once. Truth be told, John Chaney is a father to dozens, perhaps hundreds, of his former players. His affect on their lives is lasting.

It is said that the college game has passed him by. There may be some truth in that, I suppose. The Owls haven't made the NCAA Tournament since 2001 (when they got to the Elite Eight by the way), and haven't produced a first-round pick since McKie and Eddie Jones in 1994. Chaney's critics—just like Joe Paterno's at Penn State—argue that he has outlived his usefulness, ignoring that, without him there would be no glossy Liacouris Center for the team to play in and millions of fewer dollars donated to the university.

But that's not really the point. Perhaps the matchup-zone defense no longer confounds the slicked-back geniuses who patrol the opposing sidelines. Perhaps his "turnovers-are-the-devil's-work" mantra doesn't appeal to enough kids in the era of Sports Center highlights. The sad reality is that John Chaney may never again see the Elite Eight.

It doesn't matter. As long as he's still patrolling the sidelines—his tie falling out of its knot, his face twisted with emotion—Temple will be a winner. Because John Chaney is more than just a sports treasure.

He is a civic treasure.

Q: Who's the worst coach in our history?

Glen says: We've had more than our share of bad leaders over the years. Bumblers like Wayne Cashman. Bullies like Jim Fregosi. Company stooges like Rich Kotite. So many choices, so little space.

But only one of these guys could have been fairly convicted as a thief. And that was Doug Moe, who stole close to $3 million from owner Harold Katz and the better part of a season from 76ers fans.

Doug Moe was a con artist. At one point, he had been a successful coach in the NBA, but by the time he got to Philadelphia in 1992, he had no apparent interest in directing a team. He snookered Katz into believing his up-tempo style of basketball would work here, but neglected to tell the owner that he had no interest in actually teaching his troops how to play that style. Instead, he was like Professor Harold Hill in the play *Music Man*, selling a naive populace on the "Think System." You never actually have to practice. If you just visualize yourself playing the instrument, you'll become a great musician.

(Come to think of it, Allen Iverson would have loved this guy.)

"The passing game is basically doing whatever the hell you want," Moe explained. "Hey, if a coach gets some sort of thrill when the team runs a play right, that's good. I just happen to think differently."

Which is to say hardly at all. So Moe's Sixers were taught almost no set plays. They were expected just to act and react based on their basketball instincts. Problem is, a roster of Andrew Lang, Armon Gilliam and Manute Bol didn't exactly lead the league in basketball instincts.

"We never practice," backup center Eddie Lee Wilkins carped after a 56-point loss to the Seattle SuperSonics. "We have no offense. We have no defense. We're not prepared to play."

Asked to respond to players' criticisms, Moe said: "Are they mad at me? You think I care?"

Obviously not.

Moe clearly cared about nothing other than getting away from his team as quickly as possible each day. He spoke longingly about missing his wife (nicknamed "Big Jane") and his cabin in Colorado. Sometimes Moe would whistle a practice over midway through five-on-fives. Players would check their watches and snicker that the coach had just enough time to get to the matinée at the Narberth Theater.

The one thing Philadelphia fans won't tolerate is a lack of effort. But that's exactly what Doug Moe gave them. Late in a February game against Houston with the team down five, Moe called the requisite time out. Players gathered around to get directions. There were no plays, not even a magic marker to draw squiggles on an eraser board. Moe had nothing. "Go out there," he told them. "Whatever happens, happens."

Eventually, his lack of interest became just too obvious. After the third 40-point loss of the season, Moe told reporters—not for the first time—"We stink." Katz had no choice. He fired Moe, explaining, "I don't know if the players quit on him or he quit on the players. But we've become a non-competitive team."

Talk about an understatement. The Sixers were 19-37 at the time. The Spectrum seats —post-Barkley, pre-Iverson—were either empty or angry. It may have been the most apathetic period of basketball in this city's rich hoops history.

But even then, it wasn't over—at least not for Katz. Moe's contract cost the franchise more than $700,000 a year for the next three seasons. Never had a man earned so much to do so little in such a short amount of time.

A year later, *Daily News* reporter Phil Jasner reached Moe at his cabin outside Denver for one of those "where are they now" stories.

"I'm out of coaching," Moe said. "That's what happens—you move onto the next thing. I'm into fantasy leagues now."

The fantasy was that anyone thought he could coach in the first place.

Angelo says: No, Glen, the worst coach in Philadelphia history was Rich Kotite. He was also the biggest jackass, the biggest fraud and the biggest back-stabber. To say that I loathed Rich Kotite is to understate my true feelings.

Doug Moe was a dreadful coach, too, I readily admit. He brazenly stole the money of Harold Katz. But he wasn't around long enough to do the kind of damage Kotite did. He didn't take a very good team and systematically destroy it. In order to truly assess the work of a coach, Glen, you have to look at what kind of team he inherited, and what happened after he left.

And that's where Kotite has no peer. Kotite took an Eagles team that, by all accounts, had the talent to win a Super Bowl and, four years later, left it buried in the rubble of a seven-game losing streak. Kotite actually finished his tenure as Eagles coach with a winning record of 37-29, but he was the biggest loser in franchise history—bigger even than Joe Kuharich (28-41-1) or Ed Khayat (8-15-2) or Jerry Williams (7-22-2).

Let's start with the way Kotite politicked his way into the job. When owner Norman Braman had decided to fire Buddy Ryan, he also realized that he needed to name a new coach the very same day. Braman's thinking was that the loss of a popular coach would be neutralized if he had a new genius in place right away.

I spoke to Kotite the morning of his coup because he was a paid contributor to my WIP show that season. Before he was scheduled to go on the air, he told me that he absolutely would not discuss the rumors that Ryan was about to be dumped. When I reminded him that he was being paid to discuss those rumors, he hung up on me.

Until that day, no one had ever considered Kotite a candidate for a head-coaching job, and with good reason. The Eagles had hired him as their offensive coordinator, against Ryan's wishes, before the 1990 season. There was simply no argument that that 10-6 team failed primarily because of Kotite's offense. The idea that Rich Kotite could perform so miserably and then be promoted was laughable.

"Boy, am I in this thing over my head"

But we all underestimated Kotite's ability to kiss ass. Somehow, he convinced Braman and team president Harry Gamble that he was a better choice than defensive coordinator Jeff Fisher. Of course, Fisher went on to have an excellent coaching career in the NFL. Kotite ended up as a character actor in B-movies and bad TV commercials.

The first year under Kotite, the Eagles managed the impossible. They finished with the best defense in the league, had a 10-6 record and still failed to make the playoffs. The next year they actually won a playoff game in New Orleans, but by then the roster was atrophying under Kotite's leadership. The window of opportunity was closing right on Kotite's bald head.

By the third season, Kotite's charts were smearing in the rain, timeouts were being squandered before punts, and the entire city couldn't help but laugh at the man presiding over an 8-8 mess. Even when the 1994 Eagles started 7-2 under new owner Jeff Lurie, it was inevitable that Kotite would soon be leaving Philadelphia. The befuddled coach had the audacity to go on *Monday Night Football* to proclaim himself one of the NFL's best coaches that year. He even used his pet phrase that night: "Without question."

Yeah, right. This brilliant coach then watched his team fall apart in historic fashion. The Eagles lost the last seven games. Ray Rhodes was hired to replace Kotite, who exploited the advanced senility of Jets owner Leon Hess to win a job immediately with the New York Jets.

And this is where the true ineptitude of Rich Kotite is best seen, Glen. Under Rhodes —who was no Vince Lombardi, either—the same players who had lost seven straight jumped back up to 10-6 and made it to the second round of the playoffs. Meanwhile, Kotite was posting marks of 3-13 and 1-15 in New York before leaving the NFL forever.

Granted, Doug Moe was a con artist. Granted, his 56-game stint as Sixers coach was worse than any single season by Kotite. I'll even concede that Moe gave less effort than any coach in Philadelphia history.

But just present the two names to Philadelphia sports fans today and watch the reaction. Moe was a thief. Kotite was a laughing-stock.

Rich Kotite was the worst coach in Philadelphia history.

Without question.

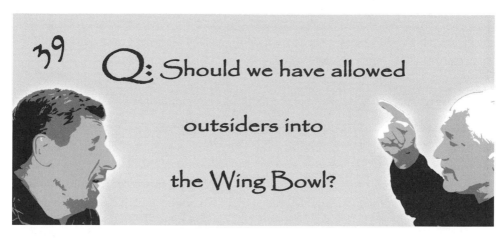

Q: Should we have allowed outsiders into the Wing Bowl?

Angelo says: I came into this world with a serious birth defect.

I wasn't born in Philadelphia.

Of course, I take no blame for this affliction, but still it is my burden to bear. No day goes by without someone scoffing at my humble beginnings in Providence, Rhode Island. Few opportunities pass without a native Philadelphian reminding me that I'm not "one of us." No credit is given for choosing the wonderful city of Philadelphia as my permanent home. Too little, too late, I guess.

I'm an outsider, maybe even a carpetbagger. I admit it.

But I never knew how distinct the city limits were drawn until I did the unthinkable in early 2004 and invited outsiders to compete in the greatest annual, single-day radio promotion in America, the Wing Bowl. I still have the emails calling for my exile back to Rhode Island, or even my execution at high noon in Love Park, after contestants from Ohio and Virginia and—gasp!—New York joined our annual tribute to bad taste.

I don't have to tell you, Glen—a Buffalo native in your own right—how tough it is to be accepted into the exclusive community of Philadelphians, even under the best of circumstances. Wing Bowl 12 was most definitely *not* the best of circumstances, believe me.

It all began innocently enough in the summer of 2003, when I started planning the promotion for the late-January event. El Wingador, a South Jersey contestant, had dominated the previous three eating competitions, and I sensed a significant downturn in the fan anticipation for a fourth straight rout.

Please understand that my primary preoccupation with every Wing Bowl is to create enough excitement to fill a 20,000-seat arena at 6 a.m.—no small achievement when the primary lure is fat guys eating chicken wings. Once those seats are filled, I hope for the kind of exciting, controversial event that will help promote the next year's contest. My only scoreboard for the Wing Bowl is the final attendance number.

I can remember the precise moment when I developed the blueprint for Wing Bowl 12. I was sitting at the Philadelphia International Airport, moments before our annual pre-Thanksgiving show, when someone came up to our broadcast table with a copy of *Maxim* magazine.

"Hey, you want to have your best Wing Bowl ever?" a stranger said. "Get this girl."

I looked down and saw a tiny article about a phenomenon, Sonya Thomas, who was confounding the country with astonishing eating feats. I knew right away that I had to have this woman in Wing Bowl 12.

To get her, I had to track down the eating association that sanctions all of Sonya's events, and it was at the International Federation of Competitive Eating (IFOCE) in New York that I learned of Ed "Cookie" Jarvis and a group of other extraordinary eaters. I got the sense right from the beginning that my chances of getting Sonya to Wing Bowl would be improved greatly if I took the New York eaters, too.

It didn't seem like a big deal at the time.

It was a *very* big deal, apparently.

The two magic words were "New York." Our city's hatred for everything New York came out with such a vengeance that I stopped answering vicious emails and, in the final days, my home phone. The most frightened I've ever been in 15 years on Philadelphia radio was when Jarvis and Sonya went into overtime tied. If the New York guy took the championship, I'm not sure I would have gotten out of the building alive that day.

As it was, I got murdered anyway—but at least it was just verbally. One fan actually screamed at me from the cheap seats, "Hey, Cataldi. You happy now, you @*$%*&#? Why don't you go home to Rhode Island?"

Well, Philadelphia is home for me now, even if I wasn't born here. The world didn't end because a 99-pound woman from Virginia won the Wing Bowl. It just made life a little more interesting.

This may make me sound like even more of an outsider, but I learned something from the debacle of Wing Bowl 12. I learned that non-natives like us might actually have more faith in Philadelphia than the people who grew up here.

We know what an amazing city this is, Glen.

Why don't the people who grew up here?

Glen says: Before I begin, let me thank you for one thing, Angelo, and that would be not bogging down Wing Bowl with stuffy Roman numerals as the NFL has with the Super Bowl. Some day in the future, I don't want to have to decipher what Wing Bowl XLVIII means.

And I think we'll get to that day. Because, with the rest of the WIP Morning Crew, you've created and nurtured one of the signature events on Philadelphia's annual calendar.

Let me repeat that—on *Philadelphia's* annual calendar.

It doesn't matter that you were born in Rhode Island and I came from Upstate New York. We've both been here long enough to know that people in this beautiful, somewhat insecure town like to talk about all things Philadelphia. It's why we don't discuss the Red Sox and Yankees on WIP. It's why so many locals would rather summer in Cape May than Cannes.

It's why Wing Bowl worked so perfectly. It was a bunch of guys from the neighborhood battling against guys from the next neighborhood for the honor of wearing that tacky crown of bones. It's irrelevant whether they can eat more than some interlopers from Brooklyn. And it's uniquely Philadelphia—no pretense, no snootiness, just a 20,000-strong mob of loonies having a little too much fun at the crack of dawn.

Actually, it goes beyond that. One of the hallmarks of Wing Bowl is its timing—it's staged the Friday before the Super Bowl. Or, as we in the Jewish faith refer to it, *shiva* – the period of mourning.

Inevitably, it comes right after the Eagles have been knocked out of the NFL post-season. Our fans are morose, their championship dreams yet again drowned down a well of disappointment.

To that end, Wing Bowl has annually served as a great Irish wake, a chance to bury our frustration in sex and sauce and beer. Yes, the Birds may have lost again, but something's right with the world if El Wingador can put on his annual sprint to victory.

It always ends the same way. We crown our own champion, a local Rocky who outbattled two dozen opponents and the gag reflex.

At least it always ended the same way. Until 2003.

Then *you* invited the outsiders.

You're not as dumb as you look Angelo. You knew exactly what you were doing, without the help of some mysterious stranger in the airport showing you a second-rate men's magazine. Bringing in trenchermen from New York and Virginia gave Wing Bowl the one element it was missing from professional wrestling—the bad guy. You might as well have put Cookie Jarvis and Moses Lehrman in black masks and Middle Eastern robes and had them strut around spitting on our flag. Oh, wait a minute, I think that *was* one guy's gig.

And, when an outsider won (admittedly, she was the most likeable of that contingent), you set up the perfect plot line for the next Wing Bowl: Can someone from Philadelphia emerge to win back our birthright?

Now you'll be able to fill months of programming searching for the next local hero.

Good luck, but I've got bigger concerns. Like your sellout to the national spotlight. And your willingness to compromise our event to fit the rules of that self-important eating organization. Gee, Ange, do you think you could fit a few more cameras on stage? I hear there were a few fans in the seats whose view wasn't blocked.

You say your biggest concern is filling the building. Fair enough. But events can lose their soul when they grow too large. Wing Bowl was perfect because it was ours. The problem is not, as you suggest, about our local self image. And it isn't that people from Philadelphia don't think we can beat the stinking outsiders.

It's just that we don't want you inviting them to our party.

You started this, Angelo. Now it's up to you to fix it.

Q: What's the best sports movie ever?

Glen says: To suggest that *Rocky* embodies Philadelphia is cliché. But it's as true now as it was when this blue-collar anthem for the ages came out in 1976. The hard-working, down-on-his luck row home lunkhead—all grit, no grace—gets his shot at the title. There is the dream, but also the underlying knowledge that he really can't beat the champ. In the end he loses, but he wins our hearts and respect by staying on his feet.

Does that sound like anything Philadelphia fans have been through over the years?

Sure, there have been some great sports films. I love *Slapshot* for the laughs, *Bull Durham* for the sex, *Raging Bull* for the violence and *Hoosiers* for the . . . well, to be honest, I can't get that hideous scene of Gene Hackman sucking face with Barbara Hershey out of my mind.

Knowing you, Angelo, you'll pick *Field of Dreams* or *The Natural* or some other weepy chick flick crammed with greeting card sappiness. Me? I get choked up when the Italian Stallion shouts, "Cut me, Mick! C'mon, cut me!"

I'll make my case this way: No sports movie in history has been copied as often as *Rocky*, and I'm not just referring to Sylvester Stallone's unwatchable sequels. Stallone may not have invented the lovable-underdog saga, but he sure perfected it. "Rudy" is a weak copy of *Rocky*. So is *Miracle*, even if it is based on a true story. So is *Bad News Bears*. And so, for that matter, is the great *Hoosiers*, although I would have loved to have seen Coach Norman Dale scream at his players, "You're gonna eat lightning and you're gonna crap thunder!"

Rocky also inspired a great Philadelphia tradition that lives on to do this day. Who among us hasn't sprinted up the art museum steps at least once (take a breather halfway if you need one, Ange), and leaped up and down with our arms upraised? Sorry, but I never watched *Field of Dreams* and then had the urge to wander around a corn field.

Need goosebumps? Try Rocky in the training sequence performing those one-armed pushups just as "Gonna Fly Now" kicks into high gear. Cut to him dashing through the

Italian Market and then Boathouse Row (some long sprint, eh?). If that doesn't inspire you off the sofa and into the gym, nothing's going to work.

And then there are the great characters. Paulie, the Port Richmond row home loser brilliantly played by Burt Young. Mick, the octogenarian trainer with the rheumy eyes seeking one last pass at the main chance. Apollo Creed—the brash, angry Ali clone. Hell, even Joe Frazier makes a nifty cameo.

Did I mention the great fight sequence? It may not boast the brutal realism of *Raging Bull*, but the first time I first saw *Rocky* crack Creed's ribs, everyone in the movie theater hopped out of his seat in delight.

The wonderful thing about *Rocky* is how intelligent and nuanced it is. There are all kinds of tender little moments and layered dialog that make it worthy of the Best Picture Oscar it won. What's astonishing is that Stallone—of all people—wrote it (in three days, no less!) after watching Ali bat around Jersey club fighter Chuck Wepner. Stallone refused to sell the rights unless he was cast in the lead. Producers had planned to cast Ryan O'Neal as Rocky and Bette Midler as Adrian.

I honestly believe Stallone made a deal with the devil that allowed him to conceive one great work and, in return, spend the rest of his life producing schlock. Thus, we've been tortured by *Judge Dredd*, *Stop! Or My Mom Will Shoot*, and *Avenging Angelo*, which, near as I can figure, isn't about you, my friend.

But I digress. So I'll leave you with this. This inexpensively filmed ($1.2 million), feel-good story of a hardscrabble club fighter is both the best movie about Philadelphia and the best sports movie ever filmed. Anytime I'm flipping around the channels and discover *Rocky* on one of the cable stations, I'm hooked for the rest of the night.

"It really don't matter if this guy opens my head, either, Adrian. 'Cause all I wanna do is go the distance."

Excuse me, Angelo, I'm all ferklempt.

Angelo says: It is hardly my intention here to denigrate a crowd-pleaser like *Rocky* —especially in a city that has embraced that film like no other. The triumphant race up the steps of the Art Museum remains one of the most exhilarating movie moments ever.

I'll even confide to you, Glen, that one of the reasons I moved to Philadelphia is because that film portrayed it as such a magical place. The jogs through the Italian Market, the sparring sessions in grimy, inner-city gyms, the bone-chilling visits to the meat locker . . . it was all so earthy, yet so charming.

As a former boxing writer, I can also say that *Rocky* spawned a generation of boxers who wanted nothing more than to live the dream that unfolded on the screen. Sylvester Stallone didn't just hit a nerve with that movie, he struck a gold mine.

But the best sports movie ever?

Puhleeeeze.

And *Rocky* most definitely is NOT the most copied sports movie ever. In fact, it may be the most derivative film ever made. Stallone, who has never had an original thought in his life, did a great clip-and-paste job, but there was absolutely nothing new in *Rocky*.

A boxing movie that builds up to a big-fight scene? Gee, that had never been done before *Rocky*. The downtrodden neighborhood kid who gets a chance to live out his dream? Another unique theme. The ugly-duckling girlfriend, the crusty boxing manager, the creepy friend . . . all brand-new characterizations, without a doubt.

And my favorite was the evil nemesis, Apollo Creed. Where in the world would Stallone come up with a flashy, loudmouth champion like him? Certainly it couldn't have been Muhammad Ali. Naw. That's just a weird coincidence. (Heck, Glen, you even refer to Creed as an "Ali clone." Doesn't that suggest to you that he is not exactly original?)

Compare *Rocky* for a moment with a true work of genius, *Hoosiers*. I'll even do it with a boxing cliché of my own, the tale of the tape:

Stallone vs. Gene Hackman—Advantage Hackman.

Burt Young vs. Dennis Hopper—Advantage Hopper.

Talia Shire (who?) vs. Barbara Hershey—Advantage Hershey.

Need I go on? The cinematography in *Hoosiers*—that sweeping panorama of the Midwest in the 1950s—makes *Rocky* look like a school project. The subtlety of the direction by David Anspaugh compared to the sledgehammer approach of novice director Stallone is laughable. The characters in *Hoosiers* were real people, flaws and all.

The best comparison I can offer is in the climax of the two movies. *Rocky* had the absurd violence in the ring (did anyone ever hear of a standing-eight count?), the melodramatic screams for Adrian, the pounding music. *Hoosiers* had a triumphant last scene, too, but it continually cut away from the basketball court and into the hospital room where Dennis Hopper was listening on the radio.

When all other scenes are forgotten, Glen, the memory of Hopper jumping up and down on his bed after the winning shot is one for the ages.

The other sports films you mention all have something in common with *Rocky*, too, Glen. They are all considerably better. *Slapshot* was unique, *Field of Dreams* was lyrical, *Bull Durham* was nuanced, *The Natural* was a spectacular fantasy come to life.

If it's any consolation, Glen, you can probably relate better now to the ending of *Rocky*.

Like Balboa, you lost this fight.

But at least there won't be any sequels.

Q: Who was right—Larry Brown or Allen Iverson?

Angelo says: As a loud, proud enemy of Larry Brown, I relish the idea of defending him with the same zeal that Allen Iverson showed for practice.

"We talkin' 'bout practice, man. . . . . Practice!"

I'll even admit that if I had to listen to Brown's incessant whining for six years, I might have acted far worse than Iverson did. Larry Brown is a lying, back-stabbing phony who preaches doing things the right way, and then does whatever the hell he pleases.

However, in this war of wills between two men in dire need of a shrink, Larry Brown was less wrong than Iverson.

It's very simple, Glen. Larry Brown tried. Allen Iverson didn't.

Let's start with Iverson, a phony in his own right. This is a guy who babbled from the day he arrived on the Sixers that his only goal was to win a championship. He would do absolutely, positively anything to win for the beloved fans of Philadelphia.

Well, maybe not *anything*. For example, he wouldn't practice if he wasn't in the mood. In his last season playing for Brown, the unofficial count on how many practices Allen begged off was 42. What would happen if the average worker called out sick 42 times in a year, Glen? He'd be sent packing, which is exactly what the Sixers should have done with Iverson.

AI also wouldn't follow the rules. He had the audacity to appear 45 minutes before game time for a playoff contest in which his team faced elimination. Only a person with no respect for authority would do something as arrogant as that, the kind of rebel who would wear the retro uniform of the hated Boston Celtics to a news conference after a Sixers game. If he had spit in the eye of every Philadelphia fan, Iverson could not have been more disrespectful that night.

Allen Iverson would do *anything* to win a title—except, of course, sit on the bench and cheer on his teammates. If Brown tried to sit his franchise player down for just a few minutes, the pout would begin to spread across Iverson's face until it stretched from baseline to baseline. Franchise players don't get treated like that, man. Franchise players don't just get their asses kissed, they get their shoes shined until they can see their pretty faces when they look down.

That was always Iverson's attitude. I'm special, man. Treat me special.

Brown never found a way to control Iverson, but it was not for lack of effort. Amid all of the futile whining, the coach tried to befriend his star, then he tried to discipline him, then he tried to reason with him, and finally he tried to weather him. In the end, Brown said he just couldn't stand another day of trying to run a team with two sets of rules—one for 11 players and the other for the man-child superstar.

I can already anticipate your anguished cries, Glen. Brown is the one who broke his contract and left. Brown is the one who never settled on an effective way to coach Iverson. Brown is the one who went public with all of his frustrations. Allen almost never aired his grievances to the media.

All of those arguments are valid. But none of them deal with the nexus of the problem—an immature, spoiled brat who thinks a crossover dribble is the lease on a sports franchise.

I'm a bottom-line guy, Glen. You are, too. So let's decide this argument by looking at the bottom line. The season after Brown bolted for Detroit, he was back in the playoffs and winning an NBA title. Iverson was home in April, after yet another season of controversy and insubordination.

Larry Brown wasn't the only person who couldn't control Allen Iverson.

In fact, no one could control Allen Iverson.

Including Allen Iverson.

Glen says: You're right about one thing, Angelo. We're debating two very flawed characters here. Two talented, emotional, immature men who behave more like each other than either wants to admit.

The question here is, which guy was right? I'd love to say—sort of both, sort of neither. But finding middle ground is not the purpose of this book. So, forced to choose one of these man-childs, I'll go with Iverson.

That's not a popular opinion these days. As you noted, Brown left Philadelphia and latched onto a champion Detroit Pistons team. Iverson, meanwhile, found himself left aboard a leaky ship as unsteady as the S.S. Minnow.

But whose fault was that? Larry Brown did to the Sixers what Larry Brown always does. He bailed. If I can take this boat metaphor a few nauseating steps further, Captain

Brown steered the Sixers' ship into troubled waters and then, just before it crashed into the rocks, he paddled away on the only life boat.

It's a shame it ended that way. Because Brown and Iverson—together—had a great run. The Sixers' 2001 playoff push was as exciting a time as we've had around here in the last decade.

But then Brown lost his touch. His draft picks were awful. He signed 90-year-old Dikembe Mutombo for $53 million, and then sold him to New Jersey for Keith Van Horn. He even made a deal with Derrick Coleman, also known as *el Diablo*.

And then, after wringing everything he could from the team, he left. That's the deal with Larry: He always leaves.

Say what you want about Iverson (and there's much to be said), but he's all about loyalty. He has stated repeatedly that he wants to finish his career in Philadelphia, and he means it. Hell, he cried a few years back when he thought he had been traded to the Los Angeles Clippers. Of course, who wouldn't?

Brown meanwhile, threatened to jump off more ledges than a Center City pigeon. Pat Croce, and later Billy King, had to talk him out of resigning more than a dozen times.

Which one of these men is a talented genius? Which is a self-centered baby?

That was Larry's way of managing problems. I don't condone Iverson's habitual skipping of practice. But rather than deal with it directly, Brown wimped out. Usually, he'd wind up going to the media to open up his whine cellar.

A strong coach handles problems straight on. And a strong coach changes with the times. Brown harped so long and hard about "playing the right way" that even John Wooden would have lost his patience and tossed up a foolish three-pointer. I respect Larry Brown's Hall of Fame career but, hey, can we evolve past *Hoosiers* here?

All that said, I didn't really see what a phony Larry Brown was until he skipped town. For all of his moralizing, he lobbied to steal colleague Rick Carlisle's job before that Detroit coach was even fired. And when he got that position, he held one of history's most putrid news conferences.

First, the man who had strip-mined the 76ers bellyached that he never had final say on basketball issues in Philadelphia, and couldn't even recall his job title. (It was, by the way, Vice President of Basketball Operations.) Then he described his six years here as "a test," and took some veiled shots at Iverson. His behavior was so despicable that day that it would have incited Gandhi to beat him up.

Now Allen has his flaws, but he has never taken public potshots. In fact, he goes out of his way to credit Brown for his success. So who's the bigger man?

Hey Ange, if you don't believe what I say about Brown, why not ask his former boss, Pat Croce?

Oh, you did. And here's what Pat said on your radio show:

"He's narcissistic. It's all about him. I like Larry, and I love what he did for the Philadelphia franchise with me . . . . But he left the team high and dry and took shots."

Then you asked Croce what he would want to say to the wandering coach.

"Hey Larry, are you happy yet?"

Larry Brown never, ever, is happy.

42 Q: What's the worst thing ever said by a local sports figure?

Glen says: We've heard players rip coaches and coaches rip players. We simmered when bumble-headed Bill Giles reduced our city to "small market" status. We booed when Mike Schmidt labeled the locals as "jealous" and "miserable."

But no one crossed the line like Jim Fregosi.

The Phils manager was a sourpuss for his entire six-year run in Philadelphia. We didn't like him—even after the "Lightning in a Bottle" run of 1993—and he made no secret of despising us.

The depths of his animus were revealed in a post-game bull session in 1994.

Fregosi was exchanging insults with some of the newspaper toadies when one asked if he had heard an imitation of him on WIP radio. The manager, according to witnesses, stood up, zipped his trousers, buttoned his shirt and lit a cigarette.

Then he let loose.

"The people who listen to WIP are in South Philly f—ing their sisters," he blustered. "And the people who work for WIP are f—ing their mothers."

Well, okay then. Needless to say, there were no follow-up questions.

Let me allow that, as someone working for WIP, I didn't take this personally. Fregosi didn't like his on-air critics, we didn't like him. He could lambaste us as much as we lambasted him—although I believe had I used his words on air I'd have lost my job.

Regardless, Fregosi's attack on the station wasn't the issue. It was his attack on the million people who listen to the station. Those people buy tickets to Phillies games, watch them on television and care deeply about the franchise. By coarsely reducing them to sexual criminals, the ol' skipper was condemning his team's customer base.

None of the half-dozen writers at the bull session initially wrote of Fregosi's attack. But one passed it on to a WIP host and, within a few days, it became the town's hot-but-ton issue. Fregosi's reaction was not one of embarrassment or shame, it was anger—that his feelings had escaped the privacy of the manager's office.

"It's understood that any comments made during these sessions are not for public consumption," he spewed. "I've been in this game 35 years, and this is the first time that trust has been violated."

Let's see here, Jimbo. You make an obscene remark about the fans and you feel betrayed because you can't hide behind an "off-the-record" excuse? How about standing behind your words and taking the consequences?

The more Fregosi tried to stonewall, the more irate phone calls the team received. After a few days, the discomfited Phillies made him call a news conference to mumble out a statement written by the team's PR pros. It said, in part, "I'm embarrassed, and I'm embarrassed for my family. I don't deny saying it. But I must reinforce that by no means does it reflect my true feelings concerning our fans."

Fregosi concluded by saying he would take no questions. No questions? That's not how news conferences work. I was among dozens of reporters in the room, so I asked if he would clarify what he meant about feeling betrayed.

"I said no questions," he snapped.

"But Jim, what about—"

"I have nothing to add. If you want to ask me about the team, I'll take questions about the team."

Forty seconds passed. Not one reporter opened his mouth. I decided to be a wise guy.

"So how's the team?"

He turned toward me and glared. Now I know what they meant by the "Fregosi death stare."

Fregosi lasted until 1996, finishing with one winning season during his six here. He continued to bark about fans and critics, but was more circumspect about whom he spoke in front of. There were no testimonials when he left town.

There is one postscript to the story. Fregosi lived that season in the South Philadelphia Holiday Inn. One late night, at the bar, he was approached by a couple of well-connected boys from the neighborhood who asked him to elucidate his words about their sibling relationships.

Apparently, they didn't like his answers. He showed up the next day with a black eye.

Angelo says: This is a really weird situation, Glen. The worst quote ever by a Philadelphia sports figure definitely was *not* the Jim Fregosi comment—stupid though it was—but I can understand why you picked it.

165

You picked it because *you* made it a great quote with your memorable reaction in the locker room the next night. I love that you finally told the story behind "So how's the team?" It took guts that night to do what you did. Just understand that without your face-to-face challenge and your own follow-up quote, it was just another dumb remark by another dopey manager.

The worst comment in the history of Philadelphia sports came from a buffoon who would have had to douse himself in gasoline and light a match to destroy his image more quickly than he did.

"For who? For what?"

Of course, I'm referring to Ricky Watters and his infamous—and still hilarious—"For who? For what?" remark after alligator-arming a pass late in *his very first game as a member of the Philadelphia Eagles.*

The end of that sentence is in italics for a reason, Glen. Here was a guy who signed as a free-agent, tried to sell a ridiculous premise that he was coming "home" because he grew up in Harrisburg, Pennyslvania, and then alienated the entire fan base in his very first game by placing his own safety above the fortunes of the team. There is simply no faster way to infuriate Eagles fans than to suggest, even for a moment, that you won't give everything on every play.

Watters didn't just suggest it. He said it. Loud and clear. It's still hard to imagine anything more ridiculous than that remark.

Let's go back in time for one more look.

In the annals of lousy debuts, Watters established a record that will never be matched in the 1995 season opener against Tampa Bay. Not only did he rush for a mere 37 yards that day, he fumbled twice and then criticized the fans for being too noisy when the Eagles were on offense. He said he couldn't hear the quarterback because the fans were cheering for the Eagles!

And then, after the Eagles had lost, 21-6, Ricky Watters capped it all off with words that will be associated with him well beyond the grave. In fact, he wrote a book about his career. Can you guess what he called it, Glen?

Yup. *For Who? For What?*

Beautiful. In promoting his book on my TV show in 2003, Watters happily recounted the story behind his infamous comment. He actually seemed delighted to recall all of the gory details, even as some fans booed him that night on live television.

Proving that time does not necessarily bring wisdom, Watters said he knew even before the ball began its flight across the middle of the field that it was a bad play-call. He was a franchise runner at the time, at least in his own mind. The game was lost by then. Why risk it? Why place himself in jeopardy for a play that would have no bearing on the outcome?

After the game, Watters was just being honest, he said. You don't last as long as he did, or remain as healthy, if you place yourself in the line of fire during lost causes.

His exact quote when a reporter asked him why he didn't try for the pass was: "I'm not going to go out there and get knocked out. For who? For what?"

He never lived it down. Everywhere he went from that day forward, people would greet him with those four words. To his credit—or maybe because he is so clueless—Watters accepted his fate with surprisingly good cheer. History will show that he was a solid, durable NFL running back. History will also show that he was not exactly the pride of the Notre Dame educational system. As a student, Ricky Watters was a great football player.

The epilogue to the Watters quote is a surprising one, Glen. As insane as it was, as difficult as it made his tenure in Philadelphia, most fans have forgiven the remark. When someone says "For who? For what?" today, it is usually accompanied by a smile or a chuckle.

Watters was not the wimp that the quote implies. Not at all. He just said something stupid in a moment of weakness. Fregosi's quote was far more mean-spirited, but it actually seemed to enhance his image. He loved the reputation as a tough-talking, macho manager—even if it earned him a black eye once in a while.

Ironically, I got to ask Fregosi about his absurd comment on another TV show in 2001. He said he meant no ill will toward South Philadelphia. But at the time he wanted to *kill* WIP.

And then, much to my chagrin, he wouldn't tell me how the team was, either.

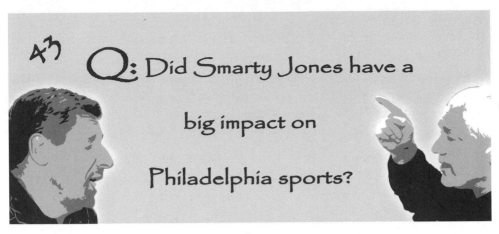

Q: Did Smarty Jones have a big impact on Philadelphia sports?

Angelo says: For many years, Philadelphia has had a reputation as a meat-and-potatoes sports city. We love the major pro sports—football, baseball, basketball, and hockey (sometimes). We pretty much shrug at everything else.

And then came a horse named Smarty Jones.

Ultimately, Smarty acted like most Philadelphia sports heroes and choked at the moment of truth, Glen. But that crazy horse taught us all a lesson about Philadelphia sports fans that no human had ever offered. He taught us that we don't mind a few carrots with our prime rib and baked potato.

We are a sucker for a great sports story.

The phenomenon of Smarty Jones occupied five weeks on the calendar in 2004, only to fade quickly from memory when the horse came up a quarter-mile short at the Belmont Stakes and lost the Triple Crown.

But few stories are like this one. Smarty's first trainer was murdered. His owner had emphysema, nearly collapsing at the end of the Kentucky Derby. His jockey was a recovering alcoholic and a card-carrying eccentric. The horse himself was a cantankerous sort with a big appetite and a bigger heart.

If you had told me that Philadelphia sports fans would embrace a sport like horse racing or an animal like Smarty, I would have told you to get back to me when you were sober. But it happened, Glen. And with the story came some surprising revelations about the fans of our city:

• Behind our crusty exterior, we embrace our own athletes like no other place, even when the superstar is just a horse.

• We are so starved for success that we'll hitch our wagon to anything that provides a chance to end our frustration.

• Once we fall in love, we'll travel long distances, pay high prices and scream our lungs out to support our heroes.

• When people like the trainer (John Servis) and the owners (the Chapman family) share their dream with the people so openly and freely, the fans respond with ardor and affection.

That last point may be the biggest lesson of all, Glen. Every day we deal with spoiled athletes who regard their own celebrity as an imposition. The Smarty family embraced the attention. The owners allowed cameras to be trained on them anywhere and everywhere, even though Roy Chapman was hooked up to an oxygen tank. The trainer was straight out of central casting—funny, candid and engaging to any and all. Even the horse never seemed to meet a camera he didn't like.

If Smarty Jones and his posse could handle the clamor for five weeks, why can't the Phillies sign a few autographs after a game or even flash a smile to the fans behind third base? Why can't Allen Iverson do something more than cupping his ear to generate cheers for himself and his team? Why does Bob Clarke always have to growl every time he's asked a tough question?

I know you hold only contempt for that horse and all that it represents, Glen, but that's only because you refuse to open your mind to new experiences. Smarty Jones was a new experience for all of us. Smarty was one of the best stories we've had in Philadelphia sports in the past decade.

The week before the Belmont Stakes, I actually traveled to Smarty's home at Philadelphia Park and got to see the trappings of his fame firsthand. While he gnawed an endless supply of hay, all of those around him savored the taste of fame. Many had lived in obscurity before this incredible story, and most are right back there now that Smarty has become a fading memory.

But the story was inspiring because it brought joy to so many people—joy that inevitably ended in sorrow, but joy nonetheless. Smarty Jones was not a hero in the end, Glen, but he reminded me of why I love sports.

Sometimes, even when you lose, you win.

Glen says: You've got me wrong, Angelo. I hold no contempt for Smarty Jones. I didn't just root for him, I bet on him. Twice. I won a couple of dollars on the Preakness, and then wagered $100 on him to win the Belmont. Like every other Philadelphian, I watched that C-Note fly away during the last 70 yards of the stretch. Why would I be bitter?

Seriously, I do believe that the five-week Smarty Jones saga was the most overblown story in Philadelphia since Randall Cunningham's $1 million, three-ring wedding in 1993.

It was a nice little tale about a nice little horse in a business that fifteen people really care about. It was a fun diversion—a well-mixed gin-and-tonic on the porch on a summer afternoon. But that's all it was.

Did we all watch the three legs of the Triple Crown? Sure, that was exciting. Did at least a few locals make a buck or two hawking "Smarty" memorabilia? Yep, and a year from now you can expect to see those T-shirts make their way through the Salvation Army donation bins to the backs of Central American peasants.

Savior of the city or candidate for the glue factory?

My point here is that while the Smarty Jones affair was an agreeable little joy ride, that's all it was. It was the fad of 2004, our sports version of the pet rock. It rode by, we cheered, it went away, we never missed it. Or have you become a regular at Philly Park, Ange?

My problem with the issue is that the few horse racing aficionados left on Earth tried to convince everyone that this was a momentous thing. For a solid month, I had to hear our airwaves co-opted by handicapping wannabes preaching that a Triple Crown by a horse would be better for local sports fans than a Stanley Cup by a hockey team (not that we'll necessarily experience either in our lifetime). A Smarty victory would end our two-decade cold streak, they insisted. It would count as a title for Philadelphia.

No, it wouldn't.

Let me give you my pecking order of local championships, and how I think they would impact the fan base:

1. The Eagles win the Super Bowl. Not even debatable. We'd party for years.

2. The Phillies win the World Series.

3. The Sixers win the NBA title. (Should be any day now.)

4. The Flyers win the Stanley Cup.

5. A local college—preferably St. Joe's or Temple—wins the NCAA Basketball Tournament.

6. A local boxer wins the heavyweight title. (I'm talking about a Joe Frazier-type pow-

erhouse here. Not some bogus cruiserweight taking a share of a split title.)

7. The horse wins.

To be honest, the Triple Crown is closer on the scale of things to having a gold medal-winning Olympic diver than it is to a professional sports championship. And the reason is simple: People root for their sports teams for decades. They follow the history. They live and die and sweat and cry as every season opens in hope and closes in disappointment.

Smarty Jones? We knew him for five weeks. I've had summer flings that lasted longer.

The problem is that too many tried to make too much of it. There were just three races, spaced weeks apart. There was nothing else, no other story line, no races to watch. But the local media—led by the *Daily News*—felt the need to fill time and space with every conceivable angle. Yes, the story of his original trainer getting murdered was a worthy read, Angelo. But did I really have to read about his love life? There was even a column in which he purported to answer reader's questions. Hell, I was waiting for the scandal in which he threatened his wife at gunpoint, followed by the weeklong media stakeout at his barn.

I agree with you that the people around Smarty Jones were terrific—from Roy Chapman telling the world, "I'm a Philly guy," to John Servis handling a nerve-wracking time with the same ease and class we'd seen from Phil Martelli.

But in the end, Smarty came, he ran, he disappeared. There was no long-term impact on the local racing industry or on us as fans. Except for that C-Note I lost.

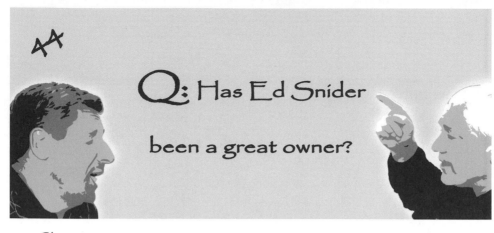

Q: Has Ed Snider been a great owner?

Glen says: I'll start with this: The guy has his faults. Ed Snider is about as warm and cuddly as a crocodile. The older he gets, the more perpetually dyspeptic he behaves. So, okay, you might not want to get stuck with him all afternoon in an elevator.

But snuggly is not a trait we usually demand in our franchise owners. I'm not looking for Mister Rogers to run my sports teams. Bill Giles is avuncular, the kind of person you'd like as a next-door neighbor. But he failed as an owner. I'll take Ed Snider and all his grouchiness.

You want a list of reasons? Let's start at the beginning. First off, the guy almost single-handedly brought the NHL to Philadelphia. Sure, the $2 million entry fee he paid back in 1967 has since been parlayed into a fortune but, at the time, it was seen as financial folly. Everything stems from Snider—from the rich history, to the team colors, to the franchise name, to kids playing street hockey and scoring for a case of Tastykakes. Name me one person in our town's history who changed the landscape of sports as much as Edward Malcolm Snider.

He also changed the landscape of the city. Other owners looking for new buildings held up the city for zillions (Jeff Lurie) or threatened to skip town (Leonard Tose). Ed Snider built his own damned arena at virtually no cost to taxpayers. He never whined about Philadelphia being a small market, never tried out potential draft picks in his driveway, never sent his players packing as soon as they reached the magic age of 30.

And what more can we ask of an owner? All we really want him to do is spend money and stay out of the way.

Ed Snider does both. The Flyers annually rank among the NHL's top five in payroll. In a league of haves and have-nots, isn't it nice to be one of the few clubs that can make the trade-deadline move to pick up a $4 million goalie? For all the mistakes made over the years with Eric Lindros, don't forget that it was Snider who initially approved spending $10 million for the kid's paycheck plus another $15 million to the Quebec Nordiques for his rights. And when the Sixers needed to rescue themselves from the Johnny Davis disaster, it was Snider who signed onto Larry Brown's $5 million-a-year salary—not to mention Brown's demands for first-class travel and five-star hotels.

Even Snider's critics will concede that he doesn't meddle. Pat Croce's divorce from the Sixers came about not because Snider interfered in his operations, but because Pat was looking to grab more responsibility (and, for the record, I agree with Croce on this one). Sixers general manager Billy King has been free to make his own mistakes—including re-upping Snider's least-favorite player, Derrick Coleman. And if you want to rip Snider for being too loyal to Flyers general manager Bob Clarke, well, there are sins worse than loyalty.

I'll take an owner who gives his GMs free reign. Would you rather have someone like his namesake—Daniel Snyder—whose interference has run the Washington Redskins into the ground? Do you really prefer someone who calls down from the owner's box to the coach—during games? Ed Snider has never been a "look-at-me" guy. He wants the focus on his team.

One last thing: Of all the current owners in this town, just one has ever won a championship. I realize that the statute of limitations on the Flyers' two Stanley Cups may be expiring, but, hey, some success beats no success.

Angelo says: The idea that Ed Snider is a good owner is laughable. He was a good owner, sure. And back then Frank Sinatra was a good singer, too. Raquel Welch was a babe. And Little Joe was doing a great job herding cattle on the Ponderosa.

But that was 30 years ago, Glen. When does the statute of limitations end on Ed Snider's two Stanley Cups? When can he be evaluated for what he's done since then? In this what-have-you-done-for-me-lately world, Ed Snider has delivered nothing but heartache and failure for a long, long time.

In fact, no individual is more responsible for the two-decade drought in Philadelphia championships than Snider. Not only has his blind loyalty to Bob Clarke strangled the Flyers, but then he went on to preside over the decay of the Sixers, too.

I'm the first one to admit that Snider has many redeeming qualities. I have worked for him in radio and television, and he truly is an honorable man. Hands off? Absolutely. He places faith in the people he hires. He lets them do their job. And no, he didn't screw over the city for funding on the arena the way other owners have. Bravo again.

In lots of ways, Snider represents a bygone era when a man's word meant something. Beneath the ornery exterior, Ed Snider is worthy of our admiration. I admit all of that.

But at the same time, I will argue forever that Snider has become a failure as an owner by his very own definition. No one should know this better than you, Glen. He made the now-infamous statement years ago on *your* radio show. He bellowed that day: "The name of the game is to win. W-I-N!"

Remember that? And he also said that day that nothing is more important to him than winning the Stanley Cup. Every move he makes, he said, is geared toward that goal.

The biggest crime is that Snider *has* always been willing to spend the money. His payroll *has* been among the highest in the NHL for many years. He is not cheap. He is just blind. And his blind spot even has a name: Bob Clarke.

In case you're conveniently forgetting the facts, Glen, it was Jay Snider—not Ed—who fired Clarke the first time. Then Ed brought back his prodigal son to perform his mad-scientist act on the roster, year after year. The implausible Chris Gratton contract didn't cost Clarke his job. The absurd Eric Lindros soap opera didn't even dent Clarke's armor. And the crass, classless remarks Clarke made about a sick but noble coach named Roger Neilson didn't even earn him a pink slip.

Someone who allows these things to happen is a good owner? You can't be serious.

And please don't blame Pat Croce for what happened after the Sixers made the NBA Finals, because everybody knows the real story. For the first time in his long career as a businessman, Snider was told the hard, painful truth by Pat Croce. Snider was told, basically, that his day had passed. He was told that it was time to let someone else have a shot. And Snider rebelled by pushing out the door the best thing that had happened to basketball in Philadelphia since 1983.

By then Snider had fallen in love with the NBA's all-time vagabond, Larry Brown. Two years later, that affection turned into anger and bitterness. As usual, Brown found the nearest exit. When Croce left in 2001, the Sixers were three games from an NBA title. In 2004, they are three lottery picks away.

I have no doubt that history will treat Ed Snider kindly. He was a generous owner who really wanted to win. He was loyal and fair and trustworthy. He really cared about the fans.

His legacy is secure, if he leaves while there are still some people alive who can remember what it was like in 1974 and 1975—when Ed Snider didn't just own the Flyers, he owned the city.

That history cannot be written, however, until he leaves.

Soon, please.

And let's hope he takes Clarke with him.

Q: What's the best trade in our history?

Angelo says: When it comes to Steve Carlton, I feel cursed. No matter how hard I try to conjure up the image of him snapping one of those devastating sliders toward the plate, all I ever see is a sad, aging lefthander hanging the damn thing and then watching it fly out of the ballpark.

Steve Carlton stayed so long past his prime that he tainted forever the memory of his masterful pitching. He didn't exactly do himself any favors with his ignorant theories on world domination, either.

But it's time to turn the dial back to the early 1970s, when there was no one better. Imagine this, Glen. You're the general manager of the Phillies, and you get a call from the GM of the St. Louis Cardinals.

"Do you have any interest in Steve Carlton?" asks Auggie Busch.

"The same Steve Carlton who won 20 games last year?" replies John Quinn, in his final act as GM of the Phils. "The same Steve Carlton who is 27 years old and is good for at least 275 innings a season? *That* Steve Carlton? . . . . Gee, let me think it over."

It would sound like a practical joke, right? Nobody trades healthy lefthanders entering their prime, even ones who are considered a little eccentric. Remember, back then all lefthanders were nuts. It added to their quirky charm.

Now comes the kicker. Auggie Busch says he wants Rick Wise in return. That's all. Rick Wise, 26, was 17-14 on the Phillies the previous season. Pretty good for a last-place club, but nothing to write Cooperstown about.

The only thing John Quinn had to do was make sure he didn't jump right through the phone that day, Glen. Carlton was awesome back then, despite a so-so 1971 season. Wise was already well on his way to baseball anonymity.

Of course, in the first season after the trade, Carlton turned in arguably the greatest season by a pitcher in baseball history—a 27-10 record for a team that won 59 games in all. Rick Wise remained a symbol of mediocrity, going 16-16.

Only later did the true story of this amazing deal—by far the best trade in Philadelphia sports history—leak out. It was even more astonishing than the deal itself.

Busch, a tightwad and a bully, dumped Carlton because the pitcher asked for $5,000 more than the Cardinals were offering. Five thousand dollars! Rather than give in to the pitcher, Busch took a noble stand. He gave away the best lefthander of his generation.

Carlton, in one of his last comments before crawling into a ten-year media shell in Philadelphia, said he was inspired by the absurdity of the deal. His goal was twenty-five wins. Not only did he top it by two, he also turned in 346 innings and a 1.96 earned run average.

All he did after that was pitch thirteen additional seasons for the Phillies, amassing 241 wins here en route to the Hall of Fame. Meanwhile, Wise lasted two seasons in St. Louis, winning 32 games before escaping to Boston and Cleveland and San Diego.

In 2003, many years after both pitchers had retired, Rick Wise appeared on my show, Glen. My second question was about the trade for Carlton.

"What took you so long to get to that?" he asked.

Wise said the deal had become a lifelong curse for him. Fans would taunt him. Writers would remind him about it constantly. Comedians would use him as a punch line.

Of course, at the end Carlton became a joke himself, playing for five different teams in his final three seasons. Then he began to speak to the media again, proving once and for all that silence is golden.

Carlton was so goofy in his final seasons and well beyond, lots of people made the same mistake I did, Glen. They began to picture Carlton at the end, not in his prime. That's why, today, the Moses Malone trade by the Sixers is often rated as a better one than Quinn's theft from Busch.

Nonsense. In a city that has had its pocket picked more times than we'd like to remember, at least we can always say we pulled off one of the greatest heists of all time.

We stole Steve Carlton.

Glen says: Wise for Carlton is a great one, Angelo. In fact, it kicked off a tremendous winning streak of trades made by our franchises. For about a decade, starting with that deal, each of the four local clubs made astonishingly bright moves. It's no coincidence that's when they all became winners.

You cited the Phils' top swap of the era. Here are, I think, the best by each of the other teams:

Eagles. Charle Young to the Rams for Ron Jaworski, 1975. Young, a tight end, played nine seasons after leaving, but never made another Pro Bowl, as he had during each of his three years here. "Jaws," of course, had a great 10-year run with the Eagles, setting seven club passing records and directing the team to the NFC title in 1980.

Flyers. A 1st-round draft pick and Doug Favell to the Maple Leafs for Bernie Parent and Larry Goodenough, 1973. Forget the pick (it became nonentity Bob Neely) and forget "Izzy" Goodenough, whose best contribution was his nickname.

Instead, focus on the goalies. Favell was a career journeyman who failed to stop a last-second shot from center ice in the last game of 1972, knocking the Flyers out of the playoffs. Parent? He can fairly be called one of the 10 greatest goalies in NHL history.

Sixers. Caldwell Jones and a 1st-round pick to the Rockets for Moses Malone in 1982. The deal was quickly arranged after the Sixers signed Moses to a free-agent offer sheet. The draft pick turned into nothing, and Jones was never more than a nice defensive player.

You dismissed this deal rather abruptly, Angelo, but don't ignore its impact. Moses came to a star-studded team and took over, winning the league's MVP Award and leading the Sixers to a title with his "fo', fo', fo' " guarantee.

So how do I choose the best trade from these three?

Well, let's set a few parameters. One would be that the player brought in led his new team to a title. Another would be that he became a Hall of Famer.

Jaworski falls a little bit short on both counts. So that deal, great as it was, is out.

Bernie and Moses, of course, are immortals among the immortals—not just Hall of Famers, but all-time bests at their positions. (So, too, is Carlton, for that matter). So that's a push.

As for the titles, both men won them and both were named playoff MVPs. The difference, of course, is that Parent won the Conn Smythe Trophy twice and the Flyers won two Stanley Cups. So Bernie gets the edge.

You could also look at longevity. Parent played six seasons with the Flyers after the trade (it was actually his second go around with the franchise), and continued to be phenomenal until an eye injury ended his career in 1979. Malone played just four years with the Sixers before one of the all-time stupidest deals (that's another chapter, eh?) sent him to Washington for a bag of magic beans.

Overall, it's close. But I'll give the nod to the Flyers deal.

You remember how it came about? Bernie was actually the first NHL player to bolt for the upstart World Hockey Association in 1972. He ended up playing one season for the Philadelphia Blazers before that debacle of a franchise folded, and his rights reverted to the Leafs. Lingering bad blood between he and Toronto owner Harold Ballard prompted the trade to Philadelphia. Within a year, Bernie was leading the first parade up Broad Street.

I'll be honest with you, Ange. You got to go first in this debate, and you might have picked the best one. But here's the bottom line: All four of the trades I cited were spectacular, franchise-turning deals that occurred within just a few years. And I could have recalled others from that era that brought in talent the likes of Garry Maddox, Tug McGraw, Bobby Jones, Rick MacLeish, Reggie Leach, Bill Bergey and Stan Walters. It's no coincidence that the period between 1974 and 1983 was the Golden Era of Philadelphia sports.

Now maybe, just maybe, the Eagles' 2004 deal for Terrell Owens will eventually prove worthy of this list. But, that aside, when's the last time one of our franchises pulled off such a masterstroke? It's been a long, dry spell, hasn't it, Angelo?

Bernie—the foundation behind two Stanley Cups.

46

Q: When did fans know more than management?

Glen says: Is this a trick question, Angelo? If there's one thing I've learned covering sports in this town for nearly 20 years, it's that the fans usually know more than they're given credit for. Management, meanwhile, almost always knows less.

You want me to limit this to one example? Okay, I'll start by giving you the date—April 22, 1995. That was, I believe, a day the Eagles could have clinched a future Super Bowl berth. Instead, they left their fans bewildered, disappointed and, ultimately, furious.

The Birds owned the 12th pick in the NFL draft. All logic said they should grab a pass-rusher, and the people's choice was University of Miami defensive tackle Warren Sapp. Problem was, it seemed unlikely Sapp would last that deep.

But things got strange. Right before the draft, rumors surfaced that Sapp had failed a marijuana test (true), as well as a cocaine test (false). His stock plummeted.

Eagles fans weren't put off. While not endorsing his pot smoking, few were shocked by a college kid having a little toke. Callers to our station were nearly unanimous: If Sapp was available, the Eagles would be insane to pass on him.

Then, on draft day, the Birds made a bold deal. They sent their first-rounder plus two second-rounders to Tampa in return for the Bucs' first pick—number seven overall. Sapp was on the board when the Eagles got their turn, and so they selected . . .

Mike Mamula!

Huh? That couldn't be right. Mamula over Sapp? That was like passing up Kobe beef for ground chuck.

Mamula was an average defensive end from Boston College. He had been projected as a 3rd-round pick until he pumped himself up before the scouting combine and wowed coaches with his ability to dance between orange cones. He certainly impressed Eagles coach Ray Rhodes, who called him "the next Charles Haley."

Eagles owner Jeff Lurie outright crowed over the pick. "We made an aggressive move," boasted Lurie, who comes from suburban Boston. "It's nice to have a New Englander, but the important thing is that it's Mamula."

Oh, shut up.

The stopwatch adored this guy. So did the weight bench. And the tape measure. One problem: He couldn't play.

That was apparent from the start. Mamula had one pass-rushing move—he'd try to beat the offensive tackle on a speed rush around the corner. But what worked against Rutgers didn't work against the New York Giants. So, time and again, he would try to angle his way to the quarterback, only to get there too late. The Eagles even invented a statistic for Mamula—"almosts"—suggest-

Mike Mamula celebrates a sack.
Probably not his own!

ing that his arrival in the backfield a half-second after the ball was thrown was quite an accomplishment.

Hey, the fans don't have a coach's pedigree, but we can recognize a bum when they see one. So Mamula became a target of booing, especially after he dropped his trousers before a female bouncer in Allentown.

Still, the club wouldn't acknowledge its mistake. We sort of understood why Rhodes was defensive about his pick. But when Andy Reid came in, he couldn't have been more complimentary if Mamula were Brigham Young. He even signed this bust to a $2.7-million-a-year contract extension, declaring, "Mike's going to be a big part of this defense's future."

Were the fans wrong? Not at all. Mamula hung around for six seasons (he was injured for one), totaling 31 sacks in a career that could generously be termed mediocre. There is no final tally on his "almosts."

And Sapp? In a great irony, the Bucs used that No. 12 pick they got from Philadelphia to pick the defensive tackle. He went on to play in seven Pro Bowls and win the NFL's Defensive MVP Award in 2000. Now with the Oakland Raiders, he had 77 sacks in his first nine seasons. And, of course, he was a big part of Tampa Bay's 2003 Super Bowl victory. You might recall, Ange, that they got there by beating the Eagles in the NFC Championship.

To be fair, not everyone wanted the Eagles to pick Sapp. My old radio partner, Jody McDonald, lobbied for a small-college pass rusher named Hugh Douglas. A few people liked Michigan cornerback Ty Law. Near as I can tell, they've done okay for themselves.

Mamula, meanwhile, is now four years out of the NFL. The fans were right from the start.

But hey, Angelo, as Jeff Lurie pointed out, he *was* a New Englander.

Angelo says: So there I sat one morning, squinting at the new rules handed down by the Eagles for their sparkling new stadium, Lincoln Financial Field. An emailer had transmitted them to me in tiny print, and I had no idea how to make the words bigger.

Were my eyes playing tricks on me or was this really possible? The Eagles were taking away the inalienable right for a football fan to bring his own sandwich to the game. In the hoagie capital of the world, no less!

Say it ain't so, Joe Banner.

When I showed the rules to my co-host, Al Morganti, he flipped. He said there was no way the fans would stand for this. Normally, the only thing that ever inspires Al to exclamations of outrage is a sudden dip in stock prices, so he had my attention.

In retrospect, the Eagles' ban of hoagies was the single worst decision I have ever seen a team exercise against its own fans. The explanation that the team was taking this action "for security reasons" was especially lame because, at that time in history, it came across as exploitation of the 9/11 tragedy.

You know the rest of the story, Glen. In 24 hours, the *Daily News* had turned the decision into a *cause celebre* like none the city has ever witnessed. My own personal favorite was the front-page photo of owner Jeff Lurie with a huge hoagie coming out of his ears.

For days in that spring of 2003, we took call after call on the air from outraged fans threatening to cancel their season tickets, picket the new stadium or even file a class-action lawsuit against the team for this infringement of their rights.

"It's one thing to give up Hugh Douglas," cried one caller. "Now we have to give up hoagies, too?"

I endorse your argument against Mike Mamula, Glen. A stiff with a great vertical reach is still a stiff. Toward the end, it was highly amusing to see his coaches defend one lousy game after another by pointing out the many "intangibles" he brought to the game. When a player gets praised for bringing intangibles, he's usually on the way out the door.

But I'm talking about *hoagies* here. From the moment the Eagles said their fans couldn't eat their own sandwiches, they were informed—in no uncertain terms—that you simply cannot do that in Philadelphia. The fans were right. The team was wrong.

Of course, before the Eagles conceded the mistake and ended Hoagiegate, they had to get some revenge against me and WIP. So they used their power in the NFL office and got me suspended. The sanction was for a diatribe against security that was inspired by the hoagie ban, and it earned me two days on the sidelines.

The fans didn't think that was right, either. Never in my life have I received so much support from anyone for anything. My backers cited the First Amendment —apparently the right to free speech is right up there with the right to bring your own hoagie to the game—and their support led to my being paid for the suspension.

I learned a lesson from Hoagiegate, Glen, just as you learned a lesson from the public reaction to drafting Mike Mamula. The fans of Philadelphia are right a lot more often than the teams would like to acknowledge. We talk to them every day. You wrote a terrific book about them.

There's this old saying that the coach who listens to the fans is soon sitting with them.

Well, if he is, at least now in Philadelphia he can eat a hoagie.

Q: Was Reggie White a big, fat phony?

Angelo says: I've done some amazingly stupid things during my decade and a half in radio, but one act of foolishness stands above all others. No, it wasn't booing Donovan McNabb at the NFL draft, nor waving a box of donuts at Derrick Coleman from the courtside seat of Sixers owner Brian Roberts, nor even trying to catch a ball dropped from a traffic helicopter on Opening Day.

Far and away the dumbest thing I've ever done in Philadelphia is sponsor a rally for Reggie White, the greatest defensive player in Eagles history—and the biggest ingrate I have ever encountered.

Reggie White didn't deserve a rally. He deserved a lynching.

The hardest part for fans is to separate the astonishing talent of White in his prime from the man of many contradictions off the field. I have no such problem with Reggie White because I knew him as well as any player I've ever covered.

The first time I ever met him was in 1985 at Oakland University, a nondescript campus in Rochester, Michigan. It was the summer training camp of the Detroit Lions, who had invited the Eagles to scrimmage against them. I was a second-year beat reporter covering the Eagles for *The Philadelphia Inquirer*.

Across the dining hall one evening sat a behemoth in a gray warm-up jacket with a fast-talking agent yammering in his ear. It was Reggie White and his alter-ego, Patrick Forte. Life would never be the same for anyone covering the Eagles that year.

A few weeks later, White defected from the dying United States Football League to the Eagles, where he spent half his time terrorizing opposing quarterbacks and the other half sermonizing on his fervent religious beliefs.

I'll never forget one time when I was interviewing him at his locker and he stopped in mid-sentence.

"When I mention Jesus, why don't you ever write what I say?" he asked. "Are you

183

afraid to write about Jesus?"

I told him I didn't think people wanted to hear about his religion. I said enough people treated football as a religion; they didn't need him adding Jesus to the equation. And I confessed that the whole thing made me uncomfortable.

When it came to Reggie White, that wasn't the only thing that made me uncomfortable. His agent, a totally outrageous negotiator, was very possibly the last man I would expect a devout man like White to hire. Patrick Forte was the most flamboyant and combative agent I ever met in eighteen years of covering sports. He was so diabolical in squeezing every penny out of that first contract that the Eagles hired him for their own front office. Norman Braman knew a penny-pincher when he met one.

Why would Reggie White employ such a money-grubbing wild man? I'll tell you why. Because Reggie White was most devout about one thing and only one thing—the almighty dollar.

Our rally attracted 7,000 fans to Center City at noon on a day months after the season had ended. Reggie was supposed to call and go on the loudspeaker—his schedule precluded a live appearance—but he must have had a higher calling that day. He blew us off.

Then he waited for word from God on whether he should consider the offers of San Francisco, Cleveland, the Eagles, or the most lucrative proposal from Green Bay. Sure enough, God spoke. He told Reggie to take the money. What a surprise.

Reggie White didn't just turn his back on the 7,000 fans at the rally that day, he bailed on millions of fans who loved him. White's high moral ground turned out to be nothing more than the mansion with the best view.

He may have been a blithering fool, but he sure could rush the passer.

The rest of the story doesn't matter to me. While Reggie got his Super Bowl ring in Green Bay, he supposedly also helped thousands with his acts of generosity. I doubt it.

The real Reggie was the hypocrite who slurred gays and minorities in an infamous speech that was far more revealing than he ever intended. The real Reggie was the player who hired the first agent who said "Show me the money." The real Reggie was the phony who used his religion to justify an act of unbridled greed in moving to Green Bay.

Sometimes, knowing an athlete as well as I knew Reggie White is the worst kind of burden to bear.

Glen says: I will not attempt here to defend Reggie White's homophobic views, which I find reprehensible. I'll only say that—misguided and ugly as they are—Reggie believes they are the scriptures of God.

So call him a fool. But he isn't a phony.

Bigotry isn't most people's argument with Reggie, anyway. Their primary beef, and yours too, Angelo, is that he took the money. Somehow that makes him a hypocrite. But exactly where does it say that religious zealots aren't supposed to be paid?

It's funny how time changes history. In Reggie White's case, he's only been gone from Philadelphia since 1993. How did we manage to forget the facts in that short a period?

Let me refresh your memory. Reggie joined the inaugural class of free agents after successfully suing the NFL to unshackle his brethren from the league's antediluvian contract rules. It was a horrible time for Eagles fans. The talent amassed by former coach Buddy Ryan was falling away, piece by piece, under cheapskate owner Norman Braman.

Still, Reggie made it clear he wanted more than anything to stay in Philadelphia. His agent, Jimmy Sexton, pleaded for the Eagles to make an offer before the free agency period began. Instead, Braman told Sexton to go test the market and get back to him. But when the contract proposals started rolling in, Braman just locked his safe, turned off his phone and went home.

(One thing we do agree on, Ange, is that White's prior agent, Patrick Forte, was a schemer. Forte, according to Reggie, has misled him about terms of his old contract, before taking a front-office job with the birds. That would seem a serious sell out.)

Regardless, in the spring of 1993, Reggie kept repeating that he wanted to stay with that Gang Green defense. He came on WIP one day and basically begged Braman to make an offer.

Braman's response: "You stay with veterans, and one day you wake up and they've all gotten old."

So, the "Reggie Over America Tour" took him to a half-dozen cities where owners didn't think he was too old to win. In truth, it became distasteful to watch wealthy barons fall over each other to lavish Reggie with gifts. But what was he supposed to do? Walk away from people handing his wife fur coats? Find me anyone who'll do that.

I covered Reggie's saga that spring for the *Philadelphia Inquirer*. I remember Sexton telling me from the start that, barring a move by the Eagles, Green Bay was the likely winner in the sweepstakes. This was curious because (A) The Packers hadn't even made an offer yet, and (B) They hadn't made the post-season in a decade. Why would Reggie move to a loser?

Turned out that he had met with Mike Holmgren, and came away convinced that the Packers' young coach was on the verge of building something. Guess he was right.

As far as that quote in which Reggie asked God what to do and was led to Wisconsin, well, remind me never to ask the Lord for directions. But seriously, I think, in his own way, Reggie was just seeking confirmation before making his decision. Hell, I know people who pray for lottery numbers to come up. Why should I begrudge anyone for looking for affirmation on a huge life decision?

It came across as greedy. And I'm not going to say that Reggie is any more or less gluttonous than anyone else. At the time, Sexton told me that one other franchise (he wouldn't say who, but my hunch was Atlanta) offered a nearly identical package.

Reggie was also chided because he said he wanted to use his money to make a difference in the community. And how many needy folks were living out there in Cheesehead Land? Well, let the record show that, by all accounts, he donated more than $1 million to charity, mostly to fund a home for unwed mothers.

Reggie wasn't a bad guy for taking the money, and he wasn't a phony for going to Green Bay. So clear your conscience, my friend. The "Rally for Reggie" was an inspired radio moment that united the fans against the scoundrel Braman.

Now *that* guy was the real phony. Do you care to debate me on that?

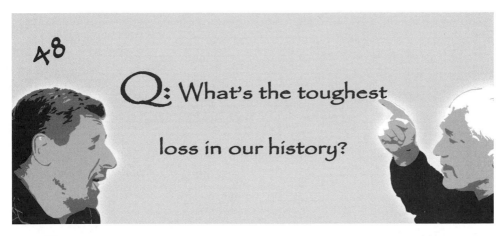

48

Q: What's the toughest loss in our history?

Glen says: The pain keeps piling up, Angelo. Year after year, our teams take turns ripping out our collective heart, doing a "Lord of the Dance" jig on it, and inviting us to come back next season.

How do I place one loss above all others?

The temptation is to go recent, one where the sting hasn't yet subsided.

But, really, this issue has to be looked at in historical terms. You eloquently wrote about the 1964 Phils' collapse earlier in this book. I'll let that go here, knowing there are middle-aged men who still wake from nightmares of Chico Ruiz stealing home.

Instead I'll nominate another shocker that was so discouraging it prompted this editorial:

"Losers. No other way to call it. Until a team wins it all, our city is represented by losers. The 76ers today. The Eagles last December. The Phillies last September. The Flyers on the horizon. More often than not, it appears that without losers Philadelphia would have no sports teams."

That sounds like many of your Monday morning shows, Ange. But it was written by *Daily News* columnist Thom Greer back in 1980, the day after the Sixers squandered an opportunity in the NBA Championship series.

You remember the setup? The 76ers and Los Angeles Lakers had split the first four games of the series before Lakers center Kareem Abdul-Jabbar sprained his ankle in the third quarter of Game 5. That was actually blown chance number one, because the Sixers somehow let Los Angeles escape that game with a win.

But Jabbar was out for Game 6 and likely the series. Without the league's Most Valuable Player, what chance did the Lakers have?

None, if you listened to the experts.

Writing in the *Daily News*, Rich Hofmann (is he really that old?) termed Lakers coach Paul Westhead's job of replacing Abdul-Jabbar, "mission impossible." When Westhead told reporters that he might let rookie point guard Magic Johnson jump center, his questioners broke into laughter at the apparent joke.

"It's a safe assumption that Billy Cunningham and Company aren't crying over that prospect," Hofmann wrote, suggesting the Lakers' coach was pulling everyone's leg and would actually play journeyman Jim Chones at center. "Nevertheless, any way Westhead lines 'em up, without Abdul-Jabbar, the odds for a Game 7 look pretty good."

This is not to pick on Hofmann, because his opinion was fairly representative. By the time fans arrived at the Spectrum that night, the biggest debate was whether the Sixers would win by 30 or just 20.

But damned if Westhead didn't confound the experts and start Magic at center.

And damned if the astounding 20-year-old rookie didn't destroy the Sixers.

Johnson led the Lakers to a 16-point victory with 42 points, 15 rebounds and 7 assists. The NBA title was won as Abdul-Jabbar cheered from his easy chair 3,000 miles away.

"The only thing Magic didn't do," mused Sixers coach Billy Cunningham, "was sell tickets and handle a camera. He could've interviewed himself."

In Los Angeles and elsewhere, the Magic moment will be remembered as one of the greatest performances in NBA history. In Philadelphia, it is recalled as a blown chance for a title. The 18,237 at the Spectrum that night kept waiting for the Sixers to come out of their malaise, but things just got worse. Other than Julius Erving, who put up 27 points, the team lumbered through the game in a fog.

Cunningham plotted a seemingly astute strategy of force-feeding the ball inside to Darryl Dawkins, but the big man responded with just eight points and four rebounds. The Sixers kept looking at each other as Magic destroyed them offensively and defensively. And, as the Lakers opened the third quarter with a 14-0 spurt, Sixers players literally began pointing fingers on the court.

"It was hard to believe how we lost it," Erving said afterward. "I think we played our poorest game of the season. Losing here today is tremendously disappointing. I'm sure it will have a lingering effect."

The effect on the Sixers was actually two more years of blown playoff opportunities before they went out and got center Moses Malone to replace Dawkins.

The effect on the fans? I'd rank this one as one of the foundation bricks in our monument to disappointment.

Angelo says: Time ultimately determines the true pain of one loss, so it's insane to choose as the worst defeat in history a contest as recent as 2003.

Well, I guess I'm insane. Because I still have not gotten over the Eagles' defeat to the Tampa Bay Buccaneers, 27-10, in the final game ever at Veterans Stadium.

Never in my experience has Philadelphia been more prepared for a celebration than on that day—January 19, 2003. Never did all of the stars line up perfectly. Never was there such a pure consensus that the wait for a Super Bowl was finally ending.

Do you remember all of the ingredients that led up to that day, Glen?

• Tampa had won only once in weather under 40 degrees. It was 37 degrees at game time.

• The Eagles had beaten the Bucs four straight times, including a playoff rout one season earlier.

• The Eagles were so good that year, they had gone 4-1 down the stretch primarily with their *third-string quarterback*. And now Donovan McNabb was back to complete a magical ride to the Super Bowl.

• Brad Johnson was brutal at QB all year for the Bucs. Mike Alstott had fumble-itis. No one on his own team was even talking to loudmouth Warren Sapp.

And then, just to build up our confidence a little more, Brian Mitchell took the opening kickoff and ran it back 70 yards. The din created by that runback and the ensuing touchdown by Duce Staley still echoes in my ears, Glen. No Philadelphia crowd has ever been louder or prouder than the fans were at that moment.

It was going to be the greatest sendoff a stadium ever had. The Vet would be a pile of rubble in a matter of months—some would say it was never much more than that anyway —but it would go out on top, home of the world

The fans faces in the front row tell the whole story.

champion Philadelphia Eagles.

The rest of the game is a blur. No matter how much I have replayed it, I still only see Joe Jurevicius running with the ball across the field and then down the far sideline. I keep telling myself that someone is going to catch him. Hell, he's not even their speed receiver. Someone is going to catch Joe Jurevicius any second now.

As far as I'm concerned, Jurevicius is still running. Supposedly, he was tackled 71 yards down the field, but I don't remember it. No one does. Moments later, the Bucs pulled ahead, 10-7. The crowd grew quiet. The funeral procession for another lost season began to assemble.

I don't have to tell you how much Philadelphia loves the Eagles, Glen. Nor do I have to remind you of the pure joy of anticipation leading up to that game. On my radio show, I was actually getting complaints by the end of the week that too many callers were singing. That's how happy the fans were.

And then, from that high, came a low so low that I'm not sure we'll ever recover. Part of me still doesn't believe the Eagles lost that game.

Your choice of the famous Magic Johnson game is an inspired one, Glen. That loss has stood the test of time, and it may have been the defining moment in the career of one of the greatest players ever.

The difference between your choice and mine is that a Hall of Fame player raised his game to new heights and carried his team to victory in your game. In mine, a nondescript wide receiver took a pass from a below-average quarterback and cut our throats. If you're going to lose, isn't it better to lose to Magic Johnson than Joe Jurevicius?

And that Bucs loss is the game that keeps on giving. Just when our pain was beginning to ebb, we got some more unwelcome news in the months that followed that Bucs debacle. Strong safety Blaine Bishop revealed that he was seriously injured before the fatal play but chose not to remove himself from the game in favor of the more talented and healthier Michael Lewis.

The reason no one could catch Joe Jurevicius is because, for most of those 71 yards, no one was chasing him. Moments later, Bishop left the game. He never played again.

On March 21, 2004 at precisely 7 a.m., Veterans Stadium became a massive cloud of concrete and steel during a spectacular implosion. I squinted into the haze that day, Glen, and I don't have to tell you what I saw.

There he was, Joe Jurevicius, still running for daylight—and taking our dreams with him.

49

Q: Should

Joe Paterno retire?

Angelo says: Two brushes with greatness involving football legend Joe Paterno . . . .

It's 1985, and I'm sitting in the office at Penn State when a secretary ushers me into the inner sanctum, the core of gridiron greatness. Joe Paterno extends his hand in friendship, remarks about my Italian heritage and proceeds to dazzle me with an hour of absolute brilliance. I have never been more in awe of a sports figure than I am that day.

Now it's 2003, and I'm the emcee of a special dinner at the Governor's Mansion in Harrisburg, Pennsylvania. Among the heroes being honored is Joe Paterno. During the cocktail hour, I refer to our prior meeting. He shakes his head. "I should remember somebody as ugly as you," he says. I'm not embarrassed for myself. I'm embarrassed for him.

What the hell has happened to this man?

It's very easy to write off my unkind appraisal of Paterno's recent work as retaliation for that inappropriate remark, Glen, but you know me better than that. People have insulted my Frankenstein look for decades. I actually encourage it on my show. It doesn't bother me at all.

What does bother me is the pathetic sight of a legend staying long after his talents have dwindled. No sadder memory exists for me than the final days of Willie Mays or Steve Carlton or Muhammad Ali. Nothing cheers me more than the perfectly timed retirements of Jim Brown and Rocky Marciano.

Joe Paterno should retire now, today, before he smudges a scrapbook of exquisite memories and leaves fans fumbling with two separate images—the bold, powerful leader who patrolled the sidelines in the 1960s, 70s, 80s and 90s, and the cranky, bitter old man trying to deny the inexorable passage of time since 2000.

I hesitate even to produce the numbers that reflect these two separate and distinct Joe Paternos, Glen, because it's too easy. To argue that this is not a different coach than the one who built his legacy is ludicrous. But I'll offer a couple of statistics that are really not even debatable:

• In the first four decades of his career, Paterno won two national titles, had five perfect seasons and compiled a record of 317-83.

• In the first four years after the millennium, his record was 22-26.

But this isn't about the numbers, Glen. With Paterno, it's never been about the numbers. He was always the coach you wanted your own son to play for, the education-first, old-school role model who understood how to build character while he was assembling a winner.

In the past few years, even the character issue is in question now. The rash of criminal charges against Paterno's players has become epidemic: Rashard Casey, Anwar Phillips, Maurice Humphrey, and Tommy McHugh are just four names that have appeared on both his roster and the police blotter since 2000. It was unfathomable that charges of assault, rape, and public drunkenness like these would have happened in Paterno's prime.

And the coach's demeanor has changed for the worse, too. His news conferences are not much more than a grumblefest now—replete with jibes at the media, whining about officiating and a feeble defense of his outdated coaching methods and his illogical strategy.

It's over, Glen—to everyone but the man himself, who agreed to a four-year contract extension in 2004 that will take him through his 81st birthday. What is he thinking? What is he trying to prove? Has he no respect for his own legacy?

The saddest part is that Paterno appears to be the last one to know that he has lost the magic that made him so extraordinary. During the 2003 season, at his usual grumpy mid-week news conference, one of the greatest coaches who ever lived made an observation that said more about himself than the targets of his criticism.

"There doesn't seem to be any glory in it when you guys write about the games anymore," he said,

He was surprised by their lack of enthusiasm, Glen.

His record at the time was 2-7.

Glen says: Well, one thing I've learned from Joe Paterno declaring you ugly, Angelo. At least we know his vision isn't failing behind those big, thick glasses.

But I worry about your vision, my friend. Because you obviously can't see the forest through the trees. The issue with Joe Pa is not a couple of losing seasons. The issue is letting the greatest coach in the history of this state—any sport, any level—go out on his terms.

He has earned that much. For this is a great man, even if he occasionally flashes grumpiness in his old age.

We could write chapters on Paterno's 339 wins at Penn State, his 55 years on the coaching staff, his 39 as head coach. We could marvel in the statistic that there have been 742 coaches in Division 1 college football since 1966, but just one for the Nittany Lions. We could debate the undefeated teams he put together in the '60s, '70s, '80s and '90s.

Is he deluding himself to believe he can build one more powerhouse in this decade? Probably, but we at least owe him the chance. In fact, all of us—most especially the Penn State community—owe Joe Paterno a lot. He, in turn, owes us nothing.

Here's the bottom line: In a business overrun by sleaze, Paterno has forever stood as a monument to integrity. It was more than 20 years ago that he was first asked if he considered retiring. "What, and leave this business to Barry Switzer and Jackie Sherrill?" he cracked.

Nothing has changed, unfortunately. In the past year alone, college sports has wallowed in the muck of coaches like Gary Barnett, Mike Price, Larry Eustachy, Rick Neuheisel, Dave Bliss, and Bob Huggins. Say what you want about Joe Pa's foibles, you know that the man who looks like your old uncle and wears pants in constant search of a flash flood will never sleaze it up by hitting on co-eds or hiring hookers for his recruits.

We can't wring our hands about the lack of honor in college athletics and then pull the plug on Joe Paterno when his program starts to decline a bit. You either believe in nobility and loyalty or you don't. You don't toss integrity overboard for one more chance to play in the Rose Bowl.

The cliché in college today is that the coaches are teachers. In most cases, that's a laugh. But when you get those rare exceptions—John Chaney, Joe Paterno—you have to hold on to the old men for their wisdom. Paterno doesn't just build football teams, he builds men. Ask anyone who's ever played for him.

I have a friend, a restaurant manager, who played offensive line for Paterno in the 1980s. Now in his forties, my friend still doesn't make a major decision without first calling "Coach." I have no reason to believe that Paterno's current batch of players don't feel the same way. You don't turn a resource like that out to pasture.

Penn State University is one of the largest, financially healthiest, most academically elite state universities in the nation. No one is more responsible for that than the football coach. It's a damn shame that many of the same alumni calling for the old man's head went to Happy Valley in the first place because of Paterno's team. And of the hundreds of million of dollars donated by alumni, Ange, how much can we chalk up to pride in the Blue-and-White?

I know that university President Graham Spanier says Paterno is the person who convinced him to set the school's recent fund-raising goal at $1 billion. When consultants argued that the goal was unrealistic, Paterno became honorary chairman of the campaign. It raised $1.4 billion.

You don't fire a man like that. Even after a 3-9 season.

Should Paterno stay on forever? No, the four-year extension gives him the proper amount of time to right the program, find a successor and begin the transition.

Then he can retire, sit in the stands with a bag of popcorn and look around at everything he built.

50

Q: Is Jeffrey Lurie a good owner?

Glen says: Likeable? No. Tuned into the Philadelphia psyche? Hardly. But if we define "good" by victories on the field, there's no way to argue that this effete Bostonian has been anything but a succcss in a town that despises him.

Since buying the Eagles in 1994 from Norman Braman (you wouldn't prefer him, would you, Angelo?), Lurie's franchise ran off six double-digit win seasons in 10 years. The Birds also won six playoff games—the most, I'm sad to say, they ever put together in one decade. They have been, and remain, one of the NFL's elite franchises, if we define elite as being in the running to win the Super Bowl.

Ah, but there's the rub. They have not won the title under Lurie—haven't even traveled to the Super Bowl. And so, if you choose to use that as the only measure of success, Lurie is on the bus to Failure City.

Of course, that's one crowded double-decker. Of this city's current owners, only Ed Snider ever captured a flag. And you already blistered him in an earlier chapter, Angelo. Who else never met that standard of excellence? Well, start with two of your idols, Leonard Tose and Pat Croce.

In the NFL, just eight of the 32 current owners can honestly wear Super Bowl rings. And two of them—Al Davis and Lamar Hunt—are so ancient that the diamonds may be turning back into carbon.

So let's look at Lurie's record on its own merits, starting with his decisions on coaches. He fired Rich Kotite (thank you), tried Ray Rhodes (brief success, then a crash), and struck gold—well, silver, anyway—with Andy Reid. Give Lurie credit for having the balls to avoid a retread and promote the untested Reid back in 1999. Andy may be tough to listen to, but even you'd concede that he's one of the brightest young coaches in the NFL.

Lurie is often accused of being cheap, but that's a bum rap. The Eagles have been successful at identifying their key players—Donovan McNabb, Brian Dawkins, Jon Runyan

—and locking them into big-money, long-term deals. Look, I've ripped Lurie, as you have, Ange, for letting popular veterans walk. But the bottom line is, the Eagles' personnel decisions usually end up being correct.

My biggest complaint about Lurie over the years (beyond that dead mackerel handshake), was his cautiousness. He seemed to believe that it's better to always keep a few chips off the table than ever go all in (You *do* play poker, don't you, Ange?). But as I write this, we await a season featuring free agents Jevon Kearse and Terrell Owens. And Lurie spent a lot of chips to land those two aces.

Lurie drew heat early in his tenure as a fantasy league wannabe, dabbling with our beloved franchise. True, perhaps. But he learned over the years to stay out of the way and retire to his luxury box with his wife, Christina. You may feel queasy every time their faces turn up on TV, but wouldn't you rather have him there than being one of those interfering Daniel Snyder types walking around with a coach's whistle?

He's placed the franchise in good hands. Reid knows how to coach, personnel director Tom Heckert knows how to find players, and president Joe Banner knows how to run the business. Now Banner may be one of the least amiable people ever to serve as the front man for a major organization, but can you really argue with his record?

And isn't that what this debate really boils down to? We may not like Lurie and Banner's personalities, Angelo. They can be petty and greedy and thin-skinned. Their attempt to ban hoagies from the new stadium showed how little they relate to Philadelphia fans. They don't like us and we don't like them.

But I don't need to like my favorite team's owner. I just have to trust that he's competent to field a good team.

And Jeff Lurie's earned that trust.

Angelo says: Shame on you, Glen Macnow.

If you had defiled my ancestors, you could not have uttered a more nauseating phrase than: "I just have to trust that he's competent to field a good team."

Is your definition of success in sports "fielding a good team?" Is that really all it takes to win your support? Is it possible that your Buffalo upbringing has conditioned you to settle for second place?

Jeff Lurie is not a good owner in Philadelphia because he was supposed to be a *great* owner. This is the Boston guy who professed his love for the passion of Philadelphia sports fans. When he first bought the team from Norman Braman, he was the anti-Braman—friendly, accessible, driven to succeed in the standings, not on the ledger sheet.

I'll never forget doing a radio show with Lurie at Suburban Station, in a dingy corridor right near the trains. It was the first year of his ownership, and he shook hands, kissed babies and pledged an era of kinship with his "compadres," the fans of Philadelphia.

By the third year, he was no longer accessible. By the fifth year, he was seen only in his luxury box during games at Veterans Stadium. By the seventh year, all indications were that Lurie had entered the Federal Witness Protection Program.

And that's just the beginning of my disappointment with Jeff Lurie, Glen.

It's more than a little ironic that I cannot even accurately rate the full scope of his ownership because I have absolutely no idea what, if anything, he actually does. No one knows.

Is he involved in player transactions? Is he consulted when the Eagles are pondering a contract offer to a top free agent? Did he oversee construction of the new stadium? Where does he go? What does he do?

We all know that Joe Banner is the money guy, and I respect Banner more than you think, Glen. He is a skilled capologist, and he knows how to run a business. We also know that Andy Reid is in charge of the players, on and off the field. Reid is very good, I agree. We even know that Lurie's wife Christina was active in designing parts of the new stadium and handles lots of the team's charitable work.

But what the hell does Jeff Lurie do all day? Can you answer that question?

In the past few years, the only evidence of Lurie's involvement that I can confirm involved my suspension at WIP in 2003 over the hoagie ban. At one point in my on-air diatribe, I compared the Eagles security force with the Gestapo—admittedly a stupid remark but hardly a suspendable offense.

At the height of the controversy, I was handed a letter from my former boss, Cecil R. Forster, that had been sent by Lurie to NFL commissioner Paul Tagliabue and then on to the top management in our corporation demanding that I be punished for the insensitivity of my comments.

On the very day that my suspension was announced, Lurie appeared in public and said he had no involvement whatsoever in the action of our bosses. If I wasn't so angry, I might have actually laughed. Eventually, the hoagie ban was lifted and I was paid for the two days I was suspended.

Now, I *can* laugh about the whole thing. I can laugh because I have seen the real Jeff Lurie. I can understand why he hides himself behind Banner and Reid and even his own wife. He hides behind them because the alternative is to show the fans the real Jeff Lurie, an owner who is out of touch with the fans and probably with the game of football, too.

Maybe now you can understand why I'm physically ill over your comment about "fielding a good team." The last Eagles championship was in 1960, Glen. The last appearance in the Super Bowl was in 1981.

"Fielding a good team" is not good enough for me, or for the fans of the most passionate football city in America.

Shame on you, Glen Macnow.

Q: Who was better—Chamberlain or Russell?

Angelo says: I was 10 years old the first time I fell in love. My older cousin had gotten us tickets to a game between the Boston Celtics and Philadelphia 76ers at the old Auditorium, a decrepit building in our hometown of Providence, Rhode Island

On the basketball court was a vision so spellbinding, so awe-inspiring, that I instantly became a fan for life. No player, before or since, has ever captivated me like the greatest athlete in American history, Wilt Chamberlain.

That night during pre-game warmups, Wilt stood about 14 feet from the basket, three steps off the baseline, and shot ball after ball off the glass and into the net. I counted 50 straight when I finally looked away for the first time. Wilt never participated in layup drills that night, or anything else his teammates were doing. He just stood there, methodically peppering the backboard with one perfect shot after another.

He didn't seem human, Glen. That's the thing about Wilt that always impressed me the most. He was not like anyone else. At 7-foot-1, he was a behemoth in those days, so much taller and stronger than anyone else. He was Shaq two generations before Shaq. Only bigger.

The other thing about Wilt that made him so compelling was his quirky nature. He holds practically every scoring record in NBA history—Michael who?—but most of those single-season marks were established early in his career, before he got bored with scoring.

Just for his own amusement, in 1968-69, Wilt led the league in assists—the only center ever to accomplish that feat. Toward the end of his career, Wilt became more of a defensive specialist. Still, every once in a while, he'd score 50 in one night, for no better reason than to prove he could.

Even writing about him right now is sending a surge of adrenalin through my veins. He was the greatest abstract artist in the history of sports—a virtuoso who could see no reason to do the same painting over and over again.

The idea that I have to soil this poignant appreciation of Wilt with the inclusion of his rival, Bill Russell, repels me. Please don't burden our readers with more tales of Russell's many championships, Glen. No one cares. On an individual basis, Wilt was superior to Russell in every way. Wilt was superior to *everyone* in every way.

I hesitate even to roll out the numbers, they are so one-sided:

• Wilt had 29 points and 29 rebounds a game in head-to-head competition with Russell. The Celtics center had 15 points and 24 rebounds.

• Wilt once had 55 rebounds in a single game. The opposing center was Bill Russell.

• Wilt averaged 30 points a game in his career. Russell 15.

• Wilt out-rebounded Russell, 30-to-23, in career stats. Wasn't Russell supposed to be the better rebounder?

• Wilt scored 100 points in a single game. Russell never came close.

Yes, Russell won 11 championships. Wilt had only two. Russell also had teammates like Sam and K.C. Jones, Tom Heinsohn, Bob Cousy, Satch Sanders, and on and on. With a few exceptions, Wilt was asked to go it alone. Hey, he was supernatural, but no one player can beat five—not even Wilt, though he came close many times.

In his years after basketball, Wilt became a successful author, an accomplished actor, a great volleyball player, a fundraiser for charitable causes, and a Renaissance man. Russell was a coach and a broadcaster for a while, but no one could ever understand what he was saying. It's a shame Wilt didn't leave him speechless, too.

This debate is so ridiculous, I'm calling a halt to it right now, Glen. Let's just declare it a TKO in the first round for Wilt. It might have been a better fight if Russell could have brought his four teammates into the ring.

Oh, yeah. One last thought about the night I fell in love a long, long time ago back home in Providence. Since the Celtics were the opponent, it figures that Bill Russell was there, too.

I'm not sure, Glen. I don't remember.

With Wilt around, it didn't really matter.

Glen says: I fell in love around the same age, Angelo. Unfortunately, Farrah Fawcett didn't reciprocate, except in my dreams.

Regardless, it's nice of you to try to dismiss my case before I even get to make it. So let me say this: That game at which you broke your cherry back in 1962? Russell's Celtics won that night. You could look it up. (Actually, I did).

Because Russell always won. And isn't that how we measure success in sports, really?

Isn't that how we determine who's better? Wilt may have been Superman, but Russell was Kryptonite.

You threw more stats into your argument than the last guy who tried to sell me life insurance. So I'll address some of those numbers. That night Wilt had 55 rebounds? Celtics won the game. The year Wilt averaged 50 points a contest? Celtics won eight of 12 games between the two teams. In fact, it was Russell, not Wilt, who was the NBA's MVP that season. And it was the Celtics who were league champions.

Russell won five MVP awards to Chamberlain's four. And, when the NBA named its all-time greatest player during its 35-year anniversary in 1980, guess who got the nod. Here's a clue: He wore No. 6 and looked good in green.

This is not to besmirch Wilt, whose talent I admire as much as you do (well, maybe not *quite* as much). And, as a lifetime Celtics hater, I always rooted for the Dipper in those matchups. So it pains me to face the reality—Wilt may have put up the glossier stats, but Russell always smoked the victory cigar. Or at least delivered it to Red Auerbach. It was a lot like the epic Ali-Frazier fights (the other great rivalry where you took the wrong side in this book). Frazier was the better puncher; Ali won most of the fights.

Wilt and Russell met head-to-head in the playoffs eight times. Russell's Celtics won seven of those series—including all four that went to seven games. Now, Angelo, you cleverly try to lay this off on Wilt having no capable teammates over the years. Let's see . . . Paul Arizin, Guy Rodgers, Al Attles, Larry Costello, Hal Greer, Chet Walker, Billy Cunningham . . . hmm, that's not exactly a JCC Bitty Ball League squad, now is it?

The problem was that, great as he was, Wilt was about Wilt. Winning didn't interest him as much as experimenting, running up numbers or, as you so appropriately put it, Angelo, trying something "just for his own amusement." I'll give you this, Ange. No one was more fun to watch than Wilt. He may have been the greatest single athlete of the 20th century.

He just wasn't the best basketball player.

Russell redefined the game. Before he joined the Celtics, NBA teams focused entirely on offense. Russell brought in defensive skills that no one had ever seen. Certainly he led the league in blocked shots every year, but that stat wasn't kept back in those days. He stifled opposing centers (yes, even Wilt), and, by playing a one-man zone, he clogged up driving lanes and prevented easy lay-ins by the guards. His astonishing rebounding and precise outlet passes then ignited Boston's fastbreak offense.

As the hated Auerbach said, "Bill put the honor in defense. He didn't bend rims. He bent minds."

And, we all know, defense wins championships. Russell initiated a mentality that remains a focal part of championship basketball at every level. Much as you may find it irrelevant, Ange, the Celtics won 11 titles during Russell's 13 seasons. Wilt's teams won just two—one of them after Russell had retired.

Russell wasn't about the numbers. Well, just one, actually. After Chamberlain signed a contract with the San Francisco Warriors in 1965 for $100,000, Russell insisted that his deal be renegotiated to $100,001.

Ange, I do not seek to besmirch the great Chamberlain here. We just need to set the record straight. The rivalry between these two great centers defined basketball in the 1960s. And the difference between the two is easy to see.

Chamberlain won the scoring titles.

Russell simply won.

"No you don't!"   "Yes I will!"

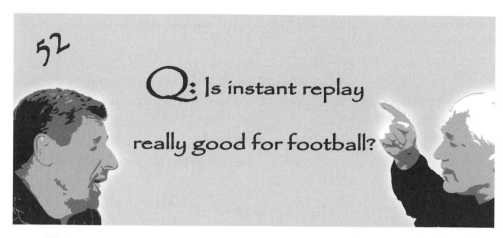

Q: Is instant replay really good for football?

Glen says: I don't need to go to the tape for this one, Angelo. The answer is clear the first time. Instant replay doesn't work, and it's time for the NFL to stop pretending it does.

I can give you more reasons than the networks have camera angles. But let's start with this one: It does virtually nothing to eliminate mistakes. If the referees are nincompoops (and I know you think they are), and the same nincompoops are studying the video replays, exactly what have we gained? Delayed incompetence?

The promise of replay was that it would end human error by using videotape to ensure that officials get the critical calls right. But what about human error involved with actually reviewing the tape? We've all seen the refs call it one way on the field, then study the film, then proceed to botch things by reversing a correct call. Fumbles are nullified, first-down yardage given or taken away, games won or lost based on the so-called "indisputable visual evidence" that's not only disputable—it's non-existent.

As John Madden said: "They stick a blanket over the guy's head and stuff his head in a hole. I don't think that works. Try it yourself. Just stuff your head in a hole and look at a television monitor, and I don't think you can see."

The camera never lies, right? Of course it does. Go stand next to a crack in the sidewalk, Angelo. Now lift your heel and shift it over the crack without actually touching it. Although you're not "out of bounds," a camera would certainly show you that way. Of course, by this time, my friend, you've probably tumbled over.

Once you recover your balance, consider this: Instant replay is doubly frustrating because it isn't used on the most-controversial calls in the NFL—holding and pass interference. Those are considered "judgment calls," as opposed to, I guess, others requiring no judgment by the refs.

And all the VCRs in the world can't reverse the dreaded quick whistle, in which a play is prematurely blown dead—usually, it seems, right before an Eagles' opponent fumbles. Not reviewable, the league says.

What is reviewable? Well, last year I saw a dozen times when officials went under the hood to debate spotting the ball. Let me fill you in on something, Ange. Every time the ball is spotted it's a rough calculation. It's not a science. Is the sport really made better by 15-minute, game-stopping discussions on where Donovan McNabb's pinkie toe touched the boundary? Just take your best stab and let's move on.

But that would mean a quicker game. And, God forbid, the last thing we want is an NFL contest to come in under three hours.

When the league reinstated replay in 1999, Paul Tagliabue promised, "There will be a noticeable positive difference in the time of the overall replay operations because there is no non-linear tape to rewind."

Translated into English, what the commissioner actually said was, "Ha, ha. The joke's on you."

Remember that 90-second time limit the league promised? Please. I've come up with a routine for each time out. I run to the bathroom, sneak to the kitchen to grab a beer and a snack, check my email, make a few calls and pay my monthly bills. Sometimes there's time left for a quick nap.

In a game in 2003, the Redskins and Giants had a 10-minute replay delay. Three days later, the NFL sent the Redskins an apology because, despite the momentum-ending holdup, the refs still blew the call.

And that, of course, became the story. My biggest gripe with replay is that it has negatively altered how we watch the sport. It's no longer about the game; it's about the refs. Fans sit in their Barcoloungers, dropping their Cheez Doodles to scream, "Andy's got to challenge that call!" Then they call us on Monday to gripe about the officiating, rather than focusing on the guys who actually play the game.

It's almost irrelevant to me whether instant replay corrects a few bad calls during the season. It's more important that it stalls my football and turns us into a fan base thinking every replay is the Zapruder film.

Guess what, Angelo. Sometimes they make bad calls. Get over it.

Angelo says: It's 2005 and the Eagles are down two points, driving in the final seconds of their fourth consecutive NFC championship game. Donovan McNabb throws the ball toward the sideline at the opponent's 25-yard line. Terrell Owens dives for it and then rolls out of bounds. Did he catch it?

If Owens makes the play, the Birds are a 42-yard field goal by David Akers away from the Super Bowl. If Owens drops it or even juggles it, the season is pretty much over.

Now what you're telling me, Glen, is that you'd rather put the season in the hands of one official standing next to the sideline making a split-second decision rather than giving a referee the chance to study the play from several angles before making the call.

Get over it, you tell me? If the official got that call wrong, none of us would ever get over it. A play like that would stay with us forever.

The strange thing about instant replay is that nothing has changed in a generation. I know. I was there at the 1986 NFL owners' meeting in Hawaii when the first instant-replay rule was approved. The same arguments, pro and con, have been rattling around ever since the rule passed that first year by the narrowest of margins.

But here's the part of the story no one ever tells: The owners of individual teams change their votes every year based on whether they were helped or hurt by the rule in the previous season. They swing back and forth, applauding only the advantage that such a rule sometimes brings. The good of the game never matters to them. It's pathetic.

You want to know why the rule isn't more all-encompassing—why it doesn't include pass interference and holding, Glen? Because they've had to cut the guts out of it every winter just to get the required twenty-one votes. Most of the time, the league office lobbies just enough teams to get a stripped-down version passed. The NFL wants instant replay because the fans want it. The last poll had seven of ten fans favoring it, warts and all.

Where your logic breaks down is in thinking an OK rule should be dumped because it isn't great. How many of the NFL rules are great? Do you like the tuck rule? Isn't holding the most arbitrary penalty in all of sports? What about grounding the ball, or roughing the passer, or taunting?

The fact is, the NFL has a much bigger problem than the weakness of its instant replay rule. What about the ineptitude of the officials themselves? I've been screaming on the radio for years that the biggest disgrace in sports is the officiating in the NFL. And you're right. Almost every week, one of the games is decided by a blatantly wrong call by an official, followed by a league-sanctioned apology. But that's not the fault of the rule, Glen. It's a problem with the people enforcing it.

The refs stink. Can I say it any more plainly? They are generally old, slow, indecisive, prone to impromptu meetings that result in bad decisions, and protected from the teams and the public by a league that's always on the defensive. It's a hard game to officiate, yes. And these guys make it seem even harder than it is.

Your other arguments hold no weight either, Glen. The father of the instant-replay rule, the late Tex Schramm of Dallas, would laugh whenever people told him that instant replay was ruining the flow of the game, as you claim.

"People are only worried about the flow of the game," he would say with that knowing drawl, "when they're losing."

There were years when (I'm pleased to report) the Cowboys were burned by their own rule, but Schramm never wavered in his belief that football was a better game when it went out of its way to get its key calls right.

As for the long delays, give me a break, please. What the heck are you doing that's so important you can't wait another minute or two? Go check your email again, or have another Cheez Doodle. I wait a week between games. I'd like to think the call they ultimately make will be right.

Of all the things you write in your essay, Glen, I am most offended by one sentence: *It's almost irrelevant to me whether instant replay corrects a few bad calls during the season.*

Do you really believe that?

OK, let's find out.

The Eagles season is on the line. Owens is near the sideline. The Super Bowl is beckoning. Millions of fans are not breathing in Philadelphia, waiting for the call.

How irrelevant is it now, Glen?

Q: Is WIP bad for
our teams?

Angelo says: When WIP became one of the first all-sports radio stations in 1988, some decisions were made that endure to this day. These decisions became the blueprint for the most popular sports station in America.

Management established right from the beginning that honest and sincere opinion would be the lifeblood of WIP. I can remember the early days when we were doing a show called *The Morning Sports Page*, Glen, and even the ads back then said we would "rattle some windows."

The premise was to take all of the great sports debates unfolding in barrooms all around Philadelphia, remove the alcohol and obscenities, and then put them right on the air. There was only one master to serve back then—the listener.

Much has changed in the years since then, but the foundation for the station remains sturdy. I know I haven't changed my approach toward sports commentary, even if I have added a few bells and whistles along the way. I still say what I think, and damn the consequences.

So the obvious question is: Have there been consequences? Has the freeform expression—much of it negative—on WIP had an adverse effect on the fortunes of Philadelphia's pro teams.

I believe it has. I believe WIP is one of many reasons for the 21-year drought (and counting) since the city's last championship. I believe the incessant second-guessing about strategy, the constant rumor-mongering over trades, the shrill tirades, and the drip, drip, drip, of dissent have all taken a toll.

Hey, I'm just doing my job. So are you, Glen. When the teams succeed, we bask in their glow. But it's not our responsibility to help them prosper.

Let me offer a few examples of how WIP has altered the fate of teams. I know for an absolute fact that our pounding drumbeat against Randy Ayers led to his firing after only

52 games with the Sixers in 2003-04. I can recall stating my case to GM Billy King right on our show. He could not ignore our cries, or—more importantly—the cries of his constituency.

Terry Francona lost his job as manager of the Phillies under similar circumstances. John Welbourn was traded three days after venting his spleen on WIP. Harold Katz and Norman Braman sold the Sixers and Eagles, respectively, and then said the relentless criticism on WIP was a factor in their decisions.

All of the above cases—and many more—are obvious examples of WIP's influence, but they weren't necessarily detrimental to the fortunes of the teams. The departure of that parade of incompetents and prima donnas was no great loss to Philadelphia or to our radio station.

But what about the departure of Buddy Ryan? It was no secret that Braman heard the angry voice of Ryan haters on WIP, and reacted. He was so determined to suppress Ryan's large army of supporters—also represented in force on our station—that he set an impossible deadline of one day to find a successor. That successor was named Rich Kotite.

Would Braman have rushed so much if WIP wasn't battering him and his franchise? I don't think so. Would Braman have realized that Ryan was poised to win a championship with that team, or that Jeff Fisher was a far superior choice to Kotite? Without question.

And then there's the case of the best third baseman of this generation, Scott Rolen. How did Rolen develop a distaste for Philadelphia? There are many reasons, but WIP must take part of the responsibility there, too. Rolen absolutely loathed the negative nature of the Philadelphia fan. Gee, I wonder where he got the impression that we tend to be negative. Maybe a certain radio station?

Need I remind you of the Eric Lindros soap opera, Glen? The Flyers sold WIP to raise the money for Lindros, then they sued the station over a report about Lindros, then they used the station to crucify the sensitive pseudo-superstar. In a more subdued setting, would Lindros have had a better chance to reach his potential? I vote yes.

I take no pride in any of this, but I offer no apologies, either. WIP is a fantastic radio station because it reflects the fans better than any other sports station in the country. We *are* the fans. We create an atmosphere that is uncomfortable for players and coaches. We don't suffer fools well.

Philadelphia has won no championships since the advent of WIP, Glen.

There are lots of reasons for this, but we are paid to tell the truth.

So here's the truth: We're one of the reasons.

Glen says: I'm sorry, I didn't know that I signed up to co-author a book with Jim

Fregosi. Who else would argue that the lack of a title in our town is not because of bad playing, stupid coaching or misguided talent evaluation—but rather the daily second-guessing offered by a half-dozen jackasses?

Clear your conscience, Angelo. We at WIP have nothing to do with the failures of our franchises—who totaled a collective 84 seasons without a parade after the Flyers' 2004 loss in the NHL Eastern Conference Finals. As Shakespeare's illegitimate son might have said about all this: "It is not in ourselves to hold our destiny, but in our stars." Or something like that. In other words, it is the actions of those millionaire on-field performers that determine success and failure; it is not the post-game commentary. The Old Bard was quite a hoops fan, by the way.

As evidence of WIP's deleterious effect, Angelo, you offer up the pressure to fire Sixers coach Randy Ayers and Phillies manager Terry Francona. Now, as we argued in an earlier debate, I don't think our input really had anything to do with these decisions, but let's say —for sake of argument—that it did. Is your position here that the Phils and 76ers would have *won* titles had these two boneheads stayed in charge? Forget the 21-year drought. If Francona kept commanding the Phillies, we'd all be older than the Queen of England by the time they sniffed the post-season.

Let's see now. We're also responsible, in your eyes, for the breakdown between Lindros and the Flyers, as well as the firing of Buddy Ryan. Hey, while you're at it, why not just blame WIP for the bad traffic after Eagles games and my skyrocketing cable bill?

Actually, I'll concede one point here. I do think that Dallas Green's appearance on our station to marinate Scott Rolen contributed to Sullen Scotty leaving town. But when you play that out, the Phils signed Jim Thome with the pile of money they had pledged to Rolen. So how did that hurt the success of our local nine? If WIP had any impact there, it ended up being positive.

There's been a lot of hand-wringing over the years as to why our teams never get to sip champagne. And there have been a lot of theories: Our fans are too tough. Our fans are too accepting. We built a skyscraper taller than City Hall. Rollie Massimino cursed us. We stuck a Flyers jersey on the Billy Penn statue.

Each of those smacked-ass suppositions is without foundation. And now, you add a new one: Let's blame the messenger. I'm supposed to believe that an army of highly skilled, tough-guy professionals wilt under the pressure of the bleating criticism that comes from our microphones.

If I follow your argument, I infer that by demanding excellence, we are creating medi-ocrity. Because we don't accept inept management or Bobby Abreu's loafing, that's exactly what we end up with.

Not buying it, Ange.

Let me break this down:

a) There are shortcomings with our teams and players.

b) They never, ever win it all.

c) We at WIP bemoan this and offer tremendously incisive opinions (well, at least during most day parts).

Now, I didn't exactly score at the top of the SAT bell curve. But it sure seems to me that B leads to C a hell of a lot more than C leads to B.

People root for sports teams because they enjoy feeling part of the collective. And when that team wins, every fan basks in the reflected glory. We believe that we're part of the effort.

Now, I've come to notice, when the teams never win, we wallow in the reflected misery. We start to blame ourselves. It's like the children of divorce feeling culpable for the breakup of their parents.

Trust me, when one of our teams finally holds a parade, Ange, they won't invite you to sit on the lead float.

And when they lose, it's not your fault. Or the fans'. Or WIP's.

Q: Is Scott Rolen better than Mike Schmidt?

Glen says: Let's be honest, Angelo. We were inspired to this debate by *Daily News* columnist Bill Conlin. When "Bill One Chair" first raised this treasonous argument, I thought he had overdosed on cabernet. But the more I studied it, the more I had to agree —the insipid Rolen is on pace to run off a better career than the greatest Phillie of all time.

It's always dangerous to compare someone who's retired with someone now in his prime. Because you can't really forecast which way a guy's career will go. Hell, I remember people projecting Richie Allen to break every home run record because of what he did before age 25. On the flip side, when the Phils traded Julio Franco back in 1982, do you think anyone expected him to still be playing 22 years later?

So any Rolen vs. Schmidt debate must be approached with the caveat that everything could become moot if Rolen broke his leg tomorrow.

Not that I'm necessarily rooting for that.

Anyway, here's the bad news, Ange: After seven full seasons in the bigs, Scott Rolen is on pace to at least challenge Mike Schmidt as the title holder of all-time, No. 1 third baseman in history. Sad, but true.

Look at the numbers. Heading into 2004, Rolen had a higher career batting average than Schmidt (.282 to .256) and also led in hits (1097 to 947) and doubles (264 to 181). Schmidt led in runs (776 to 668), RBIs (784 to 707) and, of course, home runs (282 to 192).

The key offensive numbers are basically a push. Schmidt had a slight lead in both on-base percentage (.380 to .374) and slugging percentage (.527 to .511).

Schmidt's big plus is power. There's little chance Rolen will surpass his 548 career home runs. But if Rolen keeps up his pace of 30 a year and plays, as Schmidt did, to age 38, he'll wind up with a total of 492. Not too shabby.

(Schmidt actually retired at age 39 after a frustrating 42-game season. Remember the

Memorial Day news conference in 1989 where he blubbered into the mike? I'll bet you ten bucks, Ange, that the stone-faced Rolen doesn't depart with that kind of passion.)

The area where Rolen has the biggest edge—and the toughest area to quantify—is defense. Conlin, whose baseball opinion I respect, argues that, "Rolen is the best third baseman I have covered, including Schmidt." He describes Rolen as "a 6-foot-5, 230-pound man with the quickness of a jungle cat, great range in all directions and a cannon arm."

Larry Bowa, whose baseball opinion I respect even more, agrees. "Mike was unbelievable," the man who played next to Schmidt for nine seasons told me last spring. "But Scotty's even better. He routinely steals a base hit or two every game."

Rolen won five Gold Gloves in his first seven seasons, Schmidt won four. Not much difference there. On pure fielding stats, Rolen's got a bigger edge—103 errors and a .965 fielding percentage to Schmidt's 150 errors and .961 fielding percentage.

What we don't know, again, is which direction Rolen's career will go. Schmidt won three MVP awards in his thirties; Rolen hasn't yet reached that age. But as I write this in August 2004, Rolen, at 29, is putting together an award-winning season for the St. Louis Cardinals.

What we do know is that the Phils—under pressure—gave away Rolen for a journeyman infielder (Placido Polanco), a throwaway reliever (Mike Timlin), and a sore-armed lefty (Bud Smith). Rearrange the letters in Smith's name and you get "Dumb S—t," which is exactly what Phils general manager Ed Wade was when he made this deal.

The money that would have gone to Rolen went to sign free agent slugger Jim Thome. I've got no gripe with that. But long after Thome has retired to hunt the woods of Ohio, Rolen will still be flashing leather and numbers along the Mississippi.

Like you, Ange, I despised the whiney jerk. But the truth is, he's a superstar with a chance to supplant Schmittie as the best ever.

Yep, the truth hurts. But that doesn't make it any less truthful.

Angelo says: On the day of his retirement, Scott Rolen will not step up to the microphones and "blubber" the way Mike Schmidt did. That's true, Glen. And that's exactly why Scott Rolen will never be as good as Mike Schmidt.

Scott Rolen would never think to provide a glimpse of himself to the fans who have given so much to him. Do you remember when he granted a rare interview to a Philadelphia reporter in the late 1990s, only to announce to fans that if they want to know anything personal about him, "Sorry about your luck."

I didn't like Rolen before he made that remark, and I have loathed him ever since. I don't buy into this "laid-back Midwestern boy" personality that he has hidden behind his whole career. He is a professional entertainer. He is required by the nature of that job to give something of himself, whether he likes it or not.

No one with a job likes every aspect of that profession, Glen. I love doing my radio show, but I hate the politics of the medium. I love talking sports, but I can't stomach some of the people I have to talk about. When you accept a career, you agree to fulfill all requirements of the job, not just the ones you prefer.

Scott Rolen is one of the most overrated players I've ever seen on the field, and one of the biggest ingrates off it. At a time when baseball is crying out for its stars to give something back to the fans, Rolen offers nothing. Sorry about your luck.

Let's start with his on-field contribution. Yes, his numbers are good and getting better. He is an extraordinary third baseman—probably at least the equal, defensively, of Schmidt. What I cannot recall is that he used these great numbers to win anything. I can't recall a single game in his seven-year tenure with the Phillies when he actually won a game with a clutch homer or even a big two-out hit. Can you?

The Phillies were underachievers when Rolen played here, and now the St. Louis Cardinals are underachievers, too. If you subscribe to the theory—as I do—that great players make those around them better, well, Rolen is coming up short. Scott Rolen, this fabulous player, appeared in exactly two playoff games in the first nine seasons of his career. Maybe he's afraid that the big stage will invade his privacy.

Meanwhile, Mike Schmidt won game after game, season after season, with huge hits. He won a championship in Philadelphia. He led his team—and unlike Rolen, he was truly a leader—to five division titles, two National League pennants and that precious World Series triumph in 1980. In his first nine seasons, Schmidt had already accumulated four division crowns, one pennant and the world championship.

Admittedly, Schmidt had his own personal shortcomings, but they were always more palatable to me than Rolen's. At least, as his career progressed, Schmidt began to understand his responsibility to the game. He even wore a wig one night after making some unpopular remarks about playing in Philadelphia. Hell, I was impressed that he cared enough to make those comments, even if they were negative. At least he was willing to speak his mind. That's more than Rolen would ever do.

And in the end, yes, Mike Schmidt blubbered. I loved him for it, Glen, and so did the fans. He opened himself up to Philadelphia and the baseball world on the day of his retirement. He told the fans how great it was that he got to realize his dream. He gave something back. He shared his sadness and his pride at the end of a Hall of Fame career.

The next time you and Bill Conlin are getting together, here are a few other comparisons between Schmidt and Rolen that you might like to consider:

• Mike Schmidt played his whole career in Philadelphia. Scott Rolen forced a trade to St. Louis.

• Mike Schmidt played in an era with huge cookie-cutter stadiums. Scott Rolen has profited by the bandbox fad.

• Mike Schmidt faced a great pitcher practically every night. Scott Rolen faces a great pitcher maybe once a week.

And if none of those arguments are compelling to you, Glen, I have only one other observation to make, courtesy of Scott Rolen himself.

Sorry about your luck.

55

Q: Will baseball ever be number one again in Philadelphia?

Angelo says: I've got a confession to make, Glen. I have no friends. Not a one. I have a fantastic wife and terrific kids and stepkids, but no friends. I find friends to be more trouble than they're worth. Friends are a lot like fish. After a few days, they start to smell.

For the past 30 years of my life, my best friend has been baseball. It's there every day from April through October, and it comes to visit every few days in the off-season through player trades and free-agent signings.

I talk mostly about football on the air, but I *think* mostly about baseball off the air. That's why I have to chuckle when people say that Philadelphia is a football town, and will always be a football town.

Yeah, sure. Right up until the time when the Eagles are 3-13 again. Then we'll see what kind of football town Philadelphia is. It's just human nature. We want to associate ourselves with a winner, with success. If our team is awful, we distance ourselves.

There's nothing about football that is sacred in Philadelphia. Not so many years ago —for example, in 1994 during that seven-game losing streak under Rich Kotite—I can remember entire sections at the Vet sitting empty because no one cared enough to go to one of a mere eight home football games late in the season.

It was equally amusing a few months earlier when many doomsayers predicted the permanent death of baseball in Philadelphia. The player strike in 1994 did indeed drain most of the enthusiasm and a lot of the interest out of the city for this old and beautiful game. I applaud Philadelphia for reacting so angrily to that insane act of self-destruction by the players and owners.

But gone forever? Dying a slow and painful death? Puhleeze.

Now we have an astonishing new ballpark in our city, Glen, and a good baseball team. Soon, if the Phillies dispose of an inept manager named Larry Bowa, they might be a great baseball team.

Exactly how dead is baseball when more fans bought tickets before the 2004 season than *attended* games in 2003? That's right, the Phillies sold 2.3 million tickets before their home opener at the new Citizens Bank Park in 2004, compared to a total attendance of 2.26 million in the last season at the Vet. This so-called dead sport had a chance to threaten the all-time attendance record of 3.1 million in the first season at the new park.

More importantly, the Phillies in 2004 will top that 3-million mark for the first time since—take a wild guess, Glen—1993, the season before the strike.

Baseball is not *coming* back in Philadelphia. Baseball is already back.

But will it ever supercede football in a gridiron-crazed city like Philadelphia?

Duh. Let me take a wild stab at this question myself, Glen.

Yeah, it will.

Baseball will be No. 1 in Philadelphia as soon as two simple things happen within a year of one another:

• The Phillies make the playoffs.

• The Eagles *don't* make the playoffs.

I've been talking to Philadelphia sports fans every day for 15 years, and you've been doing likewise for almost as long, Glen. Philadelphia doesn't love football any more than Pittsburgh or Denver or Green Bay. And Philadelphia doesn't like baseball less than Chicago or New York or even Boston.

If Philadelphia loves anything more than those cities, it's winning—the basic idea of scoring more points or runs or goals than the other team.

We love to win. What a shock.

I hope you'll permit one last confession, Glen. I am a Phillies fan, of course, but I am also a New York Yankees fan.

My Dad taught me an important lesson about life a long time ago.

If you're going to have only one friend, he may as well be a rich one.

Glen says: Let's see if I've got this right, Angelo. For six months of the year, spring through fall, your evenings are spent sitting alone, watching the Fightin' Phils on the old Philco? Gee whiz, and some people foolishly think you lead a mundane life, eh?

Evidenced by the fact that your routine sounds a lot like my grandfather's back in the 1950s (do you also wear a sleeveless undershirt and smoke cigars?), it seems, sad to say, a bit out of touch.

Baseball will never again be the No. 1 sport in Philadelphia.

Football is king. And the king ain't about to abdicate.

You ask me to imagine what things would be like in our city if the Eagles go 3-13. I don't have to imagine. I was there in 1998. You were too, Ange. And do you recall what people were talking about in September and October as the Eagles got off to a 1-7 start?

The Eagles, that's what. As in, when were they gonna fire Ray Rhodes? As in, who would they draft? As in, how do we get rid of Jeffrey Lurie? It was negative passion, but it wasn't apathy.

I also enjoyed the excitement surrounding the Phils' new ballpark in 2004. And do you remember the topic of most talk on WIP that April? I'll remind you: Why would the Eagles trade up in the draft for an overweight offensive lineman?

Look, I love baseball like you do. And, like you and most baseball fans, I've been blowing out more than 40 birthday candles for years. But I listen to other people. And here's what they tell me:

• The Phillies' ineptitude from, roughly, 1984 to 2001 cost this city an entire generation of baseball fans who will never come back. All of us tend to follow sports we latched onto during our youth. The average 27-year-old here was raised on a diet of Ken Howell, Gregg Jefferies and Steve Jeltz. Gee, and he never got hooked?

• That electrifying 1993 season was nothing more than a mirage that was followed by seven straight losing years. I had prom dates who didn't leave me feeling as teased.

• Sad to say, the slow-moving, thinking-person's sport will never regain its exalted status under a generation raised on Sesame Street, MTV and other attention-deficit specials. Our colleague, Al Morganti, put it best: Imagine going into a network programmer today proposing a new sport. Games take about three hours, you'd say, and the ball gets thrown about once every 30 seconds. Sometimes, the batter hits the ball; more often it just gets tossed back to the pitcher. Usually, after a batter hits it, he ends up running back to the dugout. And there's a lot of time to stand around and analyze.

You'd be laughed out of the programmer's suite.

You and I like baseball, Ange, exactly because of its relaxed pace. Kids today prefer the pinball velocity and loud noise of pseudo-sports like Arena Football and Slamball. I do not, by the way, see this as a positive step for society.

Now you mention the Phils' new park and the huge crowds that showed up opening season. Terrific, absolutely. And a positive step for the franchise. But do you know the difference between you and all those people at the park under age thirty? You're there as a fan who lives and dies with your team and loves to bore the guy in the next seat with your insights on defensive alignment. They're there because it's an outing—a building full of exciting sights and sounds and fun food and a hairy green guy dancing on the dugout.

That's why you'll sit home, alone in the dark, night after night, screaming to your wife in the kitchen that the manager is an idiot (you're wrong on that one, too, Ange.). Meanwhile, the rest of that crowd has moved on to the next event. They're not hardcore supporters who'll grow more invested in their team year after year. Their passion is as thin as Todd Pinkston's legs.

And oh, by the way, Angelo, how the hell can you root for that evil empire that is the Yankees? Boy, talk about your serious character flaws.

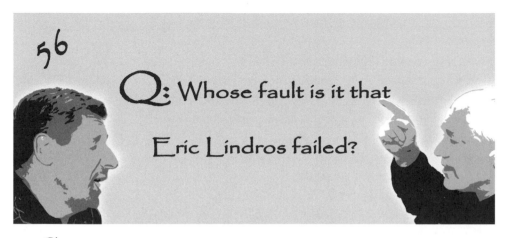

Q: Whose fault is it that Eric Lindros failed?

Glen says: No doubt, the Lindros saga was part of the most sordid period in Flyers history—an era that includes the mishandling of cancer-ridden Roger Neilson's coaching status, the public backstabbing of legend Bill Barber and even the brief employment of rapist Billy Tibbetts.

The organization that prides itself on being "family" became shockingly dysfunctional.

To that end, I don't absolve Flyers management in how it botched l'affaire Lindros. As Sonny Corleone said, "You're taking this very personal. Mr. Snider, this is business and Bob Clarke is taking it very personal."

Or something like that.

But make no mistake, Angelo. The scales of blame for this disaster tilt heavily toward the eggshell-headed hockey star and his meddlesome mommy. Rather than slog through every reason, I'll give you my top six:

1. He was unduly influenced by his parents. From the start, Eric was overprotected by Carl and Bonnie ("Mommy Dearest") Lindros. I was actually the first Philadelphia reporter to interview Eric, writing a story for the *Inquirer* about the 17-year-old junior phenom. At the time, I remember Bonnie complaining about Quebec City (too French), Eric's living conditions (too Spartan) and Wayne Gretzky (too proud).

"Boy, she's an overbearing stage mom," I thought, "but someday, she'll learn to step back."

I was half wrong.

2. He tried to get people fired. Like PR director Mark Piazza, who was accused of planting stories about Lindros' acquaintance with mobster Joey Merlino. And trainer "Sudsy" Settlemyre, whom, Bonnie Lindros said, purposely did a poor job sharpening Eric's skates during the 1996 playoffs, causing him to slip. Like coach Terry Murray, who dared accuse Eric of being slow to recover from injuries. Lindros' problems were always someone else's fault.

3. He tried to influence personnel. Again, his parents, actually. Carl Lindros allegedly called Clarke in 1999 and insisted the Flyers not trade for Mark Recchi because Recchi was represented by Eric's former agent. And, according to the Flyers, Carl tried to manipulate who played on Eric's line. He didn't want Eric paired with John LeClair, except on the power play, because—according to Carl—LeClair didn't pass the puck enough.

4. He was hypersensitive. A souring point in the relationship came in 1998 when Clarke told Lindros that if he wanted to be among the highest-paid NHL stars, he should start playing better and being a leader. You and I have been around long enough, Angelo, to see players called out hundreds of times. The adults among them respond by playing better. The children go into a funk. Lindros' parents ridiculously suggested that Clarke made the challenge because he was jealous of their son.

5. He was disingenuous. Eric's family accused the Flyers' medical staff of poor treatment (actually, one letter from Carl to Ed Snider accused them of trying to "kill" him), but part of the problem was his own tendency to hide symptoms. After one crushing hit, he denied vomiting or seeing yellow—two signs of a concussion. He played four more games before being taken off the ice, but that didn't stop his father from blaming the Flyers for the misdiagnosis.

6. He was injury prone. Not his fault, of course, but Lindros' papyrus-brittle body kept him from ever reaching his potential. Out of 626 possible regular-season games during his tenure here, Eric missed 140. More than anything, I believe, this is why the promise never came to fruition. No 50-goal seasons, no Stanley Cups, no parades.

The shame is, for most of us, the lasting image of No. 88 is of him sprawled on the ice, fetal position, after Scott Stevens delivered that shoulder to his chin in the 2000 Eastern Conference Finals.

It shouldn't have been that way. The story was supposed to end with Lindros and Clarke sharing a convertible ride down Broad Street, smiling broadly, the Cup nestled between them.

That's what we all forecast that day in 1992 when the Flyers paid $15 million, plus two first-round picks and six players for the 19-year-old center.

One of those players, I recall, was a Swedish prospect named Peter Forsberg. What ever happened to that guy anyway, Angelo?

Angelo says: This just in: The Flyers dismissed top public relations man Mark Piazza not because Eric Lindros wanted it, but because they had found a better man who worked cheaper, said nicer things about the team and showed a total dedication to Ed Snider and Bob Clarke.

That man is named Glen Macnow.

Can these Flyers do no wrong in your eyes, Glen?

Yes, Eric Lindros was, is, and always will be a baby. His parents are two boils on the ass of professional hockey. No argument.

But to absolve the Flyers from blame in this eight-year blight on Philadelphia sports is laughable. In 30 years of writing and broadcasting, I can offer no better example of a team screwing up a player than the way the Flyers mishandled Eric Lindros.

From the day they acquired him in that muddle of a deal—yes, they would have been way better off with Peter Forsberg—it's hard to find one thing the Flyers did right.

They knew from the very beginning that Lindros was a mama's boy. Hell, *we* knew it, Glen. Everyone always said Eric was part of a package deal. The Flyers coughed up six players, two draft picks and $15 million for Eric, Bonnie and Carl Lindros. It was no secret that Lindros' physical package of breathtaking power and exquisite finesse was tempered by a fragile psyche.

So how did the Flyers handle the situation? By out-babying Bonnie Lindros. I can remember those early days, during the first-blush love affair between Lindros and the Flyers, when we couldn't say a negative word about the next superstar in Philadelphia without a bitter call from the organization. WIP was the flagship station of the Flyers, and we were supposed to get behind the sensitive hero.

I was also there when Craig Carton called our show breathlessly one day to inform our audience that Lindros was scratched from a game because he was drunk. We tried in every way imaginable to discredit the story from the moment it left Carton's lips. Branding a player inebriated is one of the fastest ways to get sued, and we recognized that. Within days, the Flyers sued us.

The ensuing hubbub was symbolic of the Flyers' protectiveness in those early days of the Lindros era. Ed Snider, at his devious best, lambasted his old station—the same station he had sold to finance the acquisition of Lindros—and vowed that he would never, ever, ever, settle the suit. This was war.

A year later, Snider settled. An apology was issued. Carton departed. Lindros remained in a protective cocoon, courtesy of the Flyers.

And then everything changed. Suddenly, in his final season with the Flyers, the golden goose became a lame duck. No one has ever offered an official explanation on what happened that soured the Flyers on Lindros. I have a very simple theory, Glen. Bob Clarke got sick of him, his mother, his father, his injuries, his whining, his baby act.

How ironic is that? The Flyers created the perfect nursery for their favorite infant, then they got bitter when he didn't act his age. The smear campaign at the end was one of the worst I've ever seen or heard. There were even whispers that—gasp!—Lindros might have been drinking that night in question, after all.

Please understand, Glen, I have no sympathy for Lindros. None. He was blessed with very possibly the best hockey skills in the history of the game, and he blew it. I agree with all six of your points. He was all of those things.

Now ask yourself why. Ask yourself how different things might have been if the Flyers had treated him like a man, held him responsible for his behavior, forced him to break away from his parents and think for himself. Then ask yourself if the Flyers are the real reason for this nightmare.

One good thing has come out of all of this, Glen. I think I've got an idea for a sequel to this book. You would write it alone. Here's the title: *Why I Still Love the Flyers after 29 Lost Seasons.*

It would be sold in the mystery section of bookstores everywhere.

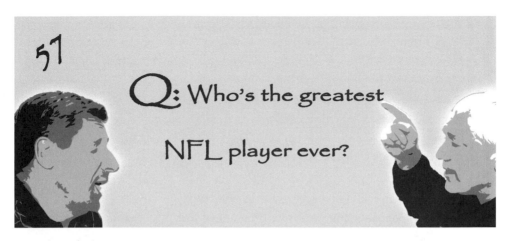

51

Q: Who's the greatest NFL player ever?

Angelo says: One of the reasons I have loved sports my whole life is that I encountered, at a very young age, the majestic talent of a man named Jim Brown. When I was 10 years old, he was the greatest football player I had ever seen. Now, 40-plus years later, he is still the best ever. By far.

For the purposes of this discussion, Glen, I need a couple of extra ground rules. First, let's keep out personal lives. Brown's struggle after football, and especially his alleged abuse of women, is contemptible if true. But it should not be a consideration here. And second, no statistics, please. In his day, Brown was the most prolific runner in history, but those numbers have no context in the offense-oriented game of today.

I could win this argument in the space of a few seconds if we had the chance to play video clips. The spectacle of just one of the pulverizing, take-no-prisoner runs by Jim Brown would render you speechless, and this argument moot. Even now, in the grainy footage of the late 1950s and early 1960s, Jim Brown has no peer. Just go to the videotape, Glen.

But Brown's impact on the game cannot be measured by the collisions that became his trademark. Very simply, Jim Brown was the most important figure in the history of pro football. At a time when the NFL was an ugly step-sister to college football in the sports pecking order in America, Jim Brown came along and ran the game right to the top.

Just consider when pro football began to captivate this nation, Glen, and you'll see a precise parallel with Jim Brown's emergence as the top attraction in all of sports. Brown started in 1957, when no one even paid attention to the NFL. He retired in 1965, when pro football was beginning to challenge baseball as the national pastime.

In the late 1950s, people would watch the games of the Cleveland Browns for no reason other than to marvel at this man's stunning ability to run over tacklers and reach the end zone. Without Jim Brown, there would have been no reason to watch. Who knows? Baseball might still be king today if not for Jim Brown.

Back when I was growing up in Rhode Island, my family would gather around the old 19-inch Admiral black-and-white TV every time Brown would go up against our beloved New York Giants. Invariably, Brown would find a way to break our hearts. My Dad actually wanted Jim Brown banned from football because he thought it wasn't fair for a player to be that much better than everybody else.

On the other hand, I quietly rooted *for* Jim Brown—just as I cheered back then for the New York Yankees and the Philadelphia 76ers. I had an instant attraction to greatness, I guess. And no one—with the exception of Wilt Chamberlain—was greater than Jim Brown.

But none of this would matter, Glen, if not for the biggest reason I love Jim Brown. In a world where everyone squeezes every drop out of their talent, at a time when fame and fortune represent the scoreboard of life, Jim Brown walked away when he was at the absolute pinnacle of his career. And he never looked back.

Think about all of the greatest players ever: Michael Jordan, Wayne Gretzky, Mark Messier, Willie Mays, Mickey Mantle, Joe Namath, Joe Montana, and Jerry Rice. Every one of them stayed too long. Every one of them diluted their legacy by going from extraordinary to ordinary. Every one of them thought about themselves before their fans.

Not Jim Brown. He retired at age 30, still in his prime, because he didn't think there was anything left to prove. He had single-handedly built the foundation of a sport that would rise bigger and taller than any other. He had carried enough defenders on his back to make his point. In people's memories, Jim Brown will always be at his very best, doing what no man before or since has ever been able to do.

And I've got one last testimonial for you to consider, Glen. My partner in my early days in radio, the legendary Tom Brookshier, often had the unenviable task of trying to tackle Jim Brown in the secondary after the greatest running back ever had blasted through the line. I asked Brookie many times to describe what it was like to hit Jim Brown.

"No one ever hit Jim Brown," Brookie often said. "He always hit us first."

Glen says: One of your key points, Angelo, is exactly what keeps Jim Brown from being the best-ever player in football: He retired too early.

Jim Brown played just nine glorious seasons in the NFL before telling Art Modell to stick it.

(If you remember the story, Brown was filming "The Dirty Dozen," and called the Browns' owner to say he might be late to training camp.

"If you're late, don't bother coming," Modell said.

"Okay, I retire," Brown countered. Way to use that leverage, Artie Baby.)

Anyway, Brown—like his '60s baseball contemporary Sandy Koufax—was a supernova, exploding on the scene, flashing unprecedented brilliance, and then disappearing too soon.

When he retired, he was the best who ever played the game. Even now, I'd take him over Payton, Sanders, Simpson or any other running back you could nominate.

But he no longer holds the title of the greatest player in history. That goes to a man who has been just as dominant as Brown was and *played twice as long a career.*

That man is Jerry Rice.

I know you don't like statistics, Angelo, so I'll just give you one:

One.

That's where Jerry Rice ranks all-time in career touchdowns, receptions, yards from scrimmage, receiving yards and touchdown receptions. He doesn't just hold records, he dominates categories. His 22,466 receiving yards going into 2004 is *51 percent more* than the second-place player, Tim Brown. Find me any other NFL category in which the record holder is that far ahead of the next guy.

You may argue, Ange, that Rice padded his records by hanging on. Not true. Do you realize that he caught 92 passes the season he turned 40? Grandpa's still got it.

You may contend, Ange, that Rice benefited from playing with Hall of Fame quarterbacks Joe Montana and Steve Young. Well, they benefited as much playing with him. He also made journeymen like Rich Gannon, Jeff Garcia and even Rick Mirer look pretty good over the years.

You may suggest, Ange, that a wide receiver gets the ball less often than a running back and so he can't be termed the best. Well, if you go with that logic, you'd have to pick a quarterback as your top dog. Beyond that, something tells me that 1,519 career receptions plus another 151 in the playoffs sort of counts as proving you've touched the ball enough.

The bottom line is this: Jerry Rice was as dominant in his time as Jim Brown was in his—except that his time lasted twice as long.

I only met Jerry Rice once, interviewing him back when I covered football for the *Inquirer* in the early 90s. I remember two things about him. First, as a workout fanatic, he was trying to see how low he could get his body fat—just as a challenge to himself. He had shrunk it to under three percent when team doctors told him to cut out the superhuman training regimen because every person should carry at least four percent body fat.

Second, I was in awe when I shook his hand. It was huge and powerful, with fingers as long as a baseball glove. He told me he had toughened his hands as a teenager by working alongside his father as a bricklayer. The only two men I had ever met with comparable hands were Julius Erving and Gordie Howe, both among the top legends in their sports.

Certainly, they were the kind of hands that could grab a football out of midair and tuck it away without losing stride. Rice caught passes at his shoelaces and three feet over his head, in his gut and behind his back.

He had moves—head shakes and shoulder rolls—that would cause a cornerback to hesitate and then find himself 15 yards behind. And he could break a linebacker's tackle on the way to a touchdown. Oh yeah, he scored more than 200 of those. No one else comes close.

And speed? Let me say, Ange, that I enjoyed Tom Brookshier's testimonial to Jim Brown. Too bad he couldn't have told us what it was like to hit Jerry Rice.

No offense to our pal Brookie, but he never would have caught Jerry Rice.

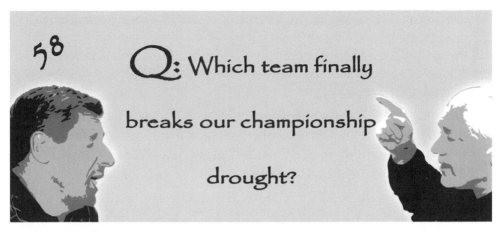

58

Q: Which team finally breaks our championship drought?

Glen says: The first show I ever hosted as a full-timer on WIP was in December 1993. The first topic I raised that day was, "Which of our four teams will be the next to win a title?"

Hell, it had been ten years since the Sixers' NBA championship—the last time a team here had won it all. It seemed like a decent subject to kick off my radio career.

Who would have dreamt that more than a decade later, we'd still be asking the same question?

This isn't a dry spell, Angelo. This is a forced march through the Sahara Desert wearing a parka and galoshes. None of the eleven other four-sport cities in America comes near our two-decade embargo on winning. In fact, only one has waited more than ten years—Minneapolis, where the last parade celebrated the Twins taking the 1991 World Series. Hell, even weenie pseudo-cities like Anaheim and East Rutherford get to party on a regular basis.

Consider it this way: If you celebrated the '83 Sixers win by conceiving a child, that youngster is now old enough to drive, vote and legally drink. You may have had a few drinks yourself awaiting the next march down Broad Street.

So, who ends the drought? I'll give you my choice through the process of elimination.

The 76ers are the easiest to rule out. The Allen Iverson era came and went without a title (yeah, I know it's not officially over, Ange, but what's the point now?). It will take years for the Sixers to build a new nucleus. And, to be honest, I have less than full faith in the acumen of Billy King and Jim O'Brien.

The Flyers have had their chances and never quite got there. As I write this, we don't know where the NHL is headed, but I'll bet my book royalties on a salary cap. If the Flyers couldn't capture the Stanley Cup with all their financial advantages over the years, what chance do they have on a level economic playing field?

The Eagles. . . well, that's probably the chalk in this horse race. Feel free to ridicule me if you're reading this chapter at the 2005 Super Bowl parade. But there's a part of me that sees the Birds as our annual heartbreaker. Donovan McNabb still has to prove he can win the Big One (or even the Next To Big One), and Andy Reid keeps looking more and more like Marty Schottenheimer.

And that leaves . . . the Phils? Well, sure, why not? It says here that the Phillies will be the next Philadelphia team to win a championship, and here's how it plays out:

Jim Thome smacks 50 homers, drives in 130 and wins the Most Valuable Player Award. Pat Burrell, batting behind Thome, adds 40 homers and 110 RBIs.

Bobby Abreu finally grows a pair and starts driving in runs at clutch time. Jimmy Rollins figures out that it makes no sense for a guy who's 5-foot-8, 165 pounds to try to drive it out of the park. He evolves into a dangerous slap hitter and uses his size to draw walks.

Randy Wolf develops the confidence to become the No. 1 starter he's capable of being. Vicente Padilla calms down his off-field partying to develop into a reliable No. 2. And Kevin Millwood, moved back in the rotation, excels in the No. 3 position as he did so well behind Greg Maddux and Tom Glavine in Atlanta.

General-Manager-for-life Ed Wade adds an on-base machine center fielder by finally trading one of those prospects that he values like gold bullion. The manager takes a step or two back and lets the veterans on the team set the mood in the clubhouse.

Billy Wagner stays healthy and becomes, well, himself. Chase Utley matures into a solid line drive hitter who can play second or third. And Mike Leiberthal fights the aging process with one more .300 season.

Wishful thinking? No doubt it is, Angelo. But when I asked this question to my very first radio audience back in 1993, the consensus then was that the Phils—fresh off their last World Series appearance—would be the next team to win it all.

Those callers haven't yet been proven wrong. I'm sticking with them.

Angelo says: If you're worried that someone is going to be reading this chapter at the 2005 Eagles championship parade, Glen, why are you picking the Phillies to end the worst drought in Philadelphia sports history?

Unlike you, I am not the least bit concerned over whether this chapter will stand the test of time. I have been saying it since the time when the Eagles acquired Terrell Owens and Jevon Kearse in the winter of 2004, and I will say it right now, in a voice that should scream off these pages:

THE EAGLES WILL WIN THE NFL CHAMPIONSHIP IN 2005.

How's that for conviction, Glen? I have never been more convinced about anything in my life than the certainty of this prediction. One of the best things about getting old is that history becomes a guide for the future as well as a reminder of the past.

There are literally dozens of signs that the Birds will end the drought with one of the greatest celebrations by a sports city in American history. I'll just share a few of the best reasons.

Entering the 2004-2005 season, the Eagles have the best team.

Don't take my word for it. Check with Vegas. The Eagles moved from 10-1 to 5-1 at most sports books the day they filled their last major need and added Terrell Owens. As I write this, in the spring of 2004, they are the choice of most sports books to win it all, slightly ahead of the reigning New England Patriots.

The Eagles probably would have won the championship in 2003-2004 if they hadn't suffered some terrible injuries at the most inopportune times. Their defensive line, one of the deepest parts of the team, was a medical nightmare by season's end. The Birds will not lose Hollis Thomas, Paul Grasmanis, Derrick Burgess, Jerome McDougal, and Jamaal Green to serious injuries all in the same season. And Kearse will give back the one thing the Birds lacked defensively, a threat to quarterbacks.

The schedule is ideal for a team with great aspirations.

Here's a first: The Eagles will be favored in no less than 14 of the 16 regular-season games in 2005—and possibly all 16. Thanks to the schedule, they are all but guaranteed a great start, during which Owens and Kearse will blend into an already excellent team. By the time the more challenging games arrive around midseason, the steamroller will be flattening everyone in sight.

Cynics like you always find things to worry about, Glen. Can Donovan McNabb throw more accurately? Who will replace Duce Staley? How will T.O. fit in with his less flamboyant teammates? Blah, blah, blah.

Better questions would be: Won't McNabb become more accurate now that he's got a great receiver like Owens? Or, just how amazing is Brian Westbrook going to be now that's he's got a couple of seasons under his belt?

It's always darkest before the dawn.

No city in America had a worse run of bad luck than Philadelphia did in the first few years of the new millennium. The luck has to change sometime. It's called the law of averages.

I will now reply to your prediction that the Phillies will be the first team to end the drought with two carefully chosen words: Larry Bowa.

Have you watched him manage a team from night to night, inning to inning? Other than Terry Francona himself—the poster boy for baseball stupidity—have you ever seen a man more poorly manage a pitching staff or a bench? Have you ever really pondered Bowa's twisted late-inning maneuvering? I honestly believe a polar bear would do a better job.

But enough about the Phillies. Let's talk Eagles.

I can see it all right now, Glen. A crowd of three million fans are squeezed into every available space along Broad Street. Confetti is everywhere. Now I hear a chuckle, building to a laugh, then a guffaw, and finally a deafening roar.

They're all laughing. They're all reading your prediction of the Phillies ending the drought, and they're laughing.

See you at the parade, Glen. Wear a disguise.

59

Q: What opposing coach did we hate the most?

Angelo says: There is no single topic in this book that I feel more qualified to address than the coach we hated the most in Philadelphia sports history. If anyone is a card-carrying coach hater, Glen, I'm your man.

In 1981, I was banished from the press table at Boston Garden by an insecure jerk named Bill Fitch because he didn't like the things I was writing about him. In 1984, I was chased around the rink by an enraged Flyers coach Bob McCammon because I had pointed out the obvious: He couldn't coach.

I'm the same guy who has a decade-long vitriol exchange program with Rich Kotite, a poison-pen relationship with Terry Francona, a blood feud with Larry Bowa and I don't think there's even a way to accurately describe my venomous association with Larry Brown.

And those are just the coaches who have been running the teams I *root* for. Imagine the festering hatred I harbor for opposing coaches and managers.

In short, I am an expert in how people react to coaches, especially how the title-starved, teeth-baring Philadelphia fans feel about the men who plot to deny us our sports dreams.

And there's no question in my mind that the most despised opposing coach ever, was Tom Landry.

If you're going to argue that the Cowboys are the most hated team ever in Philadelphia, then how can you ignore Tom Landry, Glen? Wasn't he the biggest reason for that hatred? Didn't he start the whole thing in the 1960s with his self-righteous pomposity?

Landry was more than a person to the Philadelphia fans. He was a state of mind. With that ridiculous Stetson propped on his bald head, Tom Landry was a symbol of the robotic world of the Dallas Cowboys. Landry even introduced that hitch by the offense just before the snap to reinforce this machine-like precision.

Yes, in their day they were great. That's not what Philadelphia hated about them. What we hated was the way the Cowboys felt obligated to flaunt their success, rub salt into wounds that had become scars. With his stone face and his ruthless nature, Landry was the mastermind of that torment.

How ruthless was Tom Landry? He actually ran up the score in a game against the Eagles during the strike-plagued 1987 season. Using a superior team of scabs, he blitzed Buddy Ryan's Eagles, 41-22, while the regular players were sitting out a contract dispute. Most coaches were nauseated by the scabs; Landry used them as a battering ram.

The greatest joy I ever witnessed as an Eagles fan came at the end of a contest two weeks after that scab game, on a simple play in which Randall Cunningham faked taking a knee, then snapped back up and flicked a pass that capped a 37-20 blowout of the Cowboys.

Ryan later said that was the day he truly won the love of the fans.

"I did what the fans wanted me to do," Ryan said. "I kicked their ass."

Landry coached the Cowboys from their inception in 1960 through the 1988 season, when his doom was sealed in a game against the Eagles. Down 24-23, the legendary coach lost track of the situation and tried a ridiculous pass play on fourth down. He later admitted he thought it was third down.

A few months later, he was fired. Owner Jerry Jones brought in his old buddy Jimmy Johnson to continue their reign of pomposity, and Johnson was almost as contemptible. Almost.

Like everything else, though, there's no replacement for the real thing. Tom Landry haunted and taunted Philadelphia sports fans for nearly three decades, inspiring a rivalry like few in professional sports. When Landry died at 75 in 2000, there was actually sadness in Philadelphia.

No, it wasn't because a great coach had passed away, Glen.

We just would have liked to kick his ass one more time.

Glen says: Right church, wrong pew, Angelo. In fact, you even brought up the name of the guy who replaced Tom Landry, not just as coach of the Evil Empire, but as the most despicable coach ever to lead a team into our fair town.

Jimmy Johnson is the outsider we hated the most. I'll put it to you this way: Much as we loathed Landry, I don't recall anyone ever trying to knock that ugly fedora off his head with a snowball.

Our revulsion was based on two factors—expectations and attitude. And, let's be honest here, maybe just a tiny twinge of envy.

Cowboys owner Jerry Jones hired his old crony, Johnson, to replace Landry in 1989. Sure, Johnson had been a formidable college coach at Miami, but we've all seen that ilk fail repeatedly in the NFL (Hello, Steve Spurrier). So when the Cowboys went 1-15 during Johnson's initial season, we figured it was just a matter of time before this ridge-haired, fat-faced blowhard was headed back to Enormous State U.

In our minds, the era of Eagle domination over Dallas (which began with that post-strike game you mentioned, Ange, and built to seven straight wins after 1990), was going to last a full decade. Except, it turned out, Johnson knew what he was doing. While Rich Kotite left his charts out in the rain, Johnson put together a nucleus that went to the play-offs within two years, and then reeled off two straight Super Bowl wins.

We hated him for that. We hated him more for his persona—a smug, pompous, "I'm-better-than-you-and-I-know-it" kind of demeanor. Hell, he was a chubby redneck from Port Arthur, Texas. Who was he to laugh in our faces?

The whole thing reached a boiling point in 1989, when Buddy Ryan (God bless him) was still here. In a Thanksgiving game in Dallas, a couple of Eagles players amused themselves by beating up on Luis Zendejas, the Cowboys' jockey-sized kicker. That annoyed Johnson, who whined to the commissioner, the networks, anyone who would listen. We viewed this as the act of a schoolyard sissy who tattled to the teacher when the game of Red Rover grew a little too rough.

By the time Johnson's Cowboys came into Veterans Stadium for a mid-December game, Eagles fans were primed to let him hear it. Then, God did us a favor by dumping six inches of snow on South Philadelphia the day before the game.

Fans arrived at the Vet to find their seats conveniently covered by a couple-dozen snowballs worth of fine packing powder. To be honest, the missiles were aimed at everyone, including players, cheerleaders, broadcasters and other fans. But no target proved quite as enticing as the impeccable carpet that doubled as the top of Johnson's head. Surely you remember the great photos, Ange, of the roly-poly coach running off the field, flanked by Philly cops—their hands up in the air, trying to protect his precious haircut. I'm glad to report the officers were less than successful.

Did we ever attack a visiting coach in such a hostile, yet wonderful manner? Was there ever a better day to be a Philadelphia fan?

No. Johnson inspired animus unlike any other clipboard-carrying loudmouth who ever visited our sidelines. More than the haughty Landry, more than the buffoonish Barry Switzer who, in turn, replaced him. More than basketball enemies Red Auerbach or George Karl. More than hockey goons Scotty Bowman or Glen Sather.

But I tell you what. Moving up fast in this horserace is Larry Brown. Since abandoning the Sixers in 2003, all he's done is set a personal agenda of annoying and tormenting us—including, of course, winning the NBA crown as soon as he skipped town. I'm officially laying claim now to the dyspeptic Mr. Brown for when we write Volume II of this book a few years from now.

Funny thing, though. When I think of the most-hated coaches in our history, turns out most of them coached *for* us, rather than *against* us. Neither Landry nor Johnson measure up anywhere near Kotite or Terry Francona. What does that say about our sports history?

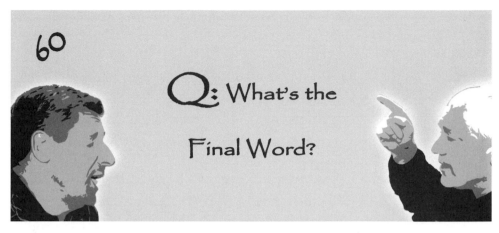

60

Q: What's the Final Word?

Glen says: I'm lucky.

I'm just an average guy. Not much to look at in my forties, with bad knees and a hair line that's well beyond receding. Not the smartest man in the world, nor the wealthiest, nor the cleverest.

I just happen to have the best job in the best city in America.

Like Angelo, I'm a transplant to Philadelphia. I ended up here after living my first three decades in Buffalo, Boston, Fort Lauderdale and Detroit. Funny thing about this town: I still find folks who believe that if you weren't spawned at Shunk and Two Street, you'll never really be a local. That's okay. I accept my handicap. Just don't ever doubt my passion for our teams.

For the last decade, I've been a host on WIP radio. I worked with two great partners —Jody McDonald and Anthony Gargano—before starting to work solo in 2002.

When people meet me, they invariably say, "What a fun job you have."

And they're right.

But their rationale is usually wrong. Most people think that being a sports talker (or a sportswriter as I was before) is exciting because you get to go to the games and hobnob with the players.

That's half correct, actually. Going to the games, as I do, is amazing. I haven't seen a championship in more than 20 years, but I saw a goalie score a goal, a pitcher throw a no-hitter and a basketball player carry an entire city on his bony shoulders. I sat in the seats (they're far better than the press box) to cheer at World Series games, Stanley Cup and NBA Finals and two NFC Championship contests.

I don't have to tell you how they all ended.

But the other part—the hobnobbing with athletes—never appealed to me. Other guys in this business enjoy the reflected glare of the spotlight, relish in comparing fur coats with the rich-and-famous. I always found our sports heroes to be as shallow in thought as they are talented on the field.

It's the fans I prefer. And I get to talk to hundreds of them every week.

Let me tell you about my favorite night on radio.

It was March 19, 2004—the night before the implosion of Veterans Stadium. Now, I know I called the Vet "a dump" earlier in this book, and I meant it. The fans of Philadelphia deserved better than that concrete donut.

At the same time, I understand what the Vet meant to everyone who spent 30-plus years cheering and booing and sweating and freezing in its seats. My show that night was a tribute to the memories—Wilbert Montgomery's run and Mitch Williams' leap off the mound and every other awe-inspiring moment. For hours, every phone line into the show was booked solid with folks who wanted to share their reminiscences.

Then it occurred to me. We needed to say goodbye in person. We needed to toast the old gray building with Cold Duck and a chorus of "Auld Lang Syne" before moving on.

I asked a caller if he would join me outside the Vet when I got off the air at 11 p.m. He agreed. So did the next caller. And the next. People offered to bring champagne and cigars and cheesesteaks and whatever else seemed to make sense. A Philly cop called and said we could all park around the corner without being hassled.

So when my shift ended, I headed down. I hoped to find 30 fans as mentally deficient as I was to share in the moment.

Instead I found 300. The corner of Broad and Pattison was mobbed with folks who had listened to my show and wanted to hold an impromptu Irish wake for the joint the night before it went down. They drove in from Camden and Conshohocken, South Philly and Southampton.

For an hour, we toasted the Vet. We lit cigars and used newspapers and old programs to start a bonfire (the cops were terrific). We raised glasses of champagne and Scotch and homemade red to Buddy Ryan and Tug McGraw and Wendell Davis' knees. We toasted until there was nothing left to toast and drank until there was nothing left to drink.

We sang, too. "Fly, Eagles, Fly," at least a dozen times. One knucklehead even attempted a version of Dave Schultz's novelty song, "Penalty Box," just for variety. For one final time, the Vet was a magnet, drawing people of all races, educations and backgrounds.

We hugged and then went home. The next day they blew the place up.

Athletes come and go. Even the biggest stars are just visitors here. Coaches get fired. Owners sell out to the next rich guy.

But the fans stay forever. They're the lifers.

To me, they've always been the real heroes.

Angelo says: It was the most exciting night of my mediocre TV career. The Roosevelt Hotel in Center City was crammed with hundreds of fans celebrating the seventh anniversary of *The Great Sports Debate*. For a bunch of estranged *Inquirer* sports writers, it was the realization of a dream. We thought the show would last forever.

A week later, at the absolute height of the program's popularity, we were dead. The old Philadelphia sports station, Prism, was being phased out. So were we.

If I were given a choice, I would still be doing that show today, with my partners Glen Macnow, Al Morganti, Jayson Stark, and Mike Missanelli. It was everything one of those studio sports programs should be, but rarely are—spontaneous, honest, raucous and funny. That show represented the cantankerous nature of the Philadelphia sports fan as well as anything we've ever done.

So when Glen came to me in the winter of 2004 and proposed a partnership for this book, he had me the moment he recited the title. It sounded like an extension of our TV work of a decade ago. It also represented to me a chance to record, in book form, some of the most spirited debates we've been involved in over the past 15 years on WIP.

Little did I know when I started this project that there were lessons still to be learned by going through this process. As I researched my end of these debates, I saw new perspectives take shape. By the end, I had a deeper appreciation for the fans who follow the Eagles, Phillies, Sixers, and Flyers.

More than ever before, I am in awe of the resiliency of the Philadelphia sports fan. How do we do it?

Just in the few months leading up to our publication date, the Eagles flopped in the NFC championship game for a third straight time, the Flyers lost to a nondescript Tampa Bay team in the playoffs, and the miracle season of St. Joe's ended with a miracle shot—by Oklahoma State.

It just kept getting worse. Smarty Jones lost his first race ever in the stretch at the Belmont Stakes, thereby failing to win the Triple Crown. Larry Brown won his first NBA title, a year after stabbing Philadelphia in the back and bailing out on his contract.

And all of that adversity was really nothing more than the continuation of a legacy that included the 1964 Phillies and the 1979 Flyers, the 1980 Eagles, and the 1993 Phillies. And please don't forget the 2001 Sixers. The truth is, we are better than ever in dealing with failure now. We've had lots of practice.

When Glen and I were putting together the topics to debate, the ones most intriguing to me invariably were the negative ones. Don't get me wrong. I could write for weeks about the '66-67 Sixers and Wilt Chamberlain, or the 1980 Phillies and Tug McGraw.

But the real fertile ground here was in rotten trades, horrible officiating, bad behavior, and world-class scoundrels. There was no greater joy for me than getting in one more shot at Larry Brown or Rich Kotite or—my personal favorite—Terry Francona. I hope we do a sequel. I've got plenty more to say about those ingrates.

What I came away with, after months of study, was that the rewards of being a Philadelphia sports fan simply do not match the pain and suffering. For every 1980, there are five years of total despair. For every Jim Thome, there are five J.D. Drews. If a sports psychologist were to study this ratio of reward vs. pain, it's a pretty safe bet that his best advice would be to find another hobby. Maybe whittling.

But onward we march, in search of a real parade. Being a Philadelphia sports fan is a tradition handed down from generation to generation, like a mutant gene. After 21 years without a single major sports championship, we still fill just about every seat for just about every game. We still hope.

Glen and I entertained tons of ideas before settling on the debates in this book. There was one debate, however, that we never considered: Which city has the best sports fans in America?

We knew the answer to that one before we started.

DID WE MISS ANYTHING?
WHAT WAS IT?

If we missed your favorite hot sports topic in *The Great Philadelphia Sports Debate*, please let us know. It may wind up in *The Great Philadelphia Sports Debate 2*.

If you have any suggestions, please email them to the following address:

sportsdebate@wwwcomm.com

or by mail to:

Middle Atlantic Press

P.O. Box 600

Moorestown, NJ 08057

Attn: Terence Doherty

PHOTO CREDITS

All photos by permission of *The Philadelphia Inquirer* and *Philadelphia Daily News*, Philadelphia Newspapers, Inc.

Greg Lanier: 14

Jerry Lodriguss: 18, 33, 162, 184

Clem Murray: 26

George Reynolds: 35, 126, 180

Andrea Mihalik: 56

INQ archives: 68, 202

Bob Sacha: 72

Michael Mercanti: 94

Gary Bogdon: 110

John Costello: 150

Don Traver: 166

Joan Fairman Kanes: 170

Ron Cortes: 188